THE MEANING OF *BRK* "TO BLESS" IN THE OLD TESTAMENT

SOCIETY
OF BIBLICAL
LITERATURE

DISSERTATION SERIES
J. J. M. Roberts, Old Testament Editor
Charles Talbert, New Testament Editor

Number 95

THE MEANING OF *BRK* "TO BLESS"
IN THE OLD TESTAMENT

by
Christopher Wright Mitchell

Christopher Wright Mitchell

THE MEANING OF *BRK* "TO BLESS" IN THE OLD TESTAMENT

Scholars Press
Atlanta, Georgia

THE MEANING OF *BRK* "TO BLESS" IN THE OLD TESTAMENT

Christopher Wright Mitchell
Ph.D., University of Wisconsin–Madison, 1983
Michael V. Fox, Dissertation Advisor

Copyright © 1987 by the Society of Biblical Literature
Reprinted 2007 by the Society of Biblical Literature

All rights reserved. No part of this work may be reproduced or transmitted in any form or by any means, electronic or mechanical, including photocopying and recording, or by means of any information storage or retrieval system, except as may be expressly permitted by the 1976 Copyright Act or in writing from the publisher. Requests for permission should be addressed in writing to the Rights and Permissions Office, Society of Biblical Literature, 825 Houston Mill Road, Atlanta, GA 30329, USA.

Library of Congress Cataloging-in-Publication Data

Mitchell, Christopher Wright
    The meaning of *brk* "to bless" in the Old Testament.

    (Dissertation series / Society of Biblical Literature ; no. 95)
    Thesis (Ph.D.)—University of Wisconsin-Madison, 1983.
    Bibliography: p.
    1. Blessing and curse in the Bible. 2. Brk (The Hebrew root) 3. Bible, O.T. — Language, style.
    I. Title. II. Series: Dissertation series (Society of Biblical Literature) ; no. 95.

BS1199.B5M57   1987   221'.4'4   86-4001
ISBN   1-55540-002-7 (alk. paper)
ISBN   1-55540-003-5 (pbk. : alk. paper)

Printed in the United States of America
on acid-free paper

Contents

ACKNOWLEDGMENTS ix
ABBREVIATIONS xi
INTRODUCTION 1

Chapter

1 METHODOLOGICAL CONSIDERATIONS AND THE
  ETYMOLOGY OF BRK 3

  1.1 Methodology 3
  1.2 The Etymology of brk 8
  1.3 Conclusions Concerning the Etymology
      of brk 15

2 HISTORY OF THE INTERPRETATION OF BLESSING 17

  2.1 Johannes Pedersen 17
  2.2 Sigmund Mowinckel 20
  2.3 Johannes Hempel 21
  2.4 Claus Westermann 23
  2.5 Gerhard Wehmeier 24
  2.6 Josef Scharbert 26

3 GOD BLESSING MAN 29

  3.1 Promises of God's Blessing 29

      3.1.1 The Patriarchal Blessing
             Promises 29
      3.1.2 The Covenantal Blessing
             Promises 36
      3.1.3 Wisdom Retribution
             Aphorisms 44

		3.1.4	The Prophetic Apocalyptic Blessing Promises 52
		3.1.5	Miscellaneous Promises 58

3.2 Statements of God's Blessing 62

    3.2.1 Statements of God's Benediction 62

        3.2.2.1 Statements of God's Benefaction in Maintaining the Creation 65

        3.2.2.2 Statements of God's Benefaction in Accordance with the Patriarchal Promises 67

        3.2.2.3 Statements of God's Benefaction in Accordance with the Covenant 71

        3.2.2.4 Statements of God's Special Blessing upon the King 72

        3.2.2.5 Statements of God's Special Blessing Upon Zion 75

        3.2.2.6 Miscellaneous Statements of God's Benefaction 76

4 MAN BLESSING MAN 79

4.1 Declarative Human Blessings 79

    4.1.1 The Testamental Blessing 79
    4.1.2 Divination Blessing Pronouncements 90
    4.1.3 Miscellaneous Declarative Blessings 94

4.2 Optative Benedictions 95

    4.2.1 The Priestly Blessing 96
    4.2.2 Prayers for Blessing 98
    4.2.3 Greetings and Farewells 106
    4.2.4 Thanksgiving Benedictions 110
    4.2.5 Benedictions of Praise and Congratulations 115
    4.2.6 Psalmodic Concluding Benedictions 119
    4.2.7 Miscellaneous Wishes 122

4.3 Human Benefaction 126

5 THE USE OF *BRK* IN THE PRAISE OF GOD 133
   5.1 *brk*, Piel in Indicative
        Statements 134
   5.2 The Vow of Praise 137
   5.3 The Imperative Call for Praise 141
   5.4 *bārûk* and *mĕbōrak* Formulas
        with God as Subject 146
        5.4.1 *bārûk* Formulas Expressing
              Praise for Protection and
              Deliverance 150
        5.4.2 *bārûk* Formulas Expressing
              Praise for Acts of Kindness 153
        5.4.3 *bārûk* Formulas Expressing
              Wonder and Admiration 155
        5.4.4 Doxological *bārûk* and
              mĕbōrak Formulas 157
   5.5 Euphemism: "Praise/Worship" for
        "Blaspheme" 161

6 CONCLUSIONS 165

   6.1 God Blessing Man 165
   6.2 Man Blessing Man 167
   6.3 Man Praising God 169
   6.4 Magic and Blessing 171
   6.5 The Power of the Spoken Word 173
   6.6 Power Transfer and Blessing 176
   6.7 Deliverance and Blessing 177
   6.8 Some Close Synonyms of God
        Blessing Man 179

Table

1 The Occurrences of *brk* "Bless" in the
   Bible 185
2 The Genesis Niphal and Hithpael Passages
   and Later Allusions to Them 186

BIBLIOGRAPHY 187

INDEX OF SYNONYMS AND ANTONYMS OF *BRK* 201

INDEX OF BIBLICAL VERSES CONTAINING *BRK* 203

Acknowledgments

I would especially like to thank my Major Professor Michael Fox for his guidance and assistance, as well as Professors Menahem Mansoor and Keith Schoville. All three have made Hebrew philology a delight to learn. I would also like to thank my wife Carol for her loving support over the many years.

Abbreviations

AB	The Anchor Bible
ANET	Ancient Near Eastern Texts Relating to the Old Testament, ed. J. B. Pritchard
BBB	Bonner biblische Beiträge
BDB	A Hebrew and English Lexicon of the Old Testament, F. Brown, S. R. Driver, and C. A. Briggs
BETL	Bibliotheca Ephemeridum Theologicarum Lovaniensium
BHS	Biblia Hebraica Stuttgartensia
Bib	Biblica
BKAT	Biblischer Kommentar Altes Testament
BT	The Bible Translator
BWANT	Beiträge zur Wissenschaft vom Alten und Neuen Testament
BZ	Biblische Zeitschrift
BZAW	Beihefte zur ZAW
CAD	The Assyrian Dictionary of the Oriental Institute of the University of Chicago
CBQ	Catholic Biblical Quarterly
EvT	Evangelische Theologie

GKC	*Gesenius' Hebrew Grammar*, ed. E. Kautzsch, tr. A. E. Cowley
HTR	*Harvard Theological Review*
HUCA	*Hebrew Union College Annual*
ICC	International Critical Commentary
IDB	*Interpreter's Dictionary of the Bible*, ed. G. A. Buttrick
Int	*Interpretation*
JAOS	*Journal of the American Oriental Society*
JBL	*Journal of Biblical Literature*
JTS	*Journal of Theological Studies*
KAT	Kommentar zum Alten Testament
KB	*Lexicon in Veteris Testamenti Libros*, L. Koehler and W. Baumgartner
NCB	New Century Bible
NICOT	New International Commentary on the Old Testament
NIV	*The Holy Bible, New International Version*
OTL	Old Testament Library
PEQ	*Palestine Exploration Quarterly*
RB	*Revue biblique*
RHR	*Revue de l'histoire des religions*
RSR	*Recherches de science religieuse*
RSV	*The Holy Bible, Revised Standard Version*
TDNT	*Theological Dictionary of the New Testament*, eds. G. Kittel and G. Friedrich
TDOT	*Theological Dictionary of the Old Testament*, eds. G. J. Botterweck and H. Ringgren

THAT	*Theologisches Handwörterbuch zum Alten Testament*, eds. E. Jenni and C. Westermann
TWOT	*Theological Wordbook of the Old Testament*, ed. R. L. Harris. Chicago: Moody Press, 1980.
VT	*Vetus Testamentum*
VTSup	Vetus Testamentum Supplements
WMANT	Wissenschaftliche Monographien zum Alten und Neuen Testament
ZAW	*Zeitschrift für die alttestamentliche Wissenschaft*
ZDMG	*Zeitschrift der deutschen morgenländischen Gesellschaft*

Introduction

The theme of blessing is an integral element of many of the biblical traditions. God's blessings of man and the animals in the primeval history are indicative of his favorable attitude toward the creation. The major concern of the patriarchal narratives is to trace the transmission and fulfillment of God's promise to Abraham of blessing through the succeeding generations. The attainment of blessing is the motivating factor for observing the Sinai covenant. The wisdom literature also says that man's reward for Torah piety is blessing. In their apocalyptic visions, the prophets forsee a time when God's deliverance will usher in a golden age of blessing.

Human blessings likewise play a central role in the Bible. People uttered blessings on many occasions. The patriarchs delivered their deathbed testaments in the form of blessings. The priestly blessing was a central element of cultic worship. Prayers were often uttered in the form of blessings. Blessings were also spoken in everyday life situations such as greeting and departing, marriages, thanking others, and expressing friendship.

People often expressed praise toward God by means of blessing formulas and other forms of *brk*, both in secular settings and in the cult. At times God was praised for specific actions, while at other times he was praised because of his character and qualities. The Psalms in particular encourage the joyful praise of God and assert that it is man's duty to do so.

Blessing has naturally received a good deal of scholarly attention because of its importance. Yet many scholars have uncritically adopted the interpretations proposed by the History of Religion school in the 1920's which are based upon views of language and Israelite religion that have subsequently been shown to be faulty.

This study applies to blessing the fruits of modern linguistics, particularly speech-act semantics and lexicology, as well as archeology. With these tools, blessing is freed from the magical realm to which it was relegated by misunderstandings of the functions of language and societal customs. The common feature of all the meanings of *brk* is that blessing, whether it consists of a speech act (benediction) or a physical act (benefaction), is an act freely performed which expresses the grace and goodwill of the blesser. It has the connotation of a favorable relationship between the blesser and the person blessed.

1
Methodological Considerations and the Etymology of *BRK*

1.1 Methodology

Of the branches of linguistics, semantics is the field in the greatest state of fluidity. Many fundamental issues concerning the nature of meaning are as yet unresolved. Fortunately, the state of affairs in lexicology, that practical branch of semantics whose task is the determination of word meaning, is much more stable. Lexicologists have developed a number of techniques useful for determining word meaning. Recently, several excellent publications have discussed the application of lexicology to biblical studies (see especially Kedar 1981 and Silva 1983). For the purposes of this word study, I will simply discuss those lexicographic techniques that are most useful for the study of *brk*, and will avoid the larger theoretical issues of semantics.

There are two main approaches to word meaning (for summaries of the various semantic theories see Ullmann 1972, Lyons 1977, Kempson 1977, Fodor 1980, Silva 1983). Analytical theories distinguish between 1) the word (lexical unit, significant), 2) the reference, the concept the word denotes (signifié, sense, designatum, concept), and 3) the referent (referend, denotatum), the non-linguistic entity to which the word refers.[1] There is only an indirect relationship between the word and the referent. The word brings to mind the reference (the concept of a prophecy, for example), but a further link is necessary to associate the reference with a

---

[1] Semanticists and lexicographers show a lack of uniformity in terminology. The parentheses contain alternate popular terms. I use "word" to denote a lexical unit; most lexical units discussed in this study consist of single words.

specific referent (Isaiah's prophecy). The famous Ogden-Richards triangle illustrates the relationships:

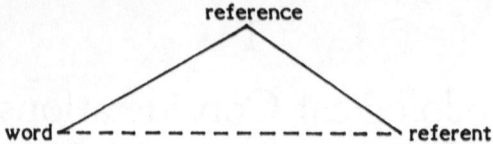

Operational theories, on the other hand, define the meaning of a word as identical with the way in which it is used. The distribution of a word in different contexts, as well as the words which occur together with it in the contexts (collocations), are studied to determine its meaning. For example, the meaning of šôr, "ox", would be inferred using this approach from its frequent occurrence in contexts discussing domesticated animals such as donkeys, sheep, and cows, and from the words and phrases such as gore, eat grass, plow, etc., that occur with it.

Modern semantics has integrated these two approaches, and lexicographic methodology draws on both of them (Zgusta 1971, Ullmann 1972, Kedar 1981, Silva 1983).

The context always plays the major role in determining word meaning. When studying a modern language, informants (native speakers) may be asked to describe a word's meaning. Since this method is not available for studying biblical Hebrew, examination of the contexts is the only reliable guide to word meaning. All languages are about fifty percent redundant (Nida 1972:74), that is, information in a spoken or written communication is repeated to a large extent to avoid misinterpretations. Examination of the contexts in which a word occurs, therefore, will usually enable a correct definition to be made of its meaning because the contexts are likely to repeat some of the information conveyed by the word. It is imperative to pay close attention to the collocations, especially synonyms and antonyms, since these indicate which meaning of a word is intended in a specific passage. The context disambiguates the meaning of a polysemous word.

Because of the large number of occurrences of brk (402; see Table 1) examination of the contexts provides a clear picture of the word meanings. It is possible to determine the usual and unusual senses. For example, the noun běrākâ occurs seventy-one times. The rare meaning "praise" (only Neh 9:5 and 2 Chr 20:26) is identified only by the collocations těhillâ and běrak "to praise."

Methodology and Etymology

When only a few contexts are available, the context still plays the major role, though it should be remembered that we are perhaps seeing only one meaning of a polysemous word, and possibly a rare meaning of the word. The word šaʿaṭnēz well illustrates the supreme importance of the context for rare words. It occurs only in Lev 19:19 and Deut 22:11. There is no definite etymological information about the word (which is not determinative anyway), but the contexts and collocations enable a certain definition to be made. It is found in apposition to "(cloth) made of two kinds of material," and with "wool and flax together" in apposition to it. Both occurrences are in contexts prohibiting mixing different kinds of animals and plants. The word therefore must mean "mixed material, material made of two kinds of fabric." However, in general, etymology usually is more important for determining the meaning of rare words (on the role of etymology see further 1.2).

Structural semanticists have developed the method of componential analysis (also called lexical decomposition), patterned after phonological analysis (Nida 1975, Lyons 1977:1.317-335, Kedar 1981:187-189, Silva 1983:132-135). This technique attempts to define the essential components of meaning that make up a word. For example, the components of ʿăqārâ "barren woman" are human, adult, female, married, and childless. Each component is usually a member of a binary opposition, i.e., animate or inanimate, male or female, etc. The similarities and differences between words are determined by comparing their components. In addition to the components, the word's connotations must be listed. Connotations are the emotions and "overtones" associated with a word. It is important for the meaning of ʿăqārâ that the word has the connotations of divine displeasure and social stigma.

Componential analysis is most useful for referential words, i.e., words such as technical terms and names that designate a specific person, thing, or other entity. With strongly referential words the reference and referent are nearly identical; there is a strong link between the word and the referent. The biblical brk derivatives are not strongly referential, so componential analysis is of limited value for their study. However, the connotations are of the utmost importance for the meanings of the brk words. The connotations distinguish their meanings from the meanings of other words which are synonyms in that they have similar referents, but which have different connotations.

Determination of the range of application of a word is often important for determining its meaning. For example, it is significant for the meanings of ptḥ and pqḥ that ptḥ can be used for opening many things besides the eyes (doors, sacks, the mouth, etc.) while pqḥ is used once for opening the ears and elsewhere always for opening the eyes. Because of the limited corpus of biblical Hebrew texts, the range of application of a word can often only be stated tentatively. We often cannot know the full range of possible contexts in which a word could occur, or all the contexts in which it could not occur. Yet because of the large number of occurrences of *brk* in the Bible (see Table 1), it is possible to define its range of application with some precision. The meaning of *brk* is to a large extent dependent on whether the blesser is God or man, and whether the object is God, or a man, or an animal, plant, or thing, so analysis of the range of application for each meaning is quite important.

Semanticists have developed the notion of the semantic field, which is of major importance for word studies (Zgusta 1971:100-111, Lehrer 1974, Vassilyev 1974, Lyons 1977:230-269, Kedar 1981:181-187, Silva 1983:161-163,176-177). A semantic field is the set of words used to denote a concept, such as blessing. The concept is designated by at least several words; languages generally never have only one word or phrase for a concept. *brk* is *not* the only root used for the concept of blessing, though it is the chief one; there are other synonymous words and phrases.

A word's meaning can be defined much more precisely when it is compared and contrasted with other words in the field than when it is considered in isolation. For example, within the concept of color, the meaning of "red" is much clearer when red is viewed in a spectrum and contrasted with the other colors than when red is viewed by itself. It is best to include in the definition of each word a comparison with the other words in the semantic field. Only by doing this can one determine why a particular word, and not a related or synonymous word, is used in a particular instance, or if another word could have been used.

Works on semantics often use the example of color to illustrate the semantic field concept because the terms and their relationships can be defined precisely. Each color can be defined as light having a wavelength within certain limits. The colors also form a continuous spectrum with no overlap and no gaps between terms.

Unfortunately, most semantic fields are considerably more complex than that of color. The meanings of words can overlap to various degrees. A word's meaning can be wholly subsumed within another word's meaning. There also can be gaps between terms, where a language has no word for a thing or an idea. Polysemous words can have meanings in several semantic fields. Care must be taken to use only those meanings of polysemous words that fall in the field under study when comparing the words in the field.

The problem of defining the relationship between words within a semantic field is further complicated in biblical Hebrew by the relatively small number of occurrences of many words. It is often difficult to discern the differences between close synonyms, or to see the similarities between distant synonyms, if the full range of a word's meaning is not visible in the limited number of occurrences.

Partially because of these problems, and partially because biblical scholars have only recently become aware of the field approach, most biblical Hebrew lexical studies have examined a single word or root, rather than one or more semantic fields. A semantic field study of *brk* has not yet been done (though see 6:8 for a discussion of works that treat synonyms and antonyms of *brk*). I will discuss synonyms and antonyms to the *brk* words in chapters three through five as they appear as collocations in the texts. In 6.8 I will discuss a few close synonyms of God blessing man.

The final development in semantics that I will mention as relevant for the study of *brk* is the area of speech-act semantics. John Austin's *How To Do Things With Words* (1962) inaugurated the study of how language performs actions (see also more recently Katz 1977, Lyons 1977:725-745, Kempson 1977:47-75, Bach and Harnish 1979, Fodor 1980:21-27, 49-58). Speech-act semantics concentrates on what utterances do, rather than on their propositional content.

An utterance used to perform an action is called a performative utterance. Such utterances have an illocutionary force, and can also have a perlocutionary force.[2] By pronouncing an illocutionary utterance, a person thereby accomplishes an action. Modern examples of illocutionary utterances are marriage ceremonies and legal oaths. When a person says "I pronounce you husband and wife," or "I swear," he thereby *does* marry a couple or put himself under oath. Other examples of illocutionary speech acts are promises, the act of naming, legal declarations, and oral blessings and curses.

Perlocutionary utterances seek to affect other people. They can be intended to elicit an action from the person addressed, as with most commands and requests, or simply to affect their mental state, as with condolences and assurances. Many utterances have both an illocutionary and a perlocutionary force. When a person says "thank you," he thereby

---

[2]Most recent semanticists reject the notion of locutionary utterances as defined by Austin (1962) because the definition uses circular reasoning. See Lyons 1977:2.730 and Fodor 1980:21-22. However, Bach and Harnish (1979) defend a definition of locutionary utterances.

does give thanks (the illocutionary force), but he does so in order to make the other person feel appreciated (the perlocutionary force). Similarly, blessings and curses, though illocutionary utterances, are often pronounced in order to affect the addressee in some way.

The fact that oral blessings are illocutionary utterances is quite important for understanding their effectiveness and how they are accomplished. Many erroneous conclusions about blessing have been drawn because the illocutionary force of blessings has been misunderstood. The perlocutionary force of blessings is also extremely important for a proper understanding of what blessing means. The significance of some blessings lies primarily in their perlocutionary force.

1.2 The Etymology of brk

The role of etymology in the determination of word meaning has been the topic of considerable debate among lexicographers. A few remarks about its role are in order here.

Biblical scholars have often misused etymology by giving it the primary or sole role in determining word meaning at the expense of the context. James Barr's *The Semantics of Biblical Language* (1961) used sound linguistic principles to refute the etymological abuse rampant in some scholarly circles.[3] Barr stressed the priority of the context over etymology, and argued that etymology was irrelevant for synchronic meaning.[4] Etymology was only important for historical studies of word meaning and lexical (meaning) change.

Many semantic theorists who are not involved in biblical studies share Barr's view. Lyons (1977:1.244), for example, remarks:

> All too often in the past, grammarians and lexicographers have taken texts from widely separated periods and treated them as samples of the same language. A particular manifestation of the failure to respect the distinction of the diachronic and the synchronic in semantics . . . is what might be called the etymological fallacy: the common belief that the meaning of words can be determined by investigating their

---

[3] Barr's work (1961) is primarily aimed at the "biblical theology" movement and *TDNT* in particular.
[4] Though Barr (1961) did recognize that "the use of words is often deeply influenced by their past history of use" (108), he generally neglected this fact throughout his book.

origins. The etymology of a lexeme is, in principle, synchronically irrelevant.

The Semantics of Biblical Language and particularly Barr's subsequent work, *Comparative Philology and the Text of the Old Testament* (1968), offer a wealth of sound methodological information in addition to appropriate rebuttals. Biblical scholars who have studied *brk* have often succumbed to a form of the etymological fallacy which Barr (1961:100-106) has dubbed the "root fallacy": the belief that meanings of all words derived from a root contain the "kernel meaning" of the root. Biblical Hebrew words derived from a root often do all have similar meanings in which one fundamental idea is present. The fallacy is to assume that there *must* be a fundamental meaning. Many groups of words have no such "kernel meaning." Word meanings should not be made to include an original root meaning unless there is good synchronic evidence that the original meaning is still present.

Words often acquire a special meaning in certain contexts. A specialized meaning acquired in a certain context is called a transferred sense, specialized sense, or contextual nuance (on these terms and their precise meanings see Zgusta 1971:62-64, 70-73). For example, *mattānâ* can denote any sort of gift or present. However, when it is used in a cultic context to denote something given to God, it specifically means "an offering." It would be wrong, though, to assume it means "an offering" when it is used in non-cultic contexts, as in Qoh 7:7 where the context indicates it means "a bribe." Assuming that different meanings of a polysemous word are in fact the same ("offering" equals "bribe") is an example of what Barr (1961:218) calls "illegitimate identity transfer." Assuming that all meanings of a word are included in a single occurrence of the word (*mattānâ* in a given verse means "present," "offering," and "bribe" all at the same time) has been labeled by Barr (1961:218) "illegitimate totality transfer."

However, etymology can play a more significant role in word meaning than Barr and Lyons indicate. The meaning of certain types of words can be strongly influenced by their etymology (Kedar 1981:88-98, Silva 1983:38-51). While the general principle of the priority of synchronic evidence (such as context, range of application, etc.) over diachronic evidence for determining meaning must never be abandoned, "historical considerations may be of synchronic value, but only if we can demonstrate that the speaker was aware of them" (Silva 1983:48).

Modern scientific terms, for example, are frequently coined using Latin and Greek words, so that the etymological meaning is the basis for the modern meaning. Transparent words are words whose origins have helped determine their later form or use, *and* whose origins are still obvious to the typical speaker. For example, *mar‘ît* "pasture" is clearly derived from *r‘h* "to tend (animals); to graze." As long as the origins of such words remain obvious to the average speaker, these words will tend to retain their etymological meaning. Finally, words that are important to a school of thought, such as a literary movement or a religious tradition, often retain a meaning from a certain period of history for a considerable length of time. The meaning of words in a revered literary work such as the Bible can become normative for later speakers.

The essential question, then, in evaluating the worth of etymological information about *brk* is whether the biblical use of the word indicates that the authors were influenced by prior use of the root. The biblical use of the root is quite similar to its use in other NW Semitic languages. However, the biblical authors give no indication that they are drawing upon other literatures for the meaning of *brk*. The root has a greater range of meaning in the Bible than in extra-biblical NW Semitic texts, indicating that the biblical authors developed to some extent the earlier NW Semitic meanings. The biblical contents are quite satisfactory by themselves for elucidating the meanings, and there is an abundance of biblical contexts. All things considered, then, the etymology is useful for background information and for comparison to biblical use, but it is *not* useful for determining the biblical meanings of the *brk* derivatives.[5]

The meanings of the root *brk* "to bless" in Arabic, and the root *brk* "to kneel" have influenced modern interpreters much more than they influenced biblical authors; there is no evidence that the biblical authors considered *brk* "to bless" related to *brk* "to kneel," or that they were influenced by the Arabic meanings of either root.

The pre-Islamic concept of blessing in Arabic was animistic (Chelhod 1955). The noun *baraka* denoted the power which gave prosperity, abundance, health, and good fortune. This power inhabited certain plants, animals, and objects. The tribal chief, or a father, or a holy man could help procure this power for the tribe. Originally, the bestowal of this power had nothing to do with any god, but the Koran, probably under Northwest Semitic influence, ascribed the bestowal of this power solely to Allah (Chelhod 1955:85, Jeffrey 1938:75). The animistic and the theistic

---

[5]There are indications within the Bible that later authors drew on the meanings of *brk* in earlier biblical books; see Isa 51:2 compared to the Abraham narratives; Ps 72:17 and Jer 4:2 compared to Gen 12:3; 18:18; 22:17; 26:4; 28:14 (see Table 2); and Ps 67:2 compared to Num 6:24-26.

conceptions coexisted in the religion of the common people (Chelhod 1955:87-88).
There is no good evidence for an etymological connection between the Arabic verbal forms of brk "to kneel," used most often of camels, and Arabic brk "to bless," or between either of these roots and the Arabic noun forms meaning "pool" (so also Scharbert 1975:284; cf. Blachère 1967:1.567-575). Wehmeier (1970:12,17) accepts Chelhod's association of brk "kneel" with brk "bless," and claims that the blessing power originally was either the bodily power to stand up, or was the power of good fortune which resulted in numerous camels (since bark could denote both a group of kneeling camels and prosperity in general, Chelhod 1955:78). However, these proposed original meanings of blessing power appear to be the result of etymologizing; there are no explicit statements which equate the blessing power with either of them.
The Akkadian verb karābu has a range of meaning strikingly similar to that of brk "to bless" in the Bible (CAD 8.192-198, von Soden 1965:1.445-446, Landsberger 1929). It is used for gods pronouncing formulas of blessing; for people blessing and greeting others, and praying to the gods; for people praising and worshipping the gods and kings; and for dedicating and consecrating offerings. The meanings of the nouns karābu and ikribu correspond to the verbal meanings; they can denote an oral blessing or benediction, a prayer, and (ikribu) and offering (CAD 7.62-66 and 8.192). However, in spite of the close similarity in meaning to NW Semitic brk "to bless," it is unlikely that the two are etymologically related; metathesis of the first and third radicals of a root is extremely rare. Akkadian krb is instead probably related to old South Arabic krb "to consecrate, to sacrifice" (see further Toll 1982:114, Wehmeier 1970:14-15, Keller 1978:353).
Akkadian provides no evidence that brk "to bless" and brk "to kneel" are etymologically related. Akkadian birku is cognate to Hebrew berek "knee." Besides the usual meaning "knee," birku can mean "strength" as well as "womb," and, euphemisticlaly, the genitals (CAD 2.255-257, von Soden 1965:1.129). Wehmeier suggests (1970:11-12) that the semantic development of běrākâ could have followed that of ʾôn, which signifies both "bodily strength, reproductive power," and "riches, wealth." However, the agreement between the meanings of birku and the meanings of běrākâ is rather limited and there is insufficient evidence for a firm etymological connection (so also Toll 1982:113-115, though his methodology relies upon the biliteral root theory and is generally suspicicious; contra Murtonen 1959:176; Keller 1978:353 is undecided).
Studies of brk in the extra-biblical Northwest Semitic languages have shown that the use of brk in these languages is quite similar to that in the

Bible (Wehmeier 1970:18-66, Schottroff 1969:178-198). *brk* occurs in verbal forms meaning "bless" as well as "kneel", and in noun forms meaning "blessing" as well as "knee," and also "pool." The relative frequency is also similar to the bibilical situation, with "bless" the most frequent meaning, then "kneel" and "knee," while "pool" is the least frequent. The studies done have found no conclusive evidence for a common original root for these three meanings (Wehmeier 1970:65-66, Schottroff 1969:178).

When *brk* "bless" is employed as a finite verb, the vast majority of passages have a god or gods as subject and a man or men as object. Blessing denotes the bestowal of long life, numerous progeny, wealth, and/or strength. When the verb is used in a greeting with a man (usually the author of a letter) as subject, blessing constitutes an entreaty for the gods to bless the person to whom the greeting is extended.

The major difference between the biblical and extra-biblical use of *brk* in NW Semitic is that the root is used for the praise of divinities only in Palmyrene dedication formulas from the second to fourth centuries A.D., aside from post-biblical Jewish literature (for the details see Wehmeier 1970:59-62,66; 1971:33-34; Schottroff 1969:186-187). The Palmyrene inscriptions use the G passive participle with a god or a god's name as subject. The most frequent form of formula is *bryk šmh lʿlmʾ*, "may his (a god's) name be praised forever", which is quite similar to the *bārûk* formula of Psalm 72:19 and the *mĕbōrak/mĕbārak* formulas of Ps 113:2 and Dan 2:20 with Yahweh's name (*šēm*) as subject. Most authors have concluded that the Palmyrene use of *brk* is due to Jewish (biblical) influence (so Wehmeier 1970:66, 1971:33-34; see the discussion in Schottroff 1969:87 note 5, who himself is undecided). The use of *brk* for the praise of God, then, is an entirely inner-biblical development.

There have been numerous unconvincing attempts to find an etymological link between *brk* "to bless" and *brk* "to kneel," and *bĕrēkâ* "pool." I will briefly mention the most important of these.

A major problem in evaluating proposed etymologies is the paucity of definitive criteria for evaluation. The area of lexical change is one of the more difficult branches of semantics. Often there is no way to prove the course of development that a word's meaning followed when the evidence is fragmentary and discontinuous, as it is in the case of the NW Semitic languages. "There are no absolute criteria for plausibility . . . one can develop a basis for plausibility judgements by comparing changes that are known to have occurred with those that are to be accepted" (Jeffers and Lehiste 1979:133, who treat a number of types of lexical change in pp 126-137; see also Bynon 1977:61-63 and Kedar 1981:134-165). Cultural

Methodology and Etymology

values and customs must be taken into account in assessing the probability of a semantic association (Bynon 1977:63).

In addition to citing analoguous examples of lexical change, a good study should trace all the words in a semantic field. Lexical change is often due to influence from other words in the field. When one word changes meaning, it may displace another word, and its former place may need to be filled, causing yet another word to change meaning (Jeffers and Lehiste 1979:129, Silva 1983:53-54; Kedar 1981:140 discusses some Hebrew examples; Silva 1983:53-97 discusses Hebrew and Greek examples and the influence of the Septuagint). These types of influences can only be detected by the field approach. Unfortunately, none of the following studies employs field theory.

Plassmann (1913) devoted a monograph to constructing an etymology of *brk* leading from Arabic usage to biblical usage. Unfortunately, the book is full of etymologizing explanations, such as the following passage where he explains how the basic meaning of *brk* denoting camels kneeling was extended:

> the Arab bedouin's life is one of idleness. In his tent he passes many an hour in drowsy reverie, as his eyes rest upon his faithful companion, the camel, lying immovably upon its breast, and affording a perfect picture of firmness, stability, and continuance. Such a picture would naturally come to his mind whenever he wished to express these qualities in reference to other objects. They thus came to constitute the dominant elements in the meanings of the verb (32).

BDB (138b-139a) associates the Piel of *brk* "bless" meaning "to praise (God)" with *brk* "to kneel" by giving the first meaning of the Piel as "bless God, adore with bended knees." This association is improbable because *brk* "bless" and *brk* "kneel" already have their distinct meanings in Ugaritic, while the meaning "praise," unattested in Ugaritic, developed later in biblical Hebrew from "bless" (see further under 5.1). "Praise" did not develop from "kneel" (see further below).

Mowvley (1965) advocates a different connection between *brk* "bless" and *berek* "knee." He develops Pedersen's (1926:204 note 1) suggestion that the expression "born on the knees" refers to children who were adopted as legitimate although born by a slave rather than by the father's legitimate wife, as in Gen 30:3, or by a non-Israelite wife, as in Gen 48:5,12. Children are born "on the knees" of their true mother (Job 3:12), and so the expression denotes the natural genetic relationship between parent and child. Mowvley concludes "the connection . . . is . . . that children were born on the knees and this was considered to be a great blessing" (1965:75).

Mowvley does not satisfactorily explain exactly why the knees would have been associated with blessing. The knees have nothing to do with the adoption or the benediction in Gen 48, though the expression clearly does signify adoption in Gen 30:3. Children certainly are viewed as blessings, but there are no verses specifically linking the adoption ceremony with this view of children. Children in general, not just those "born on the knees," or adopted, are a blessing.

It is intriguing that the idea of giving birth on the knees as a sign of adoption or legitimization is also found in classical Greek texts (Onians 1954:174-182). The meanings "knee," "generative organ," and "race, generation" are attested for Greek *gonu* and other ancient Indo-European words for "knee," a range of meaning which closely parallels that of Akkadian *birku*. There is, however, no clear evidence in the Indo-European languages either for an etymological connection between knee and blessing.

Murtonen (1959:176) suggests that *bĕrākâ* is "closely connected with the blessing brought about by rain and springs or wells." This leaves unexplained why *bĕrēkâ* is used specifically for pools and not for other sources of water, such as springs or rain, or for water itself.

It is possible that kneeling at pools to drink gave rise to the name for "pool." Gen 24:11 describes how camels were made to kneel (Hiphil of *brk*) beside a well, though the term for well there is *bĕ'ēr*, not *bĕrēkâ*. Judg 7:5-6 describes how most people knelt on their knees (*yikraʿ ʿal birkāyw*) to drink, although there *mayim*, not *bĕrēkâ*, is used to denote the water. These verses show that the practice was common, and so a semantic association is possible. Yet no biblical or extra-biblical texts explicitly associate kneeling denoted by *brk* with *bĕrēkâ*.

It is significant that three of the four occurrences of *brk* "kneel" in the Bible are in forms unattested for *brk* "bless," the finite Qal (Ps 95:5; 2 Chr 6:13), and the Hiphil (Gen 24:11). The Aramaic Peal participle occurs in Dan 6:11 with "on his knees" appended. There is little possibility of confusing the two roots because of the different forms used.

A connection between *berek* "knee" and *brk* "bless," which can have the nuance of "worship (God)" (see Chapter Five), has been postulated because of several passages where persons kneel on their knees in worship, prayer, or entreaty (1 Kgs 8:54; 18:42 (the head between the knees in prayer); 19:18; 2 Kgs 1:13; Ps 95:6; 2 Chr 6:13; Ezra 9:5; Isa 45:23). The verb used is *krʿ* except for 1 Kgs 18:42 where it is *ghr* and 2 Chr 6:13; Ps 95:6 where

Methodology and Etymology

it is *brk*. The verses describe the custom of kneeling to humble oneself before a superior and thereby show respect and reverence. Again, this is no warrant for assuming that the roots have an etymological connection.

Finally, Toll (1982) serves as an example of how fanciful etymological proposals can become, and how they can be published even in the most prestigious of journals (*ZAW*). Toll starts by proposing the meaning "penetrate, have sexual intercourse with" for *prṣ* in the obscure verse Hos 4:10. Following the biliteral root theory, the original root *pr-* is equivalent to *br-*, so that the original meaning of *brk* is also "to penetrate (sexually)", "to have sexual power or virility", which explains how blessing produces fertility! Furthermore, *běrēkâ* is derived from *brk* "to penetrate" because a pool is a hole in the ground. Toll also proposes similar semantic developments for other words denoting power.

1.3   Conclusions Concerning the Etymology of brk

The original use of *brk* in NW Semitic was for god(s) blessing man, i.e., bestowing children, wealth, etc. The other uses clearly derive from this original use.

There is really no support for the almost universal assumption that the original view of blessing in NW Semitic was an animistic conception akin to the pre-Islamic Arabic conception associated with *baraka* (contra Wehmeir 1970:17,65-66 and 1971:40, Keller 1978:355; Plassmann 1913, Pedersen 1926, Hempel 1961, Mowinckel 1961). There are hardly any NW Semitic texts where an animistic interpretation is even remotely possible. It is unwarranted to assume that Arabic preserves the original meaning simply because the religion and the concept of blessing are "more primitive", i.e., further removed from monotheism. The Arabic blessing conception was conformed to the animistic Arabic religion, and when under Islam the religion becamse monotheistic, the blessing concept followed suit. The extant extra-biblical NW Semitic texts present a thoroughly polytheistic view of blessing in conformity to the religion of the people.

The use of *brk* for man blessing man clearly developed from the first use for gods blessing man, since it constitutes an entreaty for the gods to bless the person whom the human subject "blesses." The use of *brk* in the praise of God is a subsequent, inner-biblical development arising from the use of *brk* in human benedictions (see further under 1.2, 5.1 and 5.4).

The frequency of the different meanings of *brk* changes with time. Twelve of the thirteen occurrences of *brk* in Ugaritic denote gods blessing men, with one occurrence denoting a human benediction. The frequency of human blessings increases in later NW Semitic texts. In the Bible, *brk* occurs with approximately equal frequency denoting God blessing men, men blessing others, and men praising God, with the last meaning most frequent in later biblical books. In post-biblical Hebrew, the praise of God becomes the dominant use of *brk* (see further under 5.1 and 5.4). However, this shift in distribution through time is probably not due to the development of the different meanings; all three meanings are present in the oldest biblical texts (cf. Gen 14:19-20; Deut 33:20,24; Judg 5:2,9,24). Rather, it is due to the change in subject matter of the texts.

There is no firm evidence in any Semitic language for an etymological connection between *brk* "bless" and *brk* "kneel" or *brk* "pool."

2
History of the Interpretation of Blessing

The chief questions about blessing scholars have sought to answer are:
1) What does blessing consist of?
2) What is the purpose of blessing?
3) How does blessing operate?

Some scholars have not given a single answer to each of these questions. They give separate answers depending upon whether God or man blesses, whether God or man is the object of blessing, and whether the blessing is a physical action or a speech act. In this chapter, I will only discuss the six major authors who have addressed these questions; I will not include the numerous shorter articles that repeat the results of these major authors, nor works that address other questions such as the lexical meaning of *brk* or its etymology.

The first detailed attempts to answer these questions were made in the 1920's. Pedersen (1926:182-212), Mowinckel (1961), and Hempel (1961) (originally published in 1920, 1924, and 1925 respectively) applied the methods of the History of Religion school to blessing.

2.1   Johannes Pedersen

Pedersen's work (1926) has been especially influential. To understand Pedersen's view of blessing, one must first understand his view of the soul (pp 99-181). "Soul" for Pedersen is a translation of *nepeš*, though the words *rûaḥ* and *lēb* can also denote the soul, or certain aspects of it (102). The soul is the total state of being of a person; man, in his total essence, *is* a soul (99). The soul is filled with a power which enables it to grow, thrive, and accomplish its work. The soul is a connected whole characterized by volition and action. These two are never separated, so that inactive, theoretical thinking without subsequent action is impossible for the Israelite; "the Israelite manner of thinking is of a different kind from ours" (106). All thoughts and energies of the soul are directed toward action, and "the action and its accomplishment are a matter of course, once the thought is there" (128). This notion leads to Pedersen's view of the "magical," i.e., self-fulfilling, automatic nature of blessing.

Pedersen defines blessing *(bĕrākâ)* as the power which fills the soul. It is the power of life and growth (182). At the same time, blessing denotes the success and happiness produced by the power, since the Israelite does not distinguish between the inner power and its outward manifestation. Examples of such manifestations are the giving of good counsel, wisdom, insight, prosperity, success, and military victory. Pedersen summarizes his conception of what blessing is by saying "the blessing comprises everything in life" (211); it is "the entire power of life, the strength underlying all progress and self-expansion" (212).

Pedersen does not investigate why God or people bless, except to mention that people bless each other as a necessary prerequisite for establishing relationships (202), or to influence other people by pouring their will into other people's souls (185 discussing David). Pedersen is primarily concerned with the third question, "How does blessing operate?"

Pedersen sees the act of blessing as a transfer of soul power. When God blesses a person, he increases the power of the person's soul. God's blessing is not so much a bestowal of fertility, wealth, etc., as it is a strengthening of the person's soul enabling him to promote fertility and acquire wealth by his own ability (192,195). Pedersen claims that God's power and the person's soul combine to such an extent that they can no longer be distinguished. Gideon, for example, saved the Israelites by his own power, which was the same as Yahweh's power (195).

Human blessings are also a transfer of soul power, whether they consist of a greeting, a material gift, or the benediction of a dying father. The blesser gives the recipient a part of his own soul. Physical contact, such as laying on of hands or kissing, is generally necessary for the proper transmission of the soul (200-201).

When humans bless God, they strengthen God and praise him. Blessing God signifies the "praising and corroboration of his wealth" (204). Pedersen does not expand upon these brief remarks about man blessing God.

In general, Pedersen sees blessing as a self-fulfilling power. An oral blessing cannot be revoked because it has been created by the power of the soul of the one who pronounced it. Once the blessing is uttered, "it must act by the power which has been put into it" (200). Pedersen spends a good deal of time describing how the blessing that an individual possesses determines his fate throughout his life, and uses the word "blessing" as an equivalent of "fate" and "destiny."

There are several problems with Pedersen's views. His assertions about the Israelite manner of thought and the workings of the soul are quite dubious. His terminology is mystical and at times unclear. Because he feels that the Israelites perceived of everything as "totalities" and "connected wholes," he defines nothing precisely, and his concepts run together.

Pedersen's mysticism leads to a confusion on the lexical level. He does not distinguish between the reference of a word and its referents. Pedersen equates the "manifestations" of blessing with blessing itself, when in fact they are referents of blessing only under certain conditions. For example, Pedersen views good counsel as an equivalent of blessing. This leads him to call Ahithophel (2 Sam 15-17) a blessed person, since he gave excellent counsel. David and Hushai prevailed over Ahithophel only because their blessing was greater than his (183-184). However, Ahithophel was not a blessed person; God was determined to break his counsel (2 Sam 17:14), and Ahitholphel neither succeeded nor had God with him, both of which Pedersen cites elsewhere as essential characteristics of a blessed person (194-197).

The problem with Pedersen's view, then, is that the "manifestations" are really blessings only under certain conditions. Pedersen defines everything positive in life as part of the lexical meaning of *brk* (211-212). His definition is much too broad and vague. There needs to be a clearer definition of when good things can and cannot be called blessings.

There is little evidence for Pedersen's contention that blessing operates by means of soul power. God's blessing is not normally accomplished by strengthening the souls of men. For example, Pedersen's assertion that "there is no question of any distinction between the strength of Gideon and that of Yahweh" (195) is untenable. Judg 7:13-22 emphasizes that it was God, not Gideon, who caused the Midianites to dream of defeat and who made them turn against each other. There is no indication that Gideon had the power within himself to induce dreams into the minds of the sleeping Midianites. It is also difficult to imagine how the strength of a man's soul could produce the blessings of fertility in his wife, animals, and crops.

Likewise, human blessings do not rely upon soul power. The benedictions given by the dying patriarchs, for example, hardly show that the Israelites derived their souls from their forefathers and passed on blessing "like a family heirloom through the souls" (193). Instead, these benedictions are based upon legal societal practices (see 4.1.1). Like most types of human blessings, the patriarchal benedictions usually called upon God to bless. The transfer of blessing cannot be accomplished by human power alone.

2.2 Sigmund Mowinckel

Sigmund Mowinckel (1961, originally published in 1924)[1] adopted Pedersen's views of blessings as his starting point (p 5 note 1). Mowinckel's contribution is that he gives an extended analysis of blessing in the cult, and develops Pedersen's ideas about man blessing God.

Mowinckel defines blessing as consisting of all that man desires (131). When the Psalms do occasionally specify exactly what blessings are, they are usually related to outward prosperity and consist of such things as fertility, protection from demons, and tranquility. Like Pedersen, Mowinckel sees these as manifestations of the healthy condition of the righteous man's soul (131).

Mowinckel devotes much of his attention to the purposes of human blessings. He considers the cult to be the central element of Israelite religion. The purpose of the cult, and religion in general, was to procure blessing for the people (130-131). The high point of the cult was the annual festivals. The blessing given by the cult officiant to the congregation at the conclusion was the most important part of the festivals. The words of blessing (Num 6:24-26) audibly and tangibly bestowed the divine benefits upon the people (130). Blessing was transmitted by the cult in this way because of the belief that no religious act was permanently effective. Prayers, sacrifices, and blessings had to be repeated periodically. By doing so at the annual festivals, the blessing power was continually renewed for the community (13).

The purpose of man blessing God was to increase the blessing power available to the community. The cultic praises and thanksgiving strengthened the divinity's soul, so that when the community partook of the sacrificial animals, which contained the divinity, they would ingest a greater amount of divine power (23-28). However, Mowinckel says that in time the Israelite divinity increasingly became a personal, transcendent God with independent volition. Sacrifice then became simply a testimony to the pious attitude of the worshippers (42). Blessing became a gift that God

---

[1] *Psalmenstudien V.* is Mowinckel's most thorough treatment of blessing. His more recent works give condensed versions of his views (1953:55-56,64-66; 1962:44-52).

bestowed upon the pious. The priestly blessing formulas became prayers for God to bless. All extant blessings in the Bible have been to some extent "Yahwistized" into prayers (31,50-58).

The purpose of man blessing God also changed. Because God became the sole bestower of blessing, man could no longer bless God. The meaning of brk with man as subject and God as object became purely "praise, thank" (132).

Mowinckel makes several valuable points. It is certainly correct that the acquisition of blessing was one of the chief purposes of the cult, though Mowinckel's explanation of how it was acquired is questionable. Unlike Pedersen, Mowinckel correctly recognized that blessing became solely the gift of God. It could not be acquired by magic; God only bestowed it upon the pious in accordance with the covenant and in response to prayer. Man could not increase God's power by blessing him; he could only praise and thank God.

Mowinckel's picture of the final stage of blessing in the OT represents a substantial improvement over Pedersen's unsatisfactory views. However, this "final stage" accurately describes much more of the OT than Mowinckel claims. It is unfortunate that Mowinckel applied Pedersen's ideas to the majority of the OT.

2.3 Johannes Hempel

Hempel's goal (1961, originally published in 1925) is to trace the evolution of the Israelite beliefs concerning blessing and curse throughout the OT. He believes that Mowinckel overemphasized the role of the cult (30-31).

Hempel defines blessing in a manner similar to Pedersen (55-66). He calls both the blessing power and its manifestations blessings, saying both "Segen ist Leben und Gedeihen" (55) and "Segen Leben und Gedeihen . . . bringt" (61). He also says that the entire content of blessing is summed up in the word šālôm, which he defines as the state of complete prosperity, wholeness and security (58-61).

Clearly blessing needs to be defined more precisely than Hempel does. Is blessing a force, or the physical benefits produced by a force, or is it a state of being, or some combination of these possibilities?

Hempel denies Mowinckel's claim that the purpose of blessing God in the Bible was to increase God's power, and says that although this was the original purpose of the blessing formulas, they no longer had this purpose in the biblical texts (96-97).

Hempel describes the manner in which blessing operated in three historical stages. In the period of folk religion, blessing was magical and self-fulfilling (31-55). In the cultic period, blessing was no longer magical, but still required ceremonies and oral formulas to prompt God to bless (67-100). In the period of ethical monotheism, blessing was completely independent of magic and the cult; the cult was no longer able to influence God. God requited blessing and curse based on the ethical values proclaimed by the prophets (100-113).

Hempel's three stages are practically equivalent to Mowinckel's two stages because Mowinckel claimed that ethical monotheism, with blessing being a reward for the pious, developed *within* the cult. Mowinckel marshalls convincing evidence for his view (1961:97-112,131-132).

There are two chief difficulties with Hempel's evolutionary approach. First, Hempel does not convincingly demonstrate the existence of the folk religion stage in the Bible. Although his cultic and ethical stages of blessing are based upon explicit biblical texts, Hempel relies upon emendations and unwarranted assumptions to construct the folk religion stage. For example, Hempel cites Josh 6:26 and 1 Kgs 16:34 to illustrate the self-fulfilling nature of the curse (31-32). Hiel loses two of his sons when he rebuilds Jerico. Hempel arbitrarily ascribes the phrase "before Yahweh" in Joshua's curse, which indicates that Joshua is invoking God to effect the curse, to a later redactor (75). To prove the magical origin of blessing Hempel cites Gen 48:15-22 (35). He describes Jacob's words as having a religious tone, that is, they call upon God to bless. However, Jacob proceeds to lay his hands on his grandsons, with the right hand signifying the greater blessing. Hempel sees this gesture as an indication that the rite was originally magical; the words and actions themselves imparted the blessing with no help from God. However, this gesture simply illustrates a social custom which need not have expressed magical beliefs any more than a handshake with the right hand does today.

Secondly, Hempel does not convincingly demonstrate the evolution of blessing from the level of magic to ethical monotheism. Hempel overemphasizes the differences between cultic blessings and blessings as a reward for ethical piety. The formulas and rites used with cultic blessings are based on religious traditions and social customs instead of magic. The differences that do exist do not necessarily imply that the views were incompatible; they may have coexisted. Also, just because the ethical view of blessing is farther removed from magic (according to Hempel) does not necessarily imply that the ethical view arose from the cultic view.

History of Interpretation   23

2.4   Claus Westermann

Westermann (1978, originally published in 1968) examines blessing using a tradition history approach. Like his predecessors he says that the oldest concept of blessing is visible in Gen 27, where blessing consists of the power of life, fertility, and prosperity (54). Later biblical traditions expanded the content of blessing. The Priestly blessing shows that P, which contains the latest stage in the development of the concept of blessing, included "God's friendly approach to those who will receive him" (43). Westermann recognizes that success, the presence of God, peace, and wisdom belong to the semantic field of blessing (28,37-39).

Westermann follows his predecessors' views about the magical operation of blessing in the earliest strata of the Bible (53-59). However, the Balaam narratives and J restricted the magical operation of blessing; Yahweh had the ability to control the magical power-laden words spoken by individuals and to use them to effect blessing as he wished. These two traditions theologized blessing by asserting that God was able to bless independently of magical rites. They also made blessing a part of salvation history by making God's promises of land and descendants a part of blessing (49-53).

The historical books tie the operation of blessing to the institutions of kingship and the cult. These institutions mediate God's blessing to the people (30-32). Westermann generally follows Mowinckel's views about cultic mediation of blessing in the Writings (34-37). Contrary to most scholars, Westermann sees blessing as an important part of prophecy. The purpose of the prophetic intercessions was to ensure that blessing continued for the people. The prophecies of salvation portrayed salvation as a state of blessing.

The main thesis of Westermann's work is that God blesses through his continual activity in promoting a prosperous state of being, and so blessing is a different form of God's activity than deliverance, which God accomplishes through occasional saving acts. The state of blessing is the result of an act of deliverance, and should not be equated with an act of deliverance (1-14).

I will evaluate Westermann's thesis in 6.7; it suffices to say here that the biblical traditions, particularly the patriarchal narratives, Deuteronomy, and the prophetic apocalypses, do not make such a sharp distinction between blessing and deliverance.

Westermann's work is an impressive advance over the earlier History of Religion works. Westermann's tradition history approach enables him to highlight the distinctiveness of the blessing concept found in each tradition and to describe the contribution of each tradition to the development of the concept of blessing in the Bible. Unlike Hempel, Westermann does not feel compelled to squeeze the evidence into the Procrustean bed of a rigid evolutionary scheme.

Yet by the same token, Westermann does not present an integrated picture of blessing in the OT. He simply presents a series of descriptions of blessing in various traditions. The concepts of blessing in the traditions are not so disparate as to prevent a unified description of blessing throughout the OT.

2.5   Gerhard Wehmeier

Wehmeier's published dissertation *Der Segen im Alten Testament* (1970) is the most thorough study of *brk* in the OT. He employs a tradition history approach similar to Westermann's.

Wehmeier defines blessing as a power. It is "lebensförnde Kraft," "die Kraft des Wachstums und Gedeihens" (101). Like Pedersen, he says this power manifests itself in various ways, especially as the fertility of men, animals, and crops. The noun *bĕrākâ* can denote either the blessing power or its manifestations.

Wehmeier accepts the description of blessing as self-fulfilling due to the soul power of the blesser, which Pedersen, Mowinckel, and Hempel advocated, as the original concept of the operation of blessing in the Bible. However, he says that this original concept is still visible only in the oldest strata of three narratives, Gen 27 and 32:22-32, and the Balaam narrative. Later redactors have attempted to theologize the magical picture of blessing in these passages, but have not succeeded in obliterating it (189-198).

Wehmeier sees the chief contribution of J not so much as "Yahwistizing" blessing, as Westermann saw it, but as elevating God from being the God of fertility to being the God of blessing for all mankind. In Gen 12:1-3 the blessing promised for mankind replaces the earlier curse in Gen 3, and the fact that the promise is repeated twice (Gen 18:18; 28:14) shows how central the theme is for J. J describes Israel's role as being the mediator of God's blessing for all mankind. A few passages in the prophets develop this J theme. Isa 19:18-25 is the culmination of the theme (199-204, 218-224).

Wehmeier does not perceive a blessing theme in E, although *brk* does occasionally occur (205).

In D, the primary blessings are the prosperity of Israel in the promised land and her election as God's people. God is quite clearly pictured as the bestower of these blessings although he is not mentioned as the agent in the covenantal stipulations. Some blessing statements are conditional upon obedience, while others are unconditional. There is no conflict here: Israel need not look for other sources of blessing, and as long as she does not do so, she will receive God's blessings. God freely chooses to bless Israel, but only as long as she is obedient, and so grace (election) and obedience are combined. D also unites salvation and blessing by joining the Exodus tradition to the law given at Mt. Sinai. The Deuteronomic history portrays obedience as the necessary prerequisite for blessing (206-210).

P incorporates the blessing promise of numerous descendants from J and the promised land theme from D, and applies them to all mankind. Certain passages in P, notably the priestly blessing, spiritualize the content of blessing. Blessing consists of God's protection, his gracious attention, and his beneficent *(heilschaffende)* presence (211-218).

Wehmeier does not consider blessing to be a frequent prophetic theme, though he agrees with Westermann in seeing the idealistic descriptions of the original paradise, descriptions of God's present blessing, and pictures of the future *Heilzeit*, as belonging to the category of blessing even though they usually lack *brk*. The prophets specify faithfulness and obedience as prerequisites for blessing, but they preserve God's freedom; the prophets do not consider God obligated to bless anyone (218-224).

Wehmeier approvingly quotes Pedersen's (198) statement, "Wisdom is the same as blessing," and sees success and prosperity as the inseparable result of possessing wisdom. *brk* occurs primarily in the older strata of the wisdom literature because wisdom was later hypostatized, and wisdom cannot bless man, since the wisdom literature says that God alone can bestow blessing. The goods people possess are only blessings when people receive them as gifts from God. When people acquire goods through their own effort, the goods are not blessings. Human effort can achieve prosperity only, not blessing. In the descriptions of individual retribution, the wisdom literature pictures God as only the indirect agent of blessing. The laws of retribution are activated by God, but then become self-fulfilling. Blessing and curse are then the natural consequences of each individual's actions (224-227).

Wehmeier offers a much more detailed exposition of blessing in the various traditions than Westermann. Although he makes few completely new suggestions, the thoroughness and depth of his study makes it an essential reference work for further work on both the lexical meaning of *brk* and the theology of blessing.

Wehmeier succeeds to a somewhat greater degree than Westermann in presenting an integrated study of blessing in the Bible. For example, Wehmeier traces the J theme of blessing for all mankind into the prophets, and shows how the prophets developed the theme. Yet Wehmeier's study is still largely a presentation of diverse concepts of blessing from various strata of the Bible. The concepts of blessing are really not as disparate as Wehmeier's tradition history study indicates.

Wehmeier does not convincingly demonstrate the existence of the supposedly original magical, soul-power transfer concept of blessing in the Bible. He also misunderstands the illocutionary force of God's spoken benedictions (170). Though Wehmeier's discussion of the lexical meaning of *brk* is generally good, his treatments of some passages, and especially of *bārûk* and the Hithpael, are unsatisfactory.

2.6   Josef Scharbert

Josef Scharbert has given an important answer to the question of the purpose of blessing (see especially 1958b and 1975a). While Pedersen, Mowinckel and Hempel said the main purpose of blessing was to affect others by the power of words, Scharbert emphasizes that blessing makes a statement about the relationship between the blesser and the person blessed.

Scharbert develops his thesis most fully describing people blessing other people. He says that the utterance of the *bārûk* formula "is an acknowledgement of the solidarity that exists between the speaker and the person for whom the formula is intended" (1975a:284); it "is always a manifestation of an intimate relationship . . . or an acknowledgement of communion" (288). An oral benediction uttered by a person shows "the appreciation, gratitude, respect, joint relationship, or good will of the speaker" (293). Also when God is the object of a human blessing, the blessing shows solidarity and communion between that person and God (293-294,305). The people whom God blesses must deserve blessing because of "fidelity to Yahweh and his law," except for the patriarchs, whom Yahweh blessed "out of pure grace" (294). Non-Israelites receive God's blessing only when they bless, i.e., treat well, an Israelite, except in the P creation narrative, where all mankind and in fact all creatures are blessed by God.

Scharbert correctly identifies blessing as a term of relationship. The connotations of blessing imply that the parties involved have a certain positive relationship. His thesis provides a far more satisfactory answer to the question of the reason for blessing than the History of Religion authors. Yet there are many instances where blessing is not an expression of solidarity. This study will attempt to define the relational connotations of blessing so that they are still valid for the passages which are not explained by Scharbert's thesis. In addition, there are types of blessing that are primarily perlocutionary utterances and which cannot be explained as illocutionary declarations of a certain relationship between the blesser and person blessed. This study will attempt to define the perlocutionary force of such blessings.

3
God Blessing Man

This study divides the biblical occurrences of *brk* into three categories, based upon the range of application. Chapter Three treats passages where God promises to bless men, or which state that God blessed men. Chapter Four discusses passages where men bless other men and utter speech forms such as prayers, wishes, and greetings which call for God to bless others. Chapter Five treats passages where men "bless," or praise, God.

The majority of God's blessings are promises. I will discuss the promises before the narrative statements of God's blessings because many of the statements are fulfillments of the promises.

3.1.1 The Patriarchal Blessing Promises

God's purpose in issuing the patriarchal blessing promises is to call the patriarchs into a close relationship with himself. The promises of blessing are to motivate the patriarchs to obey God, leave their residences, and enter into a covenant with God. By blessing the patriarchs God moreover intends them to acquire fame and renown. Others will seek to establish good relations with the patriarchs so as to acquire blessing too. God promises to bless those who are on good terms with the patriarchs in order to fulfill his stated goal of blessing all the peoples of the earth.

God's purposes are evident in Gen 12:1-3. The passage is the foundation of the theme of blessing which "extends through the patriarchal stories like a red line" (von Rad 1972:165; see Table 2):

> Yahweh said to Abraham, "Go from your native country and your father's household to the land which I will show you. I will make you into a great nation, bless you, and make your name great, and you will be a source of blessing. I will bless

those on good terms with you, but I will curse those hostile toward you, and so through you all the peoples of the earth shall acquire blessing."

God promised to bless Abraham as an expression of his good will toward him. Blessing here is not a reward for Abraham's prior conduct. The immediate purpose of God's promise to Abraham was to draw Abraham into a covenant with himself. Gen 17 describes how God used the promise of the blessings of descendants and land to motivate Abraham to accept the covenant of circumcision. God details the blessings (vv 2-9) before stating the requirements of the covenant (vv 10-14).

God's long range purpose for issuing the blessing promises was to bless all peoples. God called Abraham[1] to be a source of blessing (bĕrākâ, 12:2). Though the noun could denote a recipient of blessing (so Driver 1905:144, as in Ezek 34:26, Ps 37:26, Prov 10:7), or a proverbial example of a blessed person (so Scharbert 1958a:25-26 and Wehmeier 1970:88, as in Zech 8:13; cf. Gen 48:20), the most suitable meaning here is "source of blessing" (so BDB 139b and von Rad 1972:160, as in Isa 19:24). The phrase forms a bridge from the description of Abraham's personal blessings in vv 1-2 to the description of how all nations will acquire blessing in v 3.

God promises to bless (brk, Piel) those who are on good terms with Abraham (for this meaning of mĕbārăkeykā see 4.3). "Bless" is used in the general sense of "bestow benefits"; the benefits are left unspecified here. The promise of blessing is conditional. Only those on good terms with Abraham will acquire blessing, while those hostile to him will be the object of God's devastating curse.[2]

---

[1] Though GKC 110 i takes the imperative as signifying a result clause, the same imperative is used in Isaac's blessing of Jacob in Gen 27:29 parallel to jussives with a jussive force. Because God has the ability to fulfill his own jussive wish, the clause has the force of a promise.

[2] The distinction between qll and ʾrr is usually lost in translations. The term ʾrr is one of the strongest of the curse words (Brichto 1963:77-115; Scharbert 1958a:5-8; 1975c:405-418). It means "to apply a destructive spell" or "impose a ban", and the finite forms are used only with God or specially endowed persons as subject. The passive participle is the most common word used for forceful imprecations invoking God. The word therefore is not magical, but rather derives its effective power from the fact that it is God who effects the imprecation. In all its uses, the curse is applied to those who violate their relationship to God (Hamilton 1980a:75). Being hostile toward Abraham is tantamount to being hostile toward God, because of the covenant relationship between God and Abraham.

God Blessing Man 31

The result clause which employs nibrĕkû is repeated in 18:18 and 28:14, while the parallel passages 22:18 and 26:4 employ hitbārăkû (see Table 2). Both verbs have a middle meaning; all nations shall actually acquire blessing, rather than just wish for blessing or bless each other.[3] The

---

[3]There are four possible meanings of each verb: 1) passive, "be blessed"; 2) reflexive, "bless oneself, invoke/wish for blessing for oneself"; 3) reciprocal, "bless each other"; 4) middle, "acquire blessing (for oneself)."

The passive meaning has traditionally been the most popular, and is found in the LXX, the New Testament (Acts 3:25 and Gal 3:8), and many English translations. However, though the word used in the NT and in the LXX for both the Niphal and Hithpael, eneulogēthēsontai, is first future passive in form, it is not necessarily passive in meaning. The aorist and future passive forms became commonly used for the aorist and future middle forms in Hellenistic Greek (Robertson 1934:333-334,357, Funk 1961:42-43). It is quite possible, then, that the middle meaning was intended. The only other occurrence of the verb in the LXX is in the present middle-passive infinitive in 1 Sam 2:29, where it clearly has the middle meaning.

Leupold (1942:1.414) and Murtonen (1959:159-160), among others, argue for the passive meaning for the Niphal, which is also allowed for by Driver (1905:145) and von Rad (1972:160). GKC 51 f says significantly, "In cases where Qal is intransitive in meaning, or is not used, Niphal appears also as the passive of Piel," and gives kbd and khd as examples. Bergsträsser (1962:2.90), Brockelmann (1956:3), Blau (1976:51), and Bauer-Leander (1962:289-290) also recognize the Niphal as occasionally serving as the passive of the Piel.

While the passive meaning is certainly possible based on the grammar and context, if the author had intended to convey unambiguously the passive idea, the Pual would have been the most likely choice. Since the Niphal is used only in 12:3 and the parallel passages 18:18; 28:14, it is probable that the author chose the rare form (the Pual occurs fourteen times, the Hithpael seven) to convey a distinctive meaning. The fact that the other parallel passages 22:18; 26:4 have the Hithpael indicates that the author of those passages felt that the meaning of the Niphal differed from the simple passive, since although the Hithpael occasionally is passive in meaning (GKC 54 g) the Hithpael of brk elsewhere is middle or reflexive (but see Schottroff 1969:186 for a Nabatean inscription where the Hithpael of brk is passive).

The reflexive and reciprocal meanings are advocated by Scharbert (1958a:25, 1975a:297), and Speiser (1964:86) for the Niphal. Neither author can decide between the two meanings "wish blessing for oneself" or "wish blessing for each other." In either case the preposition b would be

promise envisions most people acquiring blessing, not curse.[4] Because of

attached to the example of a blessed person, as in Gen 48:20. The peoples would wish for themselves or for each other the good fortune that Abraham has experienced. The chief difficulty with these interpretations is that they do not fit the contexts. In 12:3a, God promises actually to bestow blessing upon those on good terms with Abraham, and so it would be unusual to conclude the passage with the statement that people will merely wish for Abraham's blessings. 3b is best taken as confirming and building upon 3a, affirming that others will actually receive blessing (Keil and Delitzsch *Genesis*:195, Wehmeier 1970:177).

The middle meaning of the Niphal, "acquire blessing," is the best choice (Schreiner 1962:7, Wehmeier 1970:177-179, Keller 1978:364). The middle preserves both the intended grammatical meaning of the Niphal and the structure of the passage (on the latter see Murtonen 1959:159-160). The *b* is instrumental (BDB 89b, Williams 1976:44), "through" or "by means of": "durch die Geschichte, die Gott mit ihm beginnt, nimmt Jahwe sich der 'unglüchlichen Völkerwelt' an und lasst sie teilhaben an dem Segen, den er schenkt" (Wehmeier 1970:179).

The most frequent meanings of the Hithpael are reflexive and middle, while the reciprocal and passive are much less common (though see Schottroff 1969:186 for a Nabatean inscription which uses the Hithpael of *brk* with a passive meaning).

Most authors advocate the reflexive meaning for the Hithpael (Driver 1905:220-221; Scharbert 1958a:25, though also allowing for the reciprocal, and 1975a:296; Murtonen 1959:172, who translates "will praise themselves happy because of thy seed"; Wehmeier 1970:184-186, von Rad 1972:238, Keller 1978:364). Keller's explanation is typical: "Das Hithp. bedeutet ganz allgemein 'sich selber *bārûk* machen bzw. nennen' . . . Gerne verwendet man die Formel *brk* Hithp. *bĕ* 'sich selber glüchlich machen durch Nennung eines anderen, besonders Gesegneten bzw. Gottes in einem Segensspruch', indem man deisen anderen als Modell . . . oder Quelle der heilskraft anruft."

Yet *GKC* 54 f(c) describes the middle as a frequent meaning, and in addition many of the verbs *GKC* lists under the reflexive (54 d) are really middle, as, for example, the Hithpaels of *gdl*, "act arrogantly or magnificently," not "make/show oneself great," *ḥkm*, "act shrewdly," not "make oneself a prophet," and *nqm*, "to avenge, take revenge," not "show oneself revengeful." In all these cases, as well as in those properly listed as middle, the Hithpael denotes behaving in a certain way, or doing something *for* oneself, rather than doing something *to* oneself.

As with the Niphal, the reflexive or reciprocal meanings would significantly weaken the force of the Hithpael promise. Wehmeier (1970:184-185) recognizes this and suggests that this weakening is due to the theol-

the middle meaning, there is no chance of confusing the construction for a passive with *b* of agent; it is God, not the mediator Abraham or his descendants, who is the ultimate source of blessing.

In the patriarchal promises, blessing consists of God's bestowal of descendants, fame, dominion over others, land, and God's presence and protection. In addition, God's blessing also consists of the conferral of the status of mediator of blessing upon the patriarchs.

---

ogy of the source for 22:18 and 26:4. He claims that the source is akin to, but not to be identified with, D, and shares the theology of D. D has no place for J's theology in the Niphal passages of blessing for the other nations, but rather advocates annihilation of them. However, the promise was such an integral part of the tradition that it could not be excised altogether, and so was instead weakened so that the nations merely "sich unter Nennung Israels Segen wünschten" (185).

Aside from the problems involved in identifying fragmentary sources and their theologies (it is not clear exactly which fragmentary theory Wehmeier is following), the fact remains that there is no compulsive reason for assuming that the Hithpael is reflexive, regardless of the verses' source.

The methodology followed by Driver, Wehmeier, Scharbert (1975a) and Keller is questionable. They start with Deut 29:18 and Isa 65:16, where *hitbārēk*, in their opinion, is reflexive, and conclude that the Genesis passages must therefore be reflexive. Yet Deut 29:18 and Isa 65:16 are completely unrelated to the Genesis Hithpael passages! As all authors recognize, Gen 22:18 and 26:4 allude instead to the Niphal passages, since the syntactical constructions are identical and the contexts are quite similar (see Table 2). It is most reasonable to conclude therefore that the same meaning is intended in both sets of passages (so also Scharbert 1958a:25, and 1972:7, responding to Wehmeier 1970). Different grammatical forms do not necessarily have different meanings; it is unwarranted to assume that the meaning of the Hithpael *must* differ from that of the Niphal. It is also incorrect to assume that the Hithpael *must* have the same meaning in all of its occurrences. The context and usage, not grammatical form, are the surest guide to meaning.

[4]The singular participle *mĕqallelkā* as compared to the plural *mĕbārăkeykā* is explained by most commentators as implying that more people will bless Abraham than will maltreat him, and that God desires to bless many and curse few (Wehmeier 1970:159; von Rad 1972:160). The textual evidence for the plural *mĕqallĕleykā* is weak and represents an attempt to harmonize the two participles. The use of the participle of *qll* in place of the participle of *ʾrr* to denote Abraham's enemies also envisions less hostility to Abraham because *qll* is a weaker verb (see note 2 above and cf. Gen 27:29; Num 24:9).

Decendants are the most frequently mentioned blessings. God promises to make Abraham into a great people (*gôy*, Gen 12:2; 17:16,20; 18:18) and to give the patriarchs numerous descendants (*zeraʿ*, 22:17; 26:4; 28:14). In 17:16,20, God further promises to make some of the descendants into rulers.

Fame is promised explicitly only in 12:2, but it is implied in many of the other promises. The blessings of dominion and being a mediator of blessing, for example, would certainly bring prestige and renown.

Blessing includes dominion over others in 12:3a, 18:18 (*gôy ʿāṣûm*); and 22:17, where God says "I will certainly bless you ... and so your descendants will take possession of their enemies' gate." Dominion is also implied in the promise of land, since it must be conquered. God promises land in conjunction with blessing in 12:1; 26:3,4; 28:13.

God's presence, i.e., being with (*ʿim* or *ʾēt*) the patriarchs (26:3,24; 28:15,20) is a general expression denoting God's benefaction and favorable disposition toward the one he is "with" (cf. Vetter 1971). In 28:15 God promises to reveal his presence by protecting Jacob: "Behold, I am with you and will guard you ... I will not forsake you."

God promises the status of being a mediator of blessing in 12:3; 18:18; 22:18; 26:4; and 28:14 (see Table 2). Gen 18 shows how Abraham was a mediator. In Gen 18:18 Yahweh asks "How can I conceal from Abraham what I am about to do when Abraham will certainly become a great people, and all peoples will acquire blessing through him?" God reveals his intentions to Abraham because of Abraham's status. Verses 23-33 describe Abraham's intercessions for Sodom. Abraham takes an active role as mediator, pleading for the pagan city, and through his efforts a few of his relatives are spared.

However, it is not always necessary for the patriarchs to take an active role in order for people associated with them to acquire blessing. In Gen 17:20, God promises to bless Ishmael with the same benefits he promised to Isaac in v 16. Ishmael will become a great people and will father rulers. God promises to fulfill some of his promises to Abraham in Ishmael's line simply because he is related to Abraham. For further examples of how the patriarchs mediated blessing, see below under 3.2.2.1.

The patriarchal blessing promises are unique in that they are transmitted diachronically. They are not transmitted by the soul power of the patriarchs, nor by the magical power of the spoken word. Rather, God renews his promises of blessing to each patriarch. God specifies that Isaac's line will carry on the covenant that he made with Abraham (17:16-21). God also assures Isaac, "I will bless you and make your descendants numerous for the sake of Abraham my servant" (26:24; cf. 26:3-4 and the

God Blessing Man 35

promise to Jacob in 28:13-15). The reason that the patriarchal blessings were transmitted diachronically is that they were still *promises* and were not completely fulfilled in the lifetime of the original recipients. Blessing was not a family possession or "heirloom" which people could pass on independently of God (contra Pedersen 1926:193). The other types of blessing promises could not be passed on.

In the patriarchal narratives God several times blesses by bestowing new names in conjunction with issuing the blessing promises (Gen 17:5, 15,19; cf. 32:27-29, and 2:3; 5:2; Exod 20:11). The significance of the renaming is that it denotes conferral of a new status. It marks the entrance of the patriarchs into a relationship with God in which they will be the recipients of the promised blessings. The act of renaming is more important than the meaning of the new names.[5] While the blessings were still only promises, the new names were tangible benefits that the patriarchs received immediately to help assure them of God's future blessings.

Throughout the patriarchal blessing promises God is the source of blessing. Blessing is never procured by magic or the self-fulfilling power of the spoken word. God makes promises in the first person and the narratives describe God as able to fulfill his promises directly. For example, God says to Abraham concerning Sarah, "I will bless her, and give a son to you from her" (17:16). The fulfillment is reported by the simple statement "Yahweh did to Sarah what he said he would do" (21:1). There is no mention of any means or indirect agent.

In Gen 12:3a there is a deliberate effort unambiguously to portray Yahweh as the sole originator of blessing and curse. The formula ʾōrǎreykā ʾārûr ûmĕbārǎkeykā bārûk (on which see 4.3) occurs in Gen 27:29 and (in reverse order) Num 24:9. The formula is a stereotyped

---

[5]The meaning of Sarah does not differ from that of Sarai. *śāray* is an older feminine noun formation (*GKC* 80 1, de Vries 1962:219), while *śārâ* has the usual biblical feminine ending. Both mean "royal lady" or "princess." The meaning of ʾabrām is generally agreed to be "father is exalted" or "exalted father," with "father" referring to God (Payne 1980:6, Hicks 1962:15). The meaning of ʾabrāhām, however, is disputed. Noth (1928:145 note 1), Speiser (1964:124,127) and Hicks take the element *rāhām* to be nothing more than an expansion of *rām*. Hebrew ʿayin-waw verbs often have Aramaic equivalents that are ʿayin-he. Payne (1980:6), however, points out that the Arabic noun *ruhāmun*, "multitude," provides good evidence that the meaning "father of a multitude" given in v 5 is etymologically possible (so also KB 8). Isaac's name, "he laughs," says little about his role in history.

blessing formula which declares the dominion of the addressee over his adversaries. In Gen 12:3a, however, the formula is reworded *wāʾăbārĕkā mĕbārăkeykā ûmĕqallelkā ʾāʾōr*. The passive participles which only imply God or the gods as agent have been replaced by finite verbs with God as the subject to emphasize that it is God who effects blessing and curse, rather than some magical or mechanical process.

The emphasis upon God effecting the curse is unusual for Hebrew and West Semitic texts in general. East Semitic maledictions openly and frequently invoke deities to approve of and effect curses, while Hebrew shares the West Semitic preference for constructions with passive verbs where the agent of the curse is not designated (Gevirtz 1962:750). However, Gen 12:3a shows that in the Bible at least this preference is not due to a belief in the autonomous power of the curse word versus the East Semitic belief in the power of deities (contra Gevirtz 1962:750 and Blank 1950:73:83), nor is it due to a desire to dissociate God from curses, since God is the subject of finite forms of *ʾrr* in Gen 5:29; 12:3; and twice in Mal 2:2, and is named as the agent of cursing in other passages employing *ʾārûr*. Rather, it is due to the implicit belief that it is God who effects curses as well as blessings (see further especially on Deut 27-28 under 3.1.2).

3.1.2 The Covenantal Blessing Promises

The purposes of God in issuing the covenantal blessing promises are somewhat different from the purposes of the patriarchal blessings. The main purpose of the covenantal promises is to motivate the Israelites to continue to observe the stipulations of the covenant already made, rather than to draw them into a covenant. The promises are addressed to the nation rather than to individuals.

The ultimate purpose of God's blessing is to bring himself the praise and respect of all nations. God desires to establish his people as a holy people (*gôy qādôš*, Exod 19:6, *ʿam qādôš*, Deut 7:6; 26:19; 28:9), a people whom he values a great deal (*ʿam segullâ*, Deut 7:6; 26:18). Israel naturally is grateful to God for his blessings, and serves him as a nation (*mamleket kōhănîm*, Exod 19:6). Because God blesses them they acquire fame and glory among the nations (Deut 26:19). This ultimately leads the other nations to fear and respect Yahweh, since they ascribe Israel's prosperity and dominion to Yahweh's activity (Deut 28:10). It is no wonder, then, that God enjoys (*śāś*, Deut 28:63) blessing Israel, since it accomplishes his purposes.

The covenantal blessings do not develop the patriarchal theme of Israel being a mediator of blessing. Instead, they emphasize that the reason God blesses is to give Israel dominion over other nations. However, this does not mean that the two types of blessings contain conflicting theologies (contra Wehmeier 1970:184-185). The patriarchal examples of the mediation of blessing (Gen 18:16-33; 30:27-30; 39:1-6, and the rest of the Joseph narrative; cf. Gen 21:22-34; 26:23-31) show that the Israelites could only mediate blessing when they themselves enjoyed abundant blessings and were in a position of authority over those to whom they mediated blessing.[6]

The content of blessing is expanded in the covenantal promises. As in the patriarchal narratives, God's blessing can consist of human fertility (Exod 23:25; Deut 7:13-14; 28:4,11; 30:16), but God does not promise that the descendants will be rulers or mediators of blessing. Deut 30:16 also includes longevity in the content of blessing. Moses tells the people that if they obey the covenant, "you will live long and be numerous and the Lord your God will bless you on the land to which you are traveling to inherit." The opposite, resulting from idolatry (v 17), is described in v 18: "you will die for sure; you will not live very long . . . ." Exod 23:25 mentions good health, as well as fertility and longevity, as blessings. God promises, "I will remove sickness from your midst. There will be no aborting or infertile woman in your land, and I will fill out the number of your days."

Deut 7:14-16 states that Israel will be blessed (*bārûk*) and therefore will have dominion over other nations. God will remove her diseases and place them on her enemies, and she will devour the other nations. Deut 15:6 combines dominion and prosperity: "Yahweh, your God, will bless you, as he said to you, and you will lend to many nations, but will not borrow. You will rule over many nations, but they will not rule over you" (similarly Deut 28:12). As a result of obeying the covenant, "there will not be any needy person among you, because Yahweh will bless you on the land which Yahweh, your God, is giving you" (15:4). However, this is conditional upon obedience. This statement is subsequently modified in v 11, "a more realistic appraisal" (Craigie 1976:237).

Most of the covenantal blessings promise fertility of domesticated animals and crops. The realm in which God will bless the people is often introduced by the preposition *b*. God promises to bless the people *běkōl*

---

[6]Although Jacob and Joseph were employed by Laban and Potiphar, respectively, they were in charge of the enterprises which received God's blessing. Joseph later was in authority over all Egypt when through his leadership it endured the famine.

mišlaḥ yādĕkā/yedkem (Deut 12:7; 15:10; 23:21; 28:8), and *bĕkōl ma⁽ăśēh yādĕkā* (Deut 14:29; 16:15; 24:19; similarly 15:10; 15:18; 28:12). These two expressions refer primarily to agriculture, as is clear from Gen 5:29; Deut 28:8,12. However, due to the general nature of the expressions, animal husbandry, and commerce in general, could be included, too. There are many other words which denote either the realm in which God blesses or which are the direct object of God's blessing, which likewise signify success in farming and animal husbandry.

The covenantal curses shed light on *brk* because they are antonyms of the blessings. The curse formulas in 28:16-19 are the exact opposite of vv 3-6, with *ʾārûr* in place of *bārûk*. The curse formulas describe the lack of food; human, plant and animal infertility; and in general, a dismal, unproductive, hard life. The curses in Deut 28:20-68 are quite diverse. They may, however, be subsumed under the following labels: death, population decrease, cannibalism, loss of family; sickness, anxiety; crop disease, infertile ground, no rain; military defeat, exile, oppression, suffering various sorts of abuse, loss of personal property; and general failure. The curse of worshipping wooden and stone gods (vv 36,64) signifies a complete break in the covenantal relationship.

I will discuss the meaning of *brk*, and the way in which blessing operates, in the course of the following discussion of the different constructions, since the meaning is in part dependent upon the particular construction used.

There are only two passages where God makes first person promises. In Exod 20:24 he says, "in every place where I cause my name to be remembered I will come to you and bless you." The article on *hammāqôm* is distributive (Childs 1974:447). The proper places for altars are those places where a theophany, vision, dream, or some other event has occurred which associates the place with Yahweh's name (Noth 1962:176). The passage says that the bestowal of blessing at the altars confirms that God is present at the places of worship—he has "come" (*bôʾ*) to the people there.

God wants to show that he is a God of blessing. Wherever he is present, people receive blessing. God also seeks to associate his previous activities with blessing. By making the places where he had previously done something places of blessing, he intends to show that his previous actions had the goal of bringing blessing to the people. God designates the centers of worship as the chief places where blessing is mediated to the people. Later traditions expand upon this idea (see 3.2.2.5 and 1 Kgs 8 under 4.2.2, and Pss 118:26b; 134:3 under 4.2.6).

In Lev 25:20-22, God describes how he will provide food for the

Sabbatical (seventh) year when there is to be no planting or harvesting: "I will dispatch my blessing to you in the sixth year, and it will yield enough produce for three years" (v 21). The subject of the old 3fs perfect ʿāśāt (GKC 75m) could be implied as ʾereṣ or ʾădāmâ, but since the bĕrākâ is here pictured as an independent entity to be sent by God, it is more likely that it is the subject of the verb (so also Wehmeier 1970:76 and Wenham 1979:314). This is an unusual picture (though Yahweh dispatches (ṣwh) blessing also in Deut 28:8); the Piel of brk with God as the subject is the most common construction.

Wehmeier (1970:76) sees blessing (bĕrākâ) as "die von Gott verordnete Macht, die Fruchtbarkeit und Gediehen wirkt." Snaith (1967:167) equates it with Arabic barakat, "the equivalent of mana, that supernatural power of primitive belief." But nowhere else does the noun denote an entity distinct from God which bestows benefits. There is no evidence for the existence of a "Segenskraft" as distinct from God himself. When God dispatches his blessing in Deut 28:8, this means that he himself will bless (ûbērakkā). The language of Lev 25:21 is figurative for God himself causing abundant produce, and should not be taken as a precise (and unique) statement of the Israelite theology of blessing.

Deut 28:12 illustrates the way in which God actually would bestow his blessing: "Yahweh will open up his storehouse of good things, the heavens, to bestow rain upon your land in its season and bless all that you do with your hands." God does not effect blessing by means of impersonal powers. Instead, he works through the natural processes. God usually blesses by making the natural processes work better than they normally do, rather than by circumventing them. When God blesses by promoting plant, animal, or human fertility, the offspring are still produced in the usual way.

In most of the covenantal passages Moses reports God's promises in the third person. Exod 23:25 shows that the third person promises are intended as equivalents of first person promises, since the discourse shifts from the third to the first person in the middle of the promise: "You shall serve your own God Yahweh, and he will bless your bread and water, and I will remove sickness from you . . . ." As God's mediator Moses speaks in place of God.

In the third person passages, brk occurs either in the Piel with Yahweh, the covenant God, as subject, or as the noun bĕrākâ, which is bestowed by Yahweh. People are usually the object of the Piel. The verb then means to promote the fertility of the people, their crops, and/or their animals, to promote good health and longevity, or to endow with prosperity, depending on the context. The realm of human endeavor which God's blessing affects is often introduced by the preposition b. When living things such as animals and crops are the object, the Piel verb means to make fruitful and productive. With bread, wine, and other inanimate objects as objects, the verb is used somewhat figuratively. The statement "Yahweh will bless your bread and water" (Exod 23:25) means "Yahweh will bless you by providing abundant bread and water." He will not make the bread and water reproduce.

A group of passages mentions God's blessing in the course of outlining covenantal requirements. The Piel in these passages has a future perfect meaning, i.e., it pictures God as already having blessed the Israelites. Deut 15:14 is typical: when an Israelite slave is set free, "you must generously give to him from your flocks, threshing floor, and wine vat. You should give to him that which Yahweh will have blessed you with" (similarly Deut 12:7; 14:24; 16:10). The noun occurs twice. The Israelites are told that when they slaughter animals they can eat as much as they want, "according to the blessing which your God Yahweh will have given you" (Deut 12:15; similarly 16:17). The noun here denotes the crops and animals which result from God's blessing activity.

There are seven bārûk formulas in the covenantal promises. Deut 7:14 shows that the formulas are indicative statements referring to the future: "You will be more blessed (bārûk tîhyeh) than all other nations." The context clearly shows that bārûk has the passive meaning "blessed, someone who has experienced God's blessing," rather than the stative meaning "im Besitz der bĕrākâ," "voll Segen, segensreich" (contra Wehmeier 1970: 111,118). The reason Israel will be bārûk is that God will bless her (bērak, twice in v 13), and will remove her diseases and give her dominion (vv 15-16). It is only because she will be the object of God's actions that Israel will be bārûk.

In Deut 28 the covenantal blessings and curses are outlined formally by a series of bārûk and ʾārûr formulas. The relationship between the blessings and curses of chapters 27 and 28 is not clear (Craigie 1976:327-336, Mayes 1979:340-351, Thompson 1974:259-262). There are no blessings recorded in chapter 27. Judging from the twelve curse formulas in chapter 27, the six formulas in each of 28:3-6 and 16-19 may be extracts from a longer series of formulas (Craigie 1976:335).

In any event, the formulas are indicative; they are statements of the future condition of the obedient Israelites, rather than prayers or wishes. The form used, bārûk ʾattâ, is both more frequent and more forceful than the form employing hyh (as in 7:14). bārûk again clearly means "blessed," that is, one who is the recipient of blessing bestowed by God (see vv 7-13 which stress Yahweh's agency). The first formula (v 3) does not specify what the blessings are, but describes the realms in which benefits will be received: "You will be blessed in the city, and you will be blessed in the field" (cf. Gen 39:5). The merism implies that the Israelites will experience God's blessing in all aspects of commerce and domestic life.

V 4 uses common Deuteronomic terms to describe human, plant and animal offspring as *bārûk*. A figure of speech is used here. Just as *brk* Piel with bread and the like as object means "to provide with abundant bread" (see Exod 23:25 and Deut 7:13, which use several of the same terms as this verse), the statement that "the fruit of your womb/land/animals will be blessed" means "you will be blessed with numerous and healthy offspring, and abundant good produce." The emphasis is on the reception of good benefits by the Israelites rather than on the reception of blessing by the offspring or produce. Similarly, "Your basket and kneading trough will be blessed" (v 5) could be paraphrased as "You will be blessed with a full basket and full kneading trough."

The final formula (v 6), like the first, contains a double blessing formula employing a merism: "You will be blessed when you come in and when you go out." The merism with *bô'* and *yṣ'* here means "the totality of life, all the daily activities in which one may be engaged" (Mayes 1979:352). It encompasses more than the frequent Deuteronomic expressions *běkōl mišlaḥ/ma'ăśēh yādeykā* which refer primarily to their occupations.

The antonym of *bārûk* used in the corresponding curse formulas (vv 16-19) is *'ārûr*. These two words also stand as antonyms in Gen 9:25-26; 27:29; Num 24:9; Jer 17:5,7; 20:14. *'ārûr* is the most common rubric for maledictions (Brichto 1963:77, Scharbert 1958a:5-8). It denotes someone who has been, or who shortly will be, the object of malefaction by God, as described in vivid detail in vv 20-68. It connotes divine displeasure, just as *bārûk* connotes divine affection (*'hb*, Deut 7:13).

As in the *bārûk* formulas, the agent who is to effect the curse is not specified. In the larger context of Deuteronomy, it is apparent that everywhere God is thought of as the one who effects blessing and curse, prosperity or misfortune, based on one's adherence to the covenant. In v 20 Yahweh is explicitly named as the one who sends a curse (*mě'ērâ*). Yet in the formulas it is not necessary to invoke God; *bārûk* and *'ārûr* both imply God's agency.

The noun *běrākâ* is used five times to refer both to the covenantal promises themselves and to the benefits they offer. In all cases the antonym *qělālâ* co-occurs and likewise denotes both the covenantal promises of misfortune for disobedience and the misfortune itself. In Deut 11:26-27, Moses says, "Today I am placing before you blessing and curse; the blessing if you obey Yahweh's commandments which I am commanding you today, and the curse if you do not obey the commandments of Yahweh, your God." The covenantal stipulations then follow in 12:1—26:15. Deut 30:1,19 are essentially the same as 11:26-27. Moses places the blessing and curse before the people, i.e., he outlines the two options available for them and lets them decide which course they will follow. "Neutrality on the issue is excluded" (Thompson 1974:156). The thought is reminiscent of the "two ways" theme in the wisdom literature. Blessing and curse denote two contrasting ways of life.

In Deut 28:2, Moses tells Israel that if she obeys, "all these blessings will come upon you and overtake you." The formal covenantal promises then follow in vv 3-13. The plural refers both to the individual promises and to the benefits which they offer (the antonym qĕlālôt in vv 15,45, is analogous).

The noun bĕrākâ occurs twice denoting only the promises themselves, and not their benefits. The antonym qĕlālâ again co-occurs. Deut 11:29 prescribes: "When the Lord, your God, has brought you to the land which you are approaching to possess, you shall place the blessing on Mt. Gerizim and the curse on Mt. Ebal." Here just the formal covenant formulas described in chapter 27 are meant. It is unclear exactly what the blessing formulas were, though the twelve curse formulas are given in 27:15-26. The fulfillment is described in Josh 8:34: "afterward [Joshua] read all the words of the law, the blessing and the curse." Here blessing and curse stand for the entire covenant. They are "all the words of the law." The Piel verb in Deut 27:12 and Josh 8:33 means "to pronounce orally the covenantal blessings" referred to in Deut 27.

Deut 27:15-26 specifies that all the people are to say ʾāmēn after each ʾārûr formula; it may be assumed that they did so after the bārûk formulas as well. By pronouncing the "Amen," the people put themselves under the force of the formulas. They agreed to comply with the covenantal stipulations and be blessed, or suffer the consequences if they do not comply.

It is interesting that qĕlālâ, and not mĕʾērâ, is used as the antonym for bĕrākâ, even though the qĕlālâ contains numerous ʾārûr formulas. There is no single root that is antonymous to brk in all its forms. Though ʾārûr is the usual antonym to bārûk, qĕlālâ is the usual antonym to bĕrākâ, and the finite forms of the verb brk can have forms of qll, ʾrr, ʾlh, nqb/qbb, or rarely other verbs as antonyms, depending on the meaning and context of brk.[7]

Several other stereotyped word-pairs are found in place of bĕrākâ/qĕlālâ. In Deut 30:19 haḥayyîm wĕhammāwet stands parallel to it. In Deut 30:15 Moses sets before the people haḥayyîm wĕʾet haṭṭôb wĕʾet

God Blessing Man

hammāwet wĕʾet hāraʿ. From this it is clear that *bĕrākâ* and *qĕlālâ* do not simply denote promises or predictions of good and evil, but also the actual attainment or forfeiture of a full, prosperous and happy life (so also Wehmeier 1970:90; cf. Brichto 1963:197-198).

All the convental blessing promises are contingent upon the people's obedience to the terms of the covenant. Yet blessing is not the result of a mechanical system of retribution. God blesses Israel out of his love for her (*ʾhb*, 7:13). Obedience did not merit blessing; rather, "obedience maintained the proper covenant relationship with God, and his people could experience the blessing of God only when the covenant relationship, which involved mutual responsibilities, was properly maintained" (Craigie 1976:180). Moreover, the covenantal legislation describes blessing as the normal state of affairs unless there is gross disobedience by the people. God seeks to bless the people as long as he legally can (cf. Wehmeier 1970:137).

Deut 7:7-8 states that God's love was not founded upon the desirability of the people, but upon the patriarchal promises. God's subsequent love was due to his desire to maintain his pledge of blessing in the patriarchal promises. The covenantal blessings frequently picture blessing as the

---

[7] The noun *qĕlālâ* primarily denotes material misfortune or abusive treatment, and only occasionally denotes a malediction (Brichto 1963:199). Brichto (1963:186-187) gives the meaning for these Deuteronomic passages as "misfortune, disaster." This is accurate as long as it is remembered that these result from divine displeasure rather than from human or accidental causes. *mĕʾērā* is a rarer word, occuring only five times, and denotes an effective curse wreaking material misfortune. It also does not necessarily involve a spoken imprecation or malediction (Brichto 1963:112-114). The term *mĕʾērā* does in fact occur in 28:20, where it refers to the *ʾārûr* formulas of vv 16-19. Contrary to Brichto (1963:113), it therefore does refer here to spoken maledictions.

The meaning of *mĕʾērâ* is then such that it is quite appropriate to serve as the antonym to *bĕrākâ*. The reason it does not is that *bĕrākâ* and *qĕlālâ* are a stereotyped word-pair in biblical Hebrew. The Piels of *qll* and *brk* are commonly used as antonyms, leading to the euphemistic use of *brk* and *qll* (Brichto 1963:157-172; see further 5.5). Similarly, *qĕlālâ* "derives most of its crystallized meaning by virtue of being the antonym of *bĕrākâ*" (Brichto 1963:18). The two are habitually associated with each other and frequently co-occur as antonyms, while *mĕʾērâ* never co-occurs with *bĕrākâ* as its antonym, though in meaning it is antonymous. The two are not direct antonyms in Mal 2:2; 3:9-10, though they are in Prov 28:20,27, where they occur separately.

fulfillment of the patriarchal promises by noting that God will bless Israel on the *promised* land (7:13; 15:4; 23:21; 28:8; 30:16).

2 Kgs 18:31 = Isa 36:16 contains a frequently misunderstood use of *bĕrākâ*. Sennacherib's field commander invites the people of Jerusalem to surrender: "Make a treaty (*bĕrākâ*) with me, and come out to me, so each one of you can eat from his vine and fig tree . . . until I come and take you to a land like your land . . . ."

Many commentators understand *bĕrākâ* as meaning oral benedictions given as greetings or in wishing each other well, so that making a blessing denotes entering into peaceful, friendly relations (so Young 1969:2.468). Gray (1964:620) understands the verse as saying that Sennacherib had blessing, meaning that fate was on his side. Murtonen (1959:173-174) tentatively suggests that *bĕrākâ* might stand for capitulation by denoting tribute. Then again, "perhaps it can be interpreted to mean a state in which both parties 'bless' each other, i.e., work for the benefit of one another - at least in theory." Scharbert (1975a:299) recognizes that the phrase means to make peace, but is at a loss for an explanation (similarly BDB 139b). Wehmeier (1970:94), however, correctly recognizes that the noun stands for the blessing clauses of a vassal treaty.

The meaning of *bĕrākâ* in 2 Kgs 18:31 = Isa 36:18 is quite similar to its meaning in Deut 11:26-29; 30:1,19; Josh 8:34, where the word-pair *bĕrākâ/qĕlālâ* stands for the Sinai covenant. Vassal treaties, like the Sinai covenant, normally concluded with invocations of the gods to bless or curse the vassal depending on his obedience. Sennacherib is at pains to present an optimistic picture of life under the proposed treaty (vv 31-32), so he only mentions the blessing. He asserts that such a treaty will only bring blessing for Israel.

3.1.3 Wisdom Retribution Aphorisms

The wisdom retribution aphorisms are similar to the covenantal promises in that they predict that God will bless (or curse) people based on their adherence to the standards of Torah piety. Their purpose is likewise to persuade people to obey the covenantal stipulations. The promise of blessing is the motivating factor for obedience. People only acquire blessing through God's retribution.

They differ from most of the covenantal promises in that God is usually not specified as the agent (though cf. Deut 28:3-6). Their form is also different. They are usually short poetic aphorisms, or part of a larger poem extolling those who fear God.

The content of blessing in the wisdom aphorisms is usually not spelled out. When it is, blessing consists of such things as prosperity, children, good crops, and esteem. Ps 128 describes the benefits of those who are *yĕrē˒ - yhwh* (vv 1,4). They eat what they have labored for (v 2), and have a fruitful wife with children (v 3). The phrase *wĕṭôb lāk* (v 2b) denotes general prosperity. V 4 describes these benefits as blessings: "For that is how a man who fears Yahweh is blessed (*yĕbōrak*)." Prov 10:22 says that wealth results from God's blessing (cf. Ps 112:3; Prov 28:20). Ps 112:2 says that the descendants of a man who fears God will themselves be blessed and be mighty (*gibbôr*) in the land. The context indicates that "mighty" denotes wealth and esteem, rather than dominion. The wisdom aphorisms only occasionally ascribe blessing explicitly to God's action. Prov 3:33 does so: "Yahweh's curse is on the house of the wicked man, but he blesses the house of the righteous."

Blessing and curse do not operate by the power of the spoken word. *mĕ˒ērâ* in Prov 3:33, as usual, does not signify a spoken imprecation. It denotes an "operating curse" (Brichto 1963:114), "das sichtbar gegenwärtige Verderben" (Wehmeier 1970:140). The curse is an ever present tendency toward failure which affects all that the wicked man does.

Blessing and curse result from God's attitude toward the person. God looks with scorn and disfavor (*lyṣ*, v 34a) upon the wicked, and so ruin and corruption follow them. There is no means stated through which God works; God's attitude is pictured as directly affecting reality.

In contrast, God blesses (*brk* Piel) the home of the righteous. This too is a constant condition. General prosperity and success accompany his undertakings, because of God's favorable disposition (*ḥēn*, v 34b) toward him. God's attitude toward a person is again pictured as directly and continually influencing that person's fate.

In Ps 5:13 the psalmist expresses his confidence that because of God's favor (*rāṣôn*) toward him, God will bless him with protection from his enemies:

> Surely you will bless the righteous man,
> Yahweh, you will surround him with favor as a shield.

Ps 24:3 asks,

> Who will ascend Yahweh's mountain?
> Who will stand in his holy place?

Vv 4-5 answer: the person who has clean hands and a pure heart, and has no desire for what is false (possibly idols).

> He will receive blessing from Yahweh,
> righteousness from his saving God.

The main point here is that God will look upon him with favor and reward him for his pious living. *ṣĕdāqâ,* parallel to *bĕrākâ,* denotes that God will consider the worshipper righteous, i.e., to have fulfilled his obligations under the covenant. Both *bĕrākâ* and *ṣĕdāqâ* connote the worshipper's favorable standing in God's sight (so also Leupold 1969:219, contra Wehmeier 1970:83, who argues that *ṣĕdāqâ* denotes prosperity).

Prov 10:22 asserts:

> It is Yahweh's blessing that gives wealth;
> toil can add nothing to it.[8]

taʿăšîr describes God's blessing as giving money as well as goods and other things of value. The point is not that all who are rich must therefore have God's blessing, for the wicked also can be wealthy. Rather, only God's blessing gives *lasting* wealth. Goods acquired by dishonest means, or simply by one's own labors without God's sanction, are fleeting (as in Ps 127:1; Prov 20:21; 21:5; 28:20,22).

Ps 37 contrasts good and evil people who are designated by a variety of common wisdom terms. V 22 states:

> Those he blesses will possess the land,
> but those he curses will be cut off.

In vv 9b, 11a, and 29a, *qōwê-yhwh,* *ʿănāwîm,* and *ṣaddîqîm,* respectively, are also said to possess the land, so it is clear that *mĕbōrākāyw* is a general term for pious people. The psalm describes them as receiving various benefits from Yahweh, such as food, vv 19,25, protection, v 28, answered prayers, v 14, *rōb šālôm,* v 11, and *tĕšûʿa,* v 39. The phrase "possess (*yrš*) the land" is "the standing phrase [in the Psalms] . . . for the

---

[8] There are two possible translations of the second line: as above, or "he does not add toil to it." This second possibility is adopted by the Targum, Syriac Peshitta, and McKane (1970:422). The idea would then be that God, when he gives wealth, also takes away labor. This, however, is not consistent with most blessing passages. God's blessing usually does not enable one to sit idly by, but rather enables one's labors to be fruitful and successful. The first translation is advocated by Scott (1965:82) and Wehmeier (1970:84).

holding of the land of promise," and refers to God fulfilling the covenantal blessing promises (Leupold 1969:303).

The antonymous participle $mĕqullālāyw$ is equivalent to $rĕšāʿîm$ in vv 28d, 38b. The participle denotes those who are "in the Deity's ill graces" and are "unfavored," without denoting an oral imprecation (Brichto 1963:125).

Both brk and qll are terms of relationship here. brk denotes a favorable relationship. Divine approval (hps, v 23) is evidenced by divine bestowal of benefits, while qll denotes a hostile relationship. God laughs ($śhq$, v 13) at the evil man.

The context of the entire psalm clearly implies Yahweh as the agent of the passive participles (contra Hempel 1961:97 note 304).[9]

Two passages imply God's agency by the descriptions of the person blessed. Ps 128:4 states that it is those who fear $Yahweh$ who are blessed, implying that Yahweh blesses them (cf. Ps 112:2). Jer 17:7 states that the man who trusts in $Yahweh$ will be blessed.

The other passages simply assert that certain people will be blessed, without naming an agent. However, in the larger context of the wisdom literature it is obvious that God is always intended as the agent of retribution. The following five verses are concerned with individual retribution.

Prov 22:9 states:

> A generous person will be blessed,
>   because he gives some of his food to the poor.

The generous person, $ṭôb-ʿayin$, is opposite to the stingy person, $raʿ-ʿayin$ (Prov 23:6; 28:22), and similar to a $nepeš-bĕrākâ$ (11:25, on which see under 4.3.2). The references to Yahweh's retribution in vv 4,12,14 clearly imply him as the agent. As often in Proverbs, blessing is given as a reward for "a keen social conscience and a concern for the poor which finds practical expression" (McKane 1970:59).

Prov 28:20 echoes the thought of Prov 20:21 (on which see below; cf. also 10:22; 11:25; 22:9):

---

[9]Hempel (1961:97 note 304) follows the LXX in reading both participles as active and claims that they were pointed as passives to avoid God being the object of qll. This, however, would give the verse a rather unusual meaning; as it stands, it is in perfect harmony with the thought of the rest of the psalm.

A faithful man obtains many blessings,
but he who tries to get rich quickly will not go unpunished.

rab-bĕrākôt describes the faithful man as obtaining wealth (cf. v 20b) as well as other types of blessings. Though he obtains them by his own diligence, it is God's sanction of his lifestyle that enables him to retain the fruit of his labors. The *bĕrākôt* are parallel and antonymous to *lōʾ yinnāqeh*, so that blessings are implied as God's reward for being *nāqî*, legally innocent in God's court.

Conversely, the greedy man tries to get rich quickly. As in 20:21, "quickly" has the connotation of "dishonestly," and so the greedy man will be held accountable. *lōʾ yinnāqeh* belongs to the language of theodicy. "Such a person is subject to Yahweh's infallible review and will be found guilty; he has no hope of a 'not guilty' verdict, for he is a *rāšāʿ*, not a *ṣaddîq*" (McKane 1970:626). The expression *rab mĕʾērôt* in v 27 is antonymous to *rab-bĕrākôt*. The expression primarily denotes material misfortune, as its parallel *maḥsôr* shows. There is no hint of any "Fluchspruch" here (so also Brichto 1963:114, contra Wehmeier 1970:86).

Prov 24:23-25 deals with just judgement:

It is not good to show partiality in judgement.
He who tells a wicked man, 'you are righteous',
people will curse him,
nations will revile him.
But for those who convict, things will go well;
a good blessing will come upon them.

The two curse-words in v 24 are *qbb* and *zʿm*. Though Brichto (1963:200-202) is skeptical, *qbb* does denote "curse" in the sense of "utter an imprecation."[10]

---

[10]Seven of the seventeen occurrences of *qbb/nqb* are in the Balaam narrative (Num 22:11,17; 23:8,11,13,14,27), where it is parallel to *ʾrr* (Num 22:6,12; 23:7; 24:9) and clearly denotes the pronouncement of an imprecation. Scharbert (1958a:14) cannot decide between "schimpfen über" and "verfluchen."

While *zʿm* can be used for imprecating, here it probably has the slightly weaker meaning "revile." It is found parallel to *ʾrr* (Num 23:7) and *qbb* (Num 23:8; Prov 24:24). Scharbert (1958a:15) argues for the meaning "voll Unmut sein," and Brichto (1963:203) correctly states that the verb denotes hostility and in some contexts at least does not denote an utterance.

For those who convict the guilty, however, impersonal constructions are used. This implies that their blessing comes from God, not from man (so also Wehmeier 1970:87). The statement is therefore stronger than a simple assurance that "society blesses those who bless it and curses those who curse it" (McKane 1970:573); just judges receive the approval of God. *birkat-ṭôb* is an attributive genitive (*GKC* 128 p) denoting a blessing consisting of good, i.e., desirable things. Prosperity and success are the visible signs of God's approval.

Prov 11:26 is quite similar:

> People curse the man who hoards grain,
> but blessing comes on the head of him who sells it.

The curse word is *qbb*, as in 24:24. *mōnēaᶜ* probably denotes "holding out for the highest price without regard for the common good" (McKane 1970:434), rather than refusing to sell at all. The question here is whether the *bĕrākâ* comes from God or man. By the parallelism, one might expect that it denotes "Segenssprüche die ihnen von Mitmenschen zuteil werden" (Wehmeier 1970:86; so also Scott 1965:86, Kidner 1964:94). However, the impersonal construction implies that blessing comes from a higher source. The construction with *lĕrōʾš* is elsewhere used only of God's blessings (Gen 49:26; Deut 33:16; Prov 10:6). The statement is stronger than merely saying that people appreciate one who sells his grain. The point is that *God* will reward such a person.[11]

Prov 10:6 also employs *lĕrōʾš* in an impersonal construction:

> Blessings come upon the head of the righteous man,
> but the mouth of the wicked man conceals violence.

The LXX correctly interprets the impersonal construction as *eulogia kuriou* (contra Scott 1965:81, "Men call down blessings"; Kidner 1964:85 and Wehmeier 1970:86 cannot decide between the two possibilities).[12]

---

[11] The blessing would likely include a bountiful grain harvest to replace that sold, as well as prosperity to make up any loss taken in selling the grain at a less-than-optimum price. God's blessing often includes bestowal of those very things used in fulfilling God's requirements (Deut 12:7,15; 14:24; 16:10,15,17; Joel 2:14). In Mal 3:10 God promises to replace food given as a tithe.

[12] The relation of v 6b to 6a is unclear. 6b is also found in 11b, where it

Prov 20:21 speaks of God blessing possessions:

> An inheritance quickly gained at the beginning,
> in the end will not be blessed.

The "inheritance quickly gained"[13] probably refers to property or money acquired dishonestly (so Kidner 1964:139). It probably does not denote the family inheritance obtained by patricide (contra McKane 1970:539). The similar ideas in 21:5, 28:20,22 imply that "not be blessed" means "to be lost"—the money is spent, the goods used up, or the land taken by another.

Ps 37:25-26 extends the usual doctrine of individual retribution:

> I have been young, and now I am old.
> I have never seen a righteous man forsaken,
> or his children seeking food.
> All day he shows mercy and lends,
> and his children will be blessed.

There are three possible interpretations of *wĕzarʿô libĕrākâ. bĕrākâ* could denote a source of blessing, as in Gen 12:2 and Isa 19:24. The righteous man is described in v 26a as lending to others, and so his children in v 26b would carry on his tradition of doing good to others (so BDB 139b, and Weiser 1962:313,321, "his seed becomes a blessing").

The second possibily is that the noun denotes a "Beispiel in Segensformeln" (Wehmeier 1970:100), as it does in Zech 8:13. The idea of a proverbial example of a blessed person is clearly described in Gen 48:20. The phrase would then be translated something like "and his children become proverbial examples of blessed people."

The third possibility is the best. By metonymy *bĕrākâ* denotes the recipient of God's blessing, as in Ezek 34:26. The phrase then means that "his children are destined for blessing" (Dahood 196:226, similarly Leupold 1969:303; cf. Prov 10:7 where *libĕrākâ* means that a righteous man's memory will be the object of human blessings and praise). The entire psalm is concerned with God's retribution. It would be odd, then, to have

---

forms an appropriate parallel to 11a. 6b seems unrelated to 6a (so also McKane 1970:422).

[13]The ketib *mĕbōhelet*, "acquired by greed," a *hapax*, makes good sense, but the qere *mĕbōhelet* has the support of the versions and agrees with the idea of 21:5; 28:20, which employ *ʾûṣ*, and 28:22, which employs the Niphal of *bhl*.

the righteous man, let alone his children, be the source of blessing. There is also no warrant for assuming that the noun has the specialized meaning of "proverbial example." The children are blessed, but not to an extreme degree. The verse is a statement of the principle of diachronic collective retribution, as in Exod 20:5-6. God's beneficent activity carries over to descendants of the righteous, as in v 25, where his children (zeraʿ) do not lack bread. The converse is also true. V 22b states that "those he (God) curses are cut off," and v 28d states that "the children (zeraʿ again) of the wicked are cut off."

Prov 11:11 discusses synchronic collective retribution:

> By the blessing given to the upright a city stands high,
> but by the mouth of the wicked it is destroyed.

The question here is whether *birkat yĕšārîm* refers to God's blessing bestowed upon the upright, or to "benedictions and pious prayers" (Keil and Delitzsch *Proverbs*:1.236) spoken by the upright. Wehmeier (1970:97-98) says *bĕrākâ* denotes human benedictions as well as the friendly interactions of the citizens. Several of the surrounding proverbs (vv 9,12,13) are concerned with speech, as is v 11b. However, all these verses describe the destructive power of speech; none ascribe any beneficial power to it at all, except when it is silenced!

The immediately preceding verse (10a) states: "a town rejoices in the prosperity (*ṭûb*) of the righteous." *bĕrākâ*, then, refers to this same prosperity (so also BDB 139b).

The city prospers because of the prosperity God gives to its upright citizens, though it can also be destroyed by the speech of the wicked (associated with *ḥāmās* in Prov 10:6,11).

In summary, the Piel of *brk* with God as subject denotes God bestowing benefits upon the pious (Ps 5:13; Prov 3:33). The Pual is the passive of the Piel. The people who are the subjects of the Pual are the recipients of benefits given by God (Pss 37:22; 112:2; 128:4; Prov 22:9). In Prov 20:21 possessions are not blessed (*brk*, Pual) in that their owner quickly loses possession of them.

The Qal passive participle denotes a person who regularly receives benefits from God (Jer 17:7). Jer 17:7-8 is quite similar to Ps 1:1-3, both in thought and language (cf. also Ps 40:5). Ps 1 begins with ʾašrê. A comparison of the two passages shows that *bārûk* and ʾašrê are completely synonymous; there is no discernible difference in meaning (on ʾašrê see further under 6.8). Furthermore, both ʾašrê and *bārûk* in these wisdom aphorisms are synonymous with the Pual when the Pual has a durative meaning describing the condition of a person, as in Ps 37:22; 112:2; 128:4. In Ps 128, the man who fears God is twice the subject of the ʾašrê formula (vv 1,2). The Pual is then used in v 4 to describe the condition of the man who is ʾašrê; he is yĕbōrak, "blessed, a man whom God constantly blesses." The description of the people denoted by the Pual participle in Ps 37 (mĕbōrākāyw, v 22) is quite similar to the descriptions of the pious who are elsewhere called bārûk or ʾašrê. However, when the Pual refers to a specific period of time (Prov 20:21; 22:9), it is not synonymous with bārûk or ʾašrê, unless one of the latter words is used in a verbal clause. For example, bārûk tihyeh (Deut 7:14) is equivalent to tĕbōrak with a future meaning.

The noun usually denotes the benefits God bestows (Ps 24:5; Prov 10:6; 11:11,26; 24:25; 28:20). Usually material benefits are meant, with the connotation that God gives them out of his favor. In Ps 24:5, however, where ṣĕdāqâ is parallel to bĕrākâ, the noun primarily denotes God's favor, and only secondarily material benefits. In Prov 10:22a, "It is Yahweh's blessing that gives wealth," the noun denotes God's blessing activity. God's blessing is the source of material benefits, but is entirely distinct from them. In Ps 37:26, the noun means "a recipient of material benefits from God," with the connotation "one with whom God is pleased."

3.1.4 The Prophetic Apocalyptic Blessing Promises

The promises of blessing in the prophetic apocalypses are different from the previously discussed promises in several respects. They are made to the nation as a whole, rather than to individuals. The prophets describe the fulfillment of the promises as occurring in a future golden age, rather than in the lifetime of the recipients of the promises. Blessing often consists of fertility or prosperity, but the thought soon turns from these ordinary benefits to extraordinary and even miraculous benefits. God does not quietly effect blessing through the natural processes, nor does blessing result from God's retribution according to the covenant. Instead, blessing results from God's dramatic intervention in the course of history. God promises to deliver his people and inaugurate a golden age of blessing through his acts of deliverance.

The promise of physical benefits in these passages is of secondary importance to the other benefits God promises. The material blessings promised are often only symbols of more abstract benefits such as God's favor and peace.

In Ezek 34:26, God promises: "I will make them and the areas around

God Blessing Man   53

my hill recipients of blessing. I will make rain come down in its season; they will be rains giving blessing."[14] The first occurrence of the noun means "a recipient of blessing" as in Ps 37:26; Prov 10:7 (contra BDB 139b who takes it as "source of blessing"). The context clearly describes the nation as receiving blessing. Conversely, *gišmê-běrākâ* does not denote rains that have received God's blessing, but rains that bring God's blessing to the nation (so also Scharbert 1975a:299, Wehmeier 1970:72-73, contra Zimmerli 1979:826 "gesegnete Regen"). God's blessing here consists of agricultural fertility (vv 26-27), as often in apocalyptic prophecies (for example Hos 2:22; Joel 3:18; Amos 9:13-14; Zech 8:12).

But fertility shrinks in importance next to the other benefits God promises. God will raise up a David figure as leader over the nation (vv 23-24; on this figure cf. Zimmerli 1979:2.841-844,848-849, Taylor 1969:222-223, Eichrodt 1970:475-479). God will make a covenant giving peace (*běrît-šālôm*) with them (v 25). *šālôm* "is not a negative concept, implying absence of conflict or worry, . . . but a thoroughly positive state in which all is functioning well" (Taylor 1969:224). God will also banish predators from the land (v 25).

Isa 65:18-25 describes the future golden age as a new creation. God promises that the people will be a "generation blessed by Yahweh" (v 23). Wehmeier (1970:116-117) argues that *zeraʿ běrûkê-yhwh* means that the people have blessings and belong to Yahweh, but Isa 61:9 describes the people as *zeraʿ bērak yhwh*; they are blessed (*běrûkîm*) because Yahweh has blessed (*bērak*) them. The participle is passive in meaning and in construct with its agent, as in Gen 24:31; 26:29.

In the context (vv 19-25), God's blessing consists of fertility, longevity, prosperity, and peace. Yet these benefits are more spectacular than they are in the other types of promises. People will normally live to over one hundred (v 20). It will be assumed that anyone who dies at less than one hundred has incurred God's disfavor (cf. Gen 38:7,10; *yěqullal* is antonymous to *bārûk* in v 23). Some of the blessing benefits clearly are not intended to be taken literally; the animal behavior in v 25 is simply a figurative description of a new, complete state of peace and harmony.

Isa 51:1-2 is concerned with demonstrating how God faithfully fulfills even his most unbelievable promises. God uses Abraham as an example of such a fulfillment:

---

[14]*ntn* is used in the sense of "make into, turn into" (cf. BDB 681a). It takes a double accusative construction (*GKC* 117 ii). *ʾōtām* represents Israel, previously described as sheep (vv 2-23). There is no need to emend *sěbîbôt* to *rěbîbîm* (contra Eichrodt 1970:474, Cooke 1936:378).

> Look to the rock from which you were cut,
>   to the quarry from which you were hewn!
> Look to Abraham, your father,
>   to Sarah, who bore you!
> He was but one person when I called him,
>   but I blessed him and made him numerous.

The comparison of Abraham to a rock describes the origin of the nation as an act of creation (Pieper 1979:400, Westermann 1969:236). A rock is barren and inanimate, incapable of producing anything by itself. It was only because God fulfilled his blessing promise that Abraham fathered Isaac, leading to the emergence of the nation. Though the nation lies in ruins (v 3), Israel is encouraged to trust that just as God made one man into a multitude, so he will again rebuild the nation. The rebuilt nation in v 3 is pictured as a second creation. It will be another Eden, full of joy and praise.

In the other passages blessing consists entirely of abstract benefits which affect Israel's relationship to God and her relationship with other peoples. Other peoples are incorporated into Israel, though Israel retains her privileged position. In Isa 61:5 foreigners stand in a subservient relationship to Israel. This is not quite dominion since Israel does not conquer them. Instead, like the Gibeonites, they are incorporated into Israel and serve as her shepherds and farmers, enabling the Israelites to assume the higher duties of the priesthood (v 6). Israel occupies a position of prestige, and God blesses the Israelites to such an extent that they are strikingly different from other people (v 9):

> Their descendents will be esteemed among the nations,
>   their offspring among the peoples.
> All who see them will recognize them,
>   for they are a people whom Yahweh has blessed.[15]

---

[15] nôdaᶜ means "esteemed," as in Ps 76:2; Prov 31:23 (Pieper 1979:611). The second occurrence of zeraᶜ, in "they are a people whom Yahweh has blessed," has the meaning of "people" in the sense of a class of people. It is quite similar to dôr in Ps 112:2, "an upright generation that will be blessed," and zeraᶜ in Isa 65:23. The emphasis is not so much on the diachronic relationship of the zeraᶜ to their progenitors, though they are genetically related, but on their synchronic relationship to each other and to those outside their number. The zeraᶜ forms a homogeneous class of people. They stand out as a group from their contemporaries.

God Blessing Man 55

In Jer 4:2 and Isa 19:24-25, other nations partake of the blessings given Israel. This is seen best in Isa 19:24-25:

> On that day Israel will be third next to Egypt and Assyria, a source of blessing in the center of the land. Yahweh of hosts will bless them, saying, "Blessed is my people Egypt, and Assyria whom I made with my hands, and Israel my inheritance."

In v 24 God promises that Israel will be a *běrākâ*, a source of blessing, as he promised to Abraham in Gen 12:2 (so also BDB 139b, Leupold 1976:1.321, Wehmeier 1970:87-88, Young 1969:45). Vv 16-22 describe how Israel will be a source of blessing. Egypt will be frightened into reverence for Yahweh and even have an altar dedicated to him (vv 16-19). Yahweh will also send someone to deliver Egypt from her oppressors (v 20). This is clearly an allusion to the Exodus; Egypt will experience the same type of deliverance that Israel did.

Egypt will know (*yd^c*) Yahweh, i.e., through her deliverance Egypt will recognize Yahweh as the saving God that he is (Leupold 1976:320), and so engage in cultic worship (v 21). Yahweh will repeatedly chastise Egypt and then heal her when she repents, just as he did to Israel (especially in the period of the Judges; cf. also Lev 26:44; Deut 32:36).

The statement that Israel will be a third means that through God's blessing all three countries will have equal standing before God. This is seen in v 25 where the terms *ʿammî* and *maʿăśēh-yāday*, which elsewhere refer to Israel (on the latter term see Isa 64:7), are applied to Egypt and Assyria (on v 25 see further under 3.2.1). Yet Israel still retains her distinctive position as the mediator of blessing (cf. John 4:22b).

Jer 4:1-2 alludes to the patriarchal promises. If the people return to God and serve him faithfully, then "all nations will acquire blessing through him, and will exult in him." The Hithpael of *brk* in v 2 with *gôyim* as the subject and *bô*, "by means of/through him," is an allusion to the five patriarchal promises of blessing for all through the mediation of Abraham and his seed (so also Thompson 1980:213, Wehmeier 1970:181, Harrison 1973:68).

As seen in Table 2, it is not an exact quote of any of the passages (the Hithpael occurs only with *bězarʿăkā*, while the Niphal occurs with *bô*, *běkā*, and *bězarʿăka*). Though God is the agent in this verse,[16] Israel acts

---

[16] There is disagreement over who *bô* refers to here. Many commentators including Wehmeier (1970:181 note 24) and BHS emend both occur-

as a catalyst. If Israel repents, other nations would see the benefits Israel would then derive from her covenant relationship to God, and would seek to enter into that relationship in order to acquire blessing from Yahweh too. Jeremiah predicts the inclusion of all the nations in the worship of Yahweh also in 3:17 (on jealousy as a means of conversion, cf. Deut 32:21b; Rom 10:19; 11:11b).

Most passages, however, are concerned solely with the internal condition of Israel and her relationship to God. Isa 44:3 describes how God's blessing will renew religious commitment among the Israelites:

> For I will pour out water on the thirsty land,
>   streams on the dry ground;
> I will pour out my spirit on your descendants,
>   my blessing on your offspring.

The figure of plant fertility is used here. God's blessing activity will be like pouring water on dry ground, enabling plants to grow (v 4). But the prophet is not primarily concerned with fertility. The effect of God's blessing is described in v 5:

> One person will say, 'I belong to Yahweh',
>   another will name himself after Jacob,
> and yet another will write on his hand, 'belonging to Yahweh',
>   and take the name of Israel.

The meanings of bĕrākâ and rûaḥ transcend the notions of the "power which bestows fertility" and "the divine power which creates life in man

---

rences of bô to bĕkā, which would then refer to Israel, but there is no textual support for this. Though unexpected shifts in person do occur in Hebrew discourse, it is unlikely that Israel would be referred to in the second person in the protasis of v 2 and in the third person in the apodosis (contra Thompson 1980:205,213, Harrison 1973:68). The parallel line "exult in him" uses hll Hithpael which often takes the preposition b attached to the basis for rejoicing or boasting (BDB 239a). When the verb denotes rejoicing it always has b attached to God or Yahweh. bô, therefore, refers to Yahweh, who is referred to in the third person in v 2a. The Hithpael of brk does not merely suggest that they will wish for the blessings Israel has (contra Wehmeier 1970:181), but that they shall actually acquire them (see on Gen 22:18; 26:4 in note 3 of chapter 3). The fact that they exult or rejoice shows that they have received what they desired.

God Blessing Man 57

and nature," respectively, which they have in the metaphor of plant growth (contra Westermann 1969:136, Wehmeier 1970:76-77). They denote God's beneficent influence on the religion of the people (so also Leupold 1976:2.99-100: "blessing . . . signifies an effective form of divine enrichment" of the "spiritual life" of the people). The effect of God's blessing and spirit being "poured out" is that the people will return to the traditional faith and declare their loyalty to Yahweh (v 5). They will proudly take the names of the patriarchs to symbolize their adherence to the ancient faith.

Wehmeier (1970:77), Westermann (1969:136-137) and Leupold (1976: 2.100) all interpret the original meaning of this passage as predicting the conversion of gentiles. Yet the prophecy is addressed to the nation, called "Jacob" and "Israel" (v 1). It is *their* descendants who will receive God's blessing; gentiles are included typologically if they are incorporated into the new Israel as spiritual descendants.

Ezek 34:26 (discussed above) likewise speaks of God blessing Israel. Wehmeier (1970:89) believes that the phrase "the areas surrounding my hill" designates the heathen gentiles who would share in the blessings God gives to Israel. However, the entire chapter is devoted to internal strife within Israel and its resolution by God. The phrase simply refers to the land of Israel, which has Zion, Yahweh's hill ($gib^c\hat{a}$, as in Isa 31:4) as its focus, though again others may be incorporated into Israel.

The prophetic apocalypses, then, say God's purpose in blessing is to inaugurate a new, intimate relationship with Israel. In the new world order God will bestow amazing benefits and Israel will wholeheartedly serve him. God's blessing makes known his feelings towards his people. God rejoices over Israel (Isa 65:19), and makes a new inviolable covenant with her out of his favor ($rāṣôn$) toward her (Isa 61:2,8; Ezek 34:25). The extraordinary blessings God bestows as part of this new covenant are indicative of the intimate relationship between God and his people.

God also blesses in order to renew the religious commitment of Israel (Isa 44:5), so that they zealously serve him as priests (Isa 61:6). God uses Israel as a mediator of blessing in order to bless other nations and lead them to worship himself (Isa 19:24-25; Jer 4:2).

God promises to inaugurate the age of blessing through acts of deliverance ($hôšîa^c$, Ezek 34:22; cf. Isa 19:20; Zech 8:13; $hiṣṣîl$, Isa 19:20; 61:9; 65:23; Ezek 34:10,12,27). In Isa 51:1-3; 65:17-25, God effects blessing by performing a second creation; the blessed state is part of a "new heavens and new earth" and a "new Jerusalem" (65:17-18). In Isa 44:3 God promotes the state of blessing by pouring out his spirit ($rûaḥ$).

3.1.5 Miscellaneous Promises

A group of five prophetic blessing promises occupies an intermediate position between the covenantal promises and the apocalyptic prophetic promises. The content of blessing is the same as in the covenantal promises, but the reasons for God's blessing are not the same either as those in the covenantal promises or in the prophetic apocalypses.

God promises to bless during the second temple period in Hag 2:19; Zech 8:13; and Mal 3:10. Blessing does not result from God's retribution according to the Sinai covenant. Instead, God promises to bless as part of the restoration. The resumption of God's blessing shows that the covenantal relationship between God and Israel has been renewed.

In Hag 2:18-19, the resumption of blessing is tied to the work on the second temple:

> Give careful thought from this day on; from this twenty-fourth day of the ninth month, give careful thought to the day when the temple was refounded. Is there any seed left in the barn? Until now, the vine, the fig tree, the pomegranite tree, and the olive tree have not borne fruit. Starting today, I will bless.

God promises to bless starting three months after the commencement of work on the temple.[17] There is no need to insert the date from 1:15a into 2:15-19 to make the blessing start immediately after the temple work resumed in 520 B.C., rather than three months later, as advocated by BHS and Wehmeier (1970:219-220). The precise date given in 2:18 is important for the prophecy, since it falls in January. The seed was not in the barn (2:18), but in the ground. God's promise to bless comes right before the spring growing season. Had God promised to bless starting with the first work on the temple three months previously, there would have been no

---

[17] *ysd* in Ezra 3:10,11 and Hag 2:18 denotes the start of the restoration or rebuilding of the temple in 538 B.C., and does not imply that the entire foundation had to be rebuilt (see Baldwin 1972:53). The work on the temple started in 538 B.C. (Ezra 3:10,11), and ceased shortly thereafter until Haggai's rebuke in 520 B.C. (Hag 1:1). Darius' second year was 520/519 B.C. Work started again on the twenty-fourth of the sixth month (Hag 1:1). God's promise to bless was given three months later, on the twenty-fourth of the ninth month. The temple was finished in the spring of 515 B.C. (Ezra 6:15, Laetsch 1956:385, Baldwin 1972:31-32, 52-53).

God Blessing Man   59

evidence yet of God's fulfillment. As the MT stands, the people will see an immediate fulfillment or failure of the prophecy, and Haggai's timing proves how confident he was of fulfillment.

Haggai points out that the absence of God's blessing had caused drought, crop disease, hail, poor harvests, and animal and human infertility (1:6,10-11; 2:16-17). The picture is similar to the curse of Mal 3:9, though no specific curse words are used here. The context implies that God's blessing will bring the opposite results.

Haggai's prophecy shows that the temple was to be just as important as the source of God's blessing in the second temple period as it was in the pre-exilic period (for the pre-exilic period see especially on 1 Kgs 8 under 4.2.2). The temple was the symbol of God's presence and of the covenant between him and Israel. Haggai says that God will only bless now based on the people's desire to maintain the covenant relationship, as evidenced by their work on the temple.

Zechariah also urged the people to work on the temple so that they could receive blessing (8:9-13). God's blessing consists of a bestowal of the same benefits promised in the Sinai covenant, showing that the covenant had been restored: "The seed will grow well, the vine will yield its fruit, the ground will produce its crops, and the heavens will drop their dew" (v 12); God also promises longevity, human fertility, and tranquility (v 4-5).

In Zech 8:13, God declares,

> Just as you were the epitome of cursing among the nations,
>   O house of Judah, and house of Israel,
> So I will deliver you, and you will be the epitome of blessing!

Because of the exile, Israel was a curse, a *qĕlālâ*, meaning "a proverbial example of a cursed people" (Brichto 1963:196, contra BDB 887a, "object of curse"). People would use the name of Israel in maledictions. Jer 29:22 explains this meaning of *qĕlālâ*. God prophesies against two false prophets: "A curse (*qĕlālâ*) will be made from them by all the exiles of Judah who are in Babylon. They will say, 'May Yahweh make you like Zedekiah and Ahab, whom the king of Babylon roasted in fire!'"

In the antonymous phrase "*wihyîtem bĕrākâ*," the noun does not simply mean "a recipient of blessing" (as in Ezek 34:26; Psalm 37:26; cf. Prov 10:7), but "a proverbial example of someone who has been blessed" (contra BDB 139b, "source of blessing"; see Gen 48:20 and Ruth 4:11-12 for instances of the invocation of such proverbial examples).[18] The reversal of Israel's fortunes will be so dramatic that Israel will serve as a proverbial example of good fortune. When someone says, "May God make you like Israel," they will no longer be pronouncing a malediction, but a benediction. God says that he will make Israel a proverbial example by delivering them (ʾôšíaʿ, v 13, and môšíaʿ, v 17). These statements resemble the descriptions of how God initiates the golden age of blessing in the prophetic apocalypses. Yet the thought here is not quite apocalyptic; the blessing benefits are not extraordinary, nor do they lie too far in the future.

In Mal 3:10, God promises to bless the Israelites if they obey the covenant stipulations. He therefore makes it clear that the blessing in the second temple period will be the result of retribution according to the Sinai covenant just as it was in the pre-exilic period. Similarly, the covenantal curses will continue to remain on the people as long as they disobey: "You are cursed (nēʾārîm) by a curse (mĕʾērâ), since you are robbing me—the whole nation of you!" (v 9). God challenges the people: "'Bring the full tithe into the storehouse, so there may be food in my house. Test me in this', says Yahweh of hosts, 'See if I will not open the floodgates of heaven for you and pour down to you blessing until there is no more room for it.'"

The noun bĕrākâ here denotes the conditions which enable the produce of the land to thrive, especially rain and dew, as well as the produce itself, which will be so abundant that they will not have enough room for it. Wehmeier (1970:80) generalizes the meaning of bĕrākâ to include "ein menschenwürdiges Dasein," but the context indicates that it is limited to the natural produce of the land.

Ezekiel, too, sees blessing as God's recompense for those who obey the commandments in his vision of the future restoration: "You shall give the first portion of your ground meal to the priest so that blessing rests upon your house" (44:30). Though some commentators see a reference in the

---

[18]In addition to Zech 8:13, various authors argue for the meaning "proverbial example of a blessed person" for the noun bĕrākâ in Gen 12:2; Isa 19:24; Ezek 34:26; Pss 21:7; 37:26; Prov 10:7. Wehmeier (1970:99-100) argues for this meaning in Gen 12:2; Ps 37:26; Prov 10:7. Scharbert (1958a:25-26) argues for them all; Keller (1978:366-367) and Murtonen (1958:159-160) have trouble deciding exactly which passages have this meaning. However, the contexts make clear that the noun does not have this meaning in any of these verses.

verse to the priestly blessing (Wehmeier 1970:85-86; Zimmerli 1979: 2.1139), the impersonal construction and the similarity of the context to the covenantal blessing promises imply that God's blessing is meant (see the impersonal constructions above under 3.1.3).

Joel reminds the people that God's blessing is essential for their participation in the cult, and that participation in the cult is a privilege of the obedient covenant people (cf. Wolff 1977:50). God had hindered cultic worship by sending a locust plague which ate up the produce used for grain offerings and libations (1:4,13) to make clear that the Israelites had violated the covenant. In 2:1-11, Joel says that the locust plague is only a mild indication of the destruction coming on Yahweh's day. Yet if the people repent, "Who knows? He may turn and relent, and leave a blessing after himself, grain offerings and libations for Yahweh your God" (2:14).

The blessing (bĕrākâ) God would leave behind consists of the natural conditions which enable the produce of the land to thrive (so also in Lev 25:21; Deut 28:8; Mal 3:10). God does not promise to inaugurate an age of blessing, as in the apocalypses, but simply to restore the ravaged land.

Ps 132 is a song of ascent. Vv 13-18 are an "Erwählungserklärung" (Kraus 1961:878), a description of God's election of Zion as his eternal dwelling place. Yahweh declares in vv 14-15,

> This is where I will rest for ever and ever,
>   here I will dwell because I desire her.
> I will abundantly bless her food supply,
>   and fill her poor with food.

The passage emphasizes that it is from Zion that God blesses. God does not promise to bless because of Israel's obedience, but simply because of his favor toward her—he chose her (bḥr, v 13, as in Deut 7:7) simply because he desired her (v 14b). The promises of vv 14-18, unlike that of v 12, are unconditional.

Blessing here consists of God providing abundant food. The phrase "I will bless her food supply" means "I will bless her by providing abundant food" (cf. Exod 23:25; Deut 7:13; 28:4-5). Though this blessing is important, the other benefits God promises in conjunction with it are more significant (vv 16-18): salvation for the priests, joy for the pious, a horn and lamp for David (cf. Ezek 34:23-24), and shame upon their enemies. The thought is similar to many of the apocalyptic promises.

For God's blessing promise in Num 6:27, see under 4.2.1.

3.2 Statements of God's Blessing

Statements to the effect that God has blessed a person mean that God has in some way displayed his favorable attitude or approval toward that person. God can do this either by means of an oral benediction or by means of benefaction.

3.2.1 Statements of God's Benediction

God's benedictions are always illocutionary utterances in which God makes known his feelings toward persons or things. The statements never effect blessing by the magical power of the spoken word. Instead, because the blessings are illocutionary utterances, the pronouncement of the benediction in itself is the act of blessing.

God pronounces a benediction using imperatives of *prh* and *rbh* four times in P (Gen 1:22,28; 9:1-7; 35:9-12). After creating the animals, "God blessed them by saying, 'Be fruitful, be numerous, and fill the water in the oceans, and may the birds be numerous on the earth'." The benediction God spoke to the humans in v 28 and to Noah in 9:1 is similar: "Be fruitful, be numerous, and fill the earth," while the benediction spoken to Jacob (35:11) uses the singular imperatives *pĕrēh ûrĕbēh* instead of the plurals and lacks *ml*'.

Practically all commentators misunderstand the nature of God's oral blessings and say that God's spoken words somehow bestowed upon the people and animals the power of fertility or the ability to reproduce (so, for example, Wehmeier 1970:133,170, von Rad 1972:56, Leupold 1942: 1.81). Certainly in the creation narrative God is pictured as capable of creating and imparting life simply by means of his spoken word. The recurrent phrase *wayyō'mer 'ĕlōhîm* ... *wayyĕhî kēn* (1:6-7,9,11,14-15,24) implies that the divine word is itself sufficient to effect what it states. But the animals and people had already been created and were already capable of reproduction. In all four verses, *brk* Piel simply means "to pronounce a blessing formula." The fact that *bērak*, and not a verb of commanding or ordering, was used shows that the formula does not really constitute a command to do something which the people and animals would not otherwise have done. Rather, because the formula is a blessing, it expresses God's approval and desire that they reproduce. The formula is an illocutionary utterance equivalent in meaning to God saying: "I hereby declare my desire for you to reproduce and so fill the earth."

Similarly, the additional imperatives God addresses to man, "subdue the earth and rule over the fish . . ." (1:28) do not somehow instill within man

God Blessing Man   63

the ability to exercise dominion. Instead, by them God explains the natural order which he had already built into the creation (so also in vv 29-30). God declares that he *wants* man to exercise dominion because he had designed the creation with dominion as man's natural function. Man is to function as God's representative on earth, since he is made in God's image (1:26; von Rad 1972:59-61).

There is no indication that God's benedictions to Noah (9:1-7) and Jacob (35:9-12) imparted fertility, or that Noah and Jacob would not have been capable of reproduction if God had not blessed them (unlike Abraham and Sarah in 17:16-21). God encouraged Noah and his family to reproduce because the human population had become precariously small.

God's declaration in 9:2-3 that the animals would subsequently serve as man's food likewise did not materially alter the creation, but simply made known God's approval of the practice.

However, God's benediction of 35:9-12 contains several promises to Abraham (cf. 3.1.1). God also renamed Jacob (on the significance of renaming in conjunction with blessing, see on Gen 17:16-20 under 3.1.1). The "primary concern of our text is to show that the promise to Abraham was renewed completely to Jacob" (von Rad 1972:339). Within the context of the promises, the imperatives carry the added connotation that God will help Jacob carry out the function of which God states his approval. That is why, when Jacob looks back upon 35:9-12 in 48:3-4, he uses Hiphil forms in his quote of God's words: "El Shaddai . . . blessed me, saying to me, 'See, I will make you fruitful and numerous'." The promises elsewhere use the Hiphil forms of *rbh* and occasionally *prh* with God as the subject (Gen 17:20; 22:17; 26:4,24; cf. the prayer of 28:3).

Gen 5:2 looks back on 1:28 and states that God named man in conjunction with blessing him: "He blessed them and named them *ʾādām* at the time that they were created." The Piel of *brk* here means to pronounce the blessing formula in 1:28. The actual naming probably occurred in 1:26. Naming was an essential part of creation, since each creature, including man, must have a label to identify its place in the created order (on naming see further on Gen 17:16-20 under 3.1.1).

God twice utters declarative *bārûk* formulas over countries. *bārûk* means that the countries stand in a covenantal relationship to God (cf. 3.1.2 and 3.2.2.2), and so God is favorably disposed toward them. The participle is passive; God blesses the countries according to the covenant, and so they are recipients of blessing.

In Num 22, Balak summons Balaam to curse Israel. Balaam asks God if he should comply, and receives a nocturnal answer in v 12: "Do not curse the people, because they are blessed." Brichto (1963:100) and Wehmeier

(1970:106-107)[19] understand bārûk as meaning "immune to a spell." However, if Israel was immune to curses, there would be no need for God to prevent Balaam from cursing her. God's preventive measures indicate that Balaam's curse would indeed have had deleterious effects. Yahweh prevented Balaam from cursing Israel because such a curse would have prophesied the disfavor and anger of Yahweh upon his people and their consequent defeat in battle. Such a curse would have inaccurately represented the relationship between Yahweh and Israel, and since it is important for Yahweh that others correctly perceive this relationship, he changes the curses into declarations of his favor toward Israel (on Balaam see further under 4.1.2).

Isa 19:25 envisions a future age when Egypt and Assyria will also be blessed by God: "Yahweh of hosts will bless them by saying, 'Blessed are my people Egypt, Assyria whom I have made with my hands, and my inheritance Israel." The Piel of brk here is delocutive, meaning "to pronounce a bārûk formula."[20] bārûk means that all three countries enjoy blessings from God because they are in a covenantal relationship with him (so also Scharbert 1975a:285; see further on v 24 under 3.1.4). God does not effect blessing or bring the countries into a covenantal relationship with himself by pronouncing the formula (contra Wehmeier 1970:170). Instead, the illocutionary declaration describes the relationship that God previously brought about through his acts of judgement and deliverance described in vv 1-23.

In three verses, God's oral blessing denotes consecration (see also 1 Sam 9:13 under 4.1.4, where brk Piel denotes consecration by a person). The meaning "consecrate" is a meaning specialized from the more general meaning "pronounce a blessing formula." In consecration, God issues a declaration that changes the status of a person or thing. The declaration is effective simply because it is an illocutionary speech act, not because of any magical or self-fulfilling power inherent in the words.

At the close of the P creation narrative God blesses the seventh day: (Gen 2:3) "God blessed the seventh day and sanctified it because on it he rested from all his work which he had done in creating." brk Piel is

---

[19] Wehmeier adds that in the present edited form of the text bārûk means that Israel is destined to be a "Segensträger," both a recipient and a source of blessing.

[20] This is the only instance where the Piel denoting a benediction by God is delocutive. The Piel denoting a human benediction spoken to another person is often delocutive (see chapter 4), while the Piel denoting human praise of God occasionally is delocutive (see 5.1, 5.2, 5.3).

God Blessing Man

parallel to *qdš* Piel. As elsewhere in the primeval history, God's blessing denotes pronouncement of a formula expressing God's sentiments. *qiddēš* specifies what type of pronouncement God made. The Piel of *qdš* is declarative; God designates the seventh day as a holy day, a day special to him. Here "holy" means only that the day commemorates God's activity; the relation of man to the day is out of the picture (so also Driver 1905:35 and Leupold 1942:1.103-104). There is no indication that God empowered the day with blessing power ("Segenskraft, d.h., Kraft der Forderung und des Gelingens") which would emanate from the day onto men (contra Wehmeier 1970:133 (quoted), and Westermann 1982:237).

Exod 20:11, on the other hand, discusses the implications of the consecration of the day for man: "In six days Yahweh made the heavens, the earth, the sea, and all that is in them, and he rested on the seventh day. That is why Yahweh blessed the Sabbath day and sanctified it." As in Gen 2:3, the Piel of *qdš* stands parallel to *brk* Piel. Here the seventh day has become the Sabbath. Because man has an opportunity to rest and be refreshed, God made the Sabbath a source of blessing for man by consecrating it (cf. Cassuto 1967:244-246). The reason God consecrated the day was to remind mankind of what he had done for them in creation.

Exod 32 narrates the golden calf incident. The Levites followed Moses' command to kill those, including their relatives, who were not "for Yahweh" (vv 26-27). In v 29, Moses tells the Levites, "You have been ordained to Yahweh today, since each of you was against his son and his brother so that blessing came upon you."[21] The blessing (*běrākâ*) that the Levites acquired was consecration so that they became priests. As with the seventh/Sabbath day, God effected blessing by means of a declaration (v 29), which he issued here through Moses. By orally ordaining the Levites as priests, God bestowed the blessing upon them.

3.2.2.1 Statements of God's Benefaction in Maintaining the Creation

Isa 65:8; Gen 27:27; and Ps 65:11 employ *brk* to describe God's maintenance of the natural process of plant growth. In these verses God's blessing does not fulfill any promise, nor is it done specifically for the

---

[21] In the expression *mil'û yedkem* the indefinite plural verb functions as a passive (*GKC* 144g). The idiom *millē' yād* is the usual one for ordination to the priesthood (BDB 570b). The verb is Piel, not Qal (contra BDB 570a), since the idiom requires the Piel. The Qal is not elsewhere used of ordination.

benefit of people who stand in a special relationship to God. God simply blesses to maintain the creation for the benefit of all mankind. God's blessings evidence God's favor toward the entire creation (as in Gen 1:22,28; 5:2).

Isa 65:8 employs bĕrākâ in an analogy: "Thus says Yahweh: just as when juice is still found in a cluster of grapes, they say, 'Don't destroy it, because there is blessing in it', so I will do for the sake of my servants by not destroying them all." The analogy refers to the vintage season. When a cluster of grapes is about to be thrown away, someone objects on the grounds that it still contains juice for making wine. Once the juice is extracted, the rest is thrown away. Yet the entire cluster is kept as long as it still contains juice, just as the whole nation will be preserved for the sake of the remnant it contains.

Pedersen (1926:182-183), Mowinckel (1961:5,9), Westermann (1969:404) and Wehmeier (1970:70-71)[22] all see bĕrākâ here as having its supposed original meaning of life-power or *Lebenskraft* in a biological, non-theological sense. However, the verse merely states that bĕrākâ is in the cluster, not that it enables the grapes to grow. The cluster would have been cut off the vine in order to be pressed; it could not grow anymore, and so would no longer contain vitality. Instead, bĕrākâ denotes the tîrôš found in the grapes. While tîrôš usually denotes new wine or must, here it denotes the grape juice made into wine (so also in Micah 6:15). God's blessing (*brk*, Piel) includes the bestowal of tîrôš in Deut 7:13 and 2 Chr 31:5 (2 Chr 31:10 says that it is a product of God's blessing). Gen 27:28 is a human benediction (*brk*, Piel) which calls upon God to bestow tîrôš. Therefore, it is easy to see how tîrôš could be called a bĕrākâ. Isa 65:8 describes the juice as a precious commodity magnanimously given by God, and says that it would be a shame to throw away this valued fruit of nature. The noun has a quite similar meaning in the five passages where it denotes a freely given, unmerited material gift given by a person (see under 4.3). The blessing of grape juice is a natural component of creation and is a benefit available to all mankind, not just Israel.

Isaac's blessing of Jacob (Gen 27:27) starts with the exclamation,

---

[22]Wehmeier also understands ʾeškôl as a section of unfruitful vine, and tîrôš as its sap, and says hiṣḥît refers to trimming the vine in mid-season, not at vintage. While hiṣḥît can mean "to cut off," ʾeškôl and tîrôš elsewhere do not mean "vine" and "sap", respectively, and so his explanation of the verse is improbable.

> See, my son's smell is like the smell of a field,
> which Yahweh has blessed.

The Piel of *brk* means "to bestow those things necessary for abundant plant and animal life," such as rain, and the dew and fertile soil mentioned in the next verse. God is not pictured here as blessing to fulfill the patriarchal promises, but simply to provide food for mankind. God's blessing is a regular part of the world order and is not limited to certain times and places.

Ps 65 is a psalm of praise. Vv 10-14 describe how God provides plants and animals for man through the natural processes. The text of v 11, addressed to God, is somewhat difficult:

> You drench the earth's furrows,
> > level its ridges;
> you soften it with abundant showers,
> > you bless its plants.

The Piel of *brk* means "to make thrive." As in Gen 27:27, God clearly does not bless using the power of the spoken word, nor by bestowing a blessing power or life-power. Rather, he blesses directly by using the natural processes such as rain to make the soil conducive to growth.

3.2.2.2 Statements of God's Benefaction in Accordance with the Patriarchal Promises

The descriptions of God's benefaction toward the patriarchs seek to show that God fulfilled his blessing promises to the patriarchs (3.1.1). The descriptions make three assertions: 1) God blessed Abraham; 2) God's blessing activity continued diachronically with Abraham's line; and 3) God blessed others through Abraham's descendants. All three points are direct fulfillments of the blessing promises.

Gen 24 relates how Abraham procured a wife for Isaac. The narrative begins with the statement that "Abraham was old and well advanced in years, and Yahweh had blessed Abraham in everything" (v 1). The preposition after the Piel introduces the realms in which God effected blessing, as often in Deuteronomy (see 3.1.2). The narrative describes Abraham as blessed in all respects; his old age, too, is a blessing (cf. Exod 23:26; Deut 30:16-18; 33:24; Job 42:16 (cf. v 12); Ps 133:3).

Vv 35-36 describe Abraham's blessings in greater detail. Abraham's messenger describes to Rebekah's family how Yahweh has blessed Abraham. The context leaves no doubt about the meaning of bĕrak:

> Yahweh has abundantly blessed my lord, and so he has become wealthy. He has given him flocks and herds, silver and gold, male and female servants, camels, and donkeys. Furthermore, Sarah, my lord's wife, bore a son for my lord after she had become old.

Abraham is well on his way toward becoming a gôy gādôl (12:2); God has certainly fulfilled his promise to bless him (12:2). wayyigdal, as in 26:13, is a general term for prosperity. The son (bēn) was promised in 17:16.

Laban sees in the presents Abraham sent and in the success of the messenger's mission proof that God has indeed blessed Abraham and his messenger. After seeing the gold ring and bracelets, and hearing of how God led Abraham's servant on the journey (v 30), Laban invites the servant in: "Come in, you who have been blessed by Yahweh!" (v 31). In the phrase bĕrûk-yhwh, the participle is passive in meaning and in construct with its agent (GKC 116 l).[23] Plassmann (1913:118) and Wehmeier (1970:115-117) argue that bārûk is stative in meaning and that the construct state indicates ownership; bĕrûk-yhwh denotes a person who possesses blessings and belongs to Yahweh. Wehmeier approvingly quotes Pedersen who sees bārûk as designating a "man possessing power, a capable, vigorous man, full of bĕrākâ" (Pedersen 1926:199). The context, however, clearly indicates that the passive meaning with the agent is intended. There are two reasons why Laban calls the servant bārûk. He notices the gold ring and bracelets given to Rebekah, and he also hears Rebekah relate the servant's words to her (v 30). Wehmeier ignores this second reason. The servant had praised Yahweh for making his mission successful, saying "Yahweh has led me on the journey" (v 29). Yahweh had blessed him by making his mission successful. Furthermore, the gold ring and bracelet do not represent the servant's own wealth. Laban knows that they are from Abraham. If ownership were the intended meaning of the participle in construct, Laban would more likely have called Abraham's servant bĕrûk-'abrāhām.

Gen 25:11 is a short note in the middle of a genealogy, and is concerned solely with describing the diachronic aspect of God's blessing: "After

---

[23] bārûk occurs in construct only here and in Gen 26:29; Isa 65:23, where it also is in construct with its agent yhwh. The construction bārûk with l introducing the agent (GKC 121f) is equivalent in meaning and occurs eight times.

God Blessing Man

Abraham died, God blessed his son Isaac." From the context it is clear that the Piel of *brk* does not denote the bestowal of any specific benefit; it means that God carried on the entirety of his beneficent actions with Isaac as the new recipient. The unnecessary inclusion of *běnô* alludes to the fact that Isaac was the promised son with whom God promised to establish his covenant (17:7,16,19). God associated himself with a group of people, rather than with a certain locale, as the Canaanite deities did (von Rad 1972:272). Blessing will continue through Isaac's line regardless of their location.

Two examples of how God's blessing activity continued with Isaac occur in Gen 26. During his stay in Gerar,

> Isaac planted in that land and he reaped a hundredfold in that year, and Yahweh blessed him. The man became rich, and he continually grew more wealthy until he was exceedingly wealthy. He had flocks, herds, and many servants, and the Philistines envied him (v 12-14).

It is significant that Isaac acquired the same goods which (except for the crops) are ascribed to Abraham in 24:35; *gādal* (three times here) also describes Abraham in 24:35.

In 26:26-31 the Philistines, led by Abimelek, come to make a covenant with Isaac. In answer to Isaac's query concerning their motivation, they say,

> We clearly see that Yahweh is with you, so we said, "There ought to be a sworn agreement between us," between us and you. Let us make a treaty with you, that you will not do us any harm, just as we did not injure you but only did good to you and sent you away in peace. Now you have been blessed by Yahweh (vv 28-29).

Abimelek recognizes the favorable relationship between Isaac and Yahweh. Yahweh is with him (*ʿim*, as in 26:3; 28:15,20; Deut 2:7; and *ʾēt* in 26:24; 39:2,3), meaning that God has made known his favorable attitude toward him by conferring various benefits upon him (see further Vetter 1971). Abimelek had asked Isaac to leave because he felt threatened by Isaac's superior strength (v 16), and here Abimelek acknowledges that this strength is the result of Yahweh's blessing, as described in vv 12-14. *běrûk-yhwh* describes Isaac as a person who has been blessed by Yahweh (see on 24:31 above). The Philistines feel constrained to make a treaty[24] with Isaac since he has a powerful God on his side.

Isaac at best is only an indirect source of blessing for the Philistines. The treaty he made with them may have given them some military security, but no major benefits. Yet the narrative does show how foreigners desired the blessings which God bestowed upon his people, and how this desire led them to treat Israelites well (cf. Gen 12:3a).

Jacob and Joseph, on the other hand, clearly mediated God's blessing to others. The mediation is in fulfillment of the five patriarchal promises that all nations would acquire blessing through Abraham's line. Laban tried to persuade Jacob not to stop working for him, saying "I have learned by divination that Yahweh has blessed me on your account" (Gen 30:27). Jacob elucidates the meaning of "bless" (*brk*, Piel) in vv 29-30 where he confirms Laban's statement: "You know how I have worked for you and what has happened to your livestock under my care. For your livestock which you had before I came was small in number, but it has increased greatly, and Yahweh has blessed you everywhere I have been."

The phrase *lĕraglî* describes God's blessing as following Jacob around (cf. BDB 919b-920a). Yet blessing is not some contagious, mysterious power which a man who is *bārûk* possesses and which he exudes onto others (contra Mowinckel 1961:8-9, Pedersen 1926:199). Jacob does not possess blessing power; he possesses the blessings God has bestowed on him. Both v 27 and v 30 clearly state that it is Yahweh who has the power to bless. Jacob does, however, possess God's promises; since God has promised to bless him he can expect God to bless his undertakings even though it may benefit others more than himself.

Joseph mediated blessing in a similar way. Potiphar appointed Joseph

---

[24] The relationship of the terms *ʾālâ*, *bĕrît*, and the verb *šbʿ* is as follows: *ʾālâ* frequently denotes the imprecation pronounced upon the covenant breakers, but by synecdoche of a part for the whole, often, as here, stands for the entire oath (Brichto 1963:27-28). The Niphal of *šbʿ* denotes swearing to obey the terms of a covenant or treaty by orally pronouncing them.

Brichto (1963:28) sees *bĕrît* as standing for the oath, by synecdoche of the whole for a part, since it is followed by the *ʾim* clause. However, since it is used with *krt*, it is more likely that *bĕrît* refers to the entire treaty and that the following *ʾim* clause simply gives its main condition. Abimelek only stipulates that Isaac shall not attack him; he does not feel that it is necessary for himself to promise the same, since Isaac is more powerful.

God Blessing Man   71

as manager of his household. "From the time that he appointed him over his household and over everything that he had, Yahweh blessed the Egyptian's household on account of Joseph. Yahweh's blessing was upon everything he had, both in the house and in the field"[25] (Gen 39:5). Potiphar saw that Yahweh was with (ʾēt) Joseph, and that Joseph was successful in all that he did (vv 2-3). Joseph's success was not due to his personal possession of blessing power (contra Pedersen 1926:192-193,195, Mowinckel 1961:8). Rather, he was an ʾîš maṣlîaḥ (v 2) because all that he did, yhwh maṣlîaḥ bĕyādô (v 3). Potiphar only received blessing on account of (bigelal, as in 30:27) his association with Joseph.

Wehmeier (1970:83) interprets bĕrākâ in the phrase "Yahweh's blessing was upon everything he had" (v 5) as "die Kraft der Fortpflanzung und Vermehrung." However, the context describes God as working directly, not through the agency of forces. God's blessing here does not consist of a force or of another entity, but of an activity (cf. Lev 25:21; Deut 28:8; Prov 10:22). birkat-yhwh means "Yahweh's blessing activity." The phrase "Yahweh's blessing was upon everything" is equivalent in meaning to the preceding phrase "Yahweh blessed."

3.2.2.3 Statements of God's Benefaction in Accordance with the Covenant

Four passages report that God has fulfilled some of the covenantal blessing promises. Deut 2:7 describes God's care of the Israelites during the wilderness wanderings: "Your God Yahweh has blessed you in all that you have done with your hands. He knows how you have traveled about in this huge wilderness. During these forty years your God Yahweh has been with you so that you have not lacked a thing." God has blessed the Israelites because of his concern for them—he knows (ydʿ) their hardships, and is with (ʿim) them. The construction bērak with b introducing the realm in which blessing occurs, bĕkōl maʿăśēh yādĕkā, occurs frequently in the Deuteronomic covenantal promises (3.1.2). God's blessing consists of the bestowal of the necessities of life—they have not lacked anything they truly required.

Josh 17:14 reports that God has begun fulfilling the patriarchal and

---

[25]The merism babbayit ûbaśśādeh signifies the entirety of his undertakings, as does ʿîr / śādeh in Deut 28:3. babbayit would include such things as human fertility, the well-being of his servants, and the success of domestic enterprises such as food preparation and textile manufacture. baśśādeh would include crops and livestock.

covenantal promises of human fertility: "The descendants of Joseph asked Joshua: 'Why have you given me only one allotment and one territory for an inheritance, although I am a numerous people, since Yahweh has blessed me to such an extent?'"[26] The result of God's blessing (*brk*, Piel) is that a single tribe is an ʿ*am rab*. Joshua turns the complaint into a challenge (vv 15-17): If they are so numerous, why don't they use their strength to capture more territory?

Ps 107 praises God for a variety of beneficent actions. Vv 33-36 describe in somewhat figurative language the Exodus and Conquest (for this interpretation see Weiser 1962:687). Vv 37-38 look back on life in the promised land:

> They sowed fields and planted vineyards,
> which yielded the fruits of produce.
> He blessed them and so they became quite numerous,
> and he did not make their animals diminish.

In all of the patriarchal promises, and in many of the covenantal promises, God had promised to make the Israelites numerous. The plant and animal fertility, though not expressly described as the result of God's blessing, is still pictured as a product of God's same beneficent activity.

2 Chr 31:10 describes God's fulfillment of his covenantal promises to bless his people if they obey the stipulations for cultic worship (cf. also Ezek 44:30; Joel 2:14; Mal 3:10). The chief priest Azariah says to Hezekiah who had urged the people to tithe, "From the time that the people started to bring the offerings to Yahweh's temple, there has been enough to eat and get full, and there is quite a lot left over, because Yahweh has blessed his people, and this great amount is left over" (for the syntax of the last clause see *GKC* 121 d).

3.2.2.4   Statements of God's Special Blessing upon the King

Three verses in the Psalms are concerned with the "grace of kingship" (Weiser 1962:214). God's special blessing rests upon the king because he is God's vice regent (Ps 21:4,7; 45:3; cf. 1 Kgs 2:45). The king mediates blessing to the people (see Ps 72:17). God aids the king in battle,

---

[26] The first ʿ*ad* need not be emended to ʿ*al* (contra BDB 725a, and *BHS*; see BDB 724b3; Boling 1982:416 emends to ʿ*ōd*, and emendation inferior to ʿ*al* and also unnecessary).

in administrative and judicial duties, and in other enterprises in order to preserve the welfare of the people. The people expected God specially to bless the king. If, however, usurpation occurred or if military defeat, famine, or poverty characterized his reign, the people would conclude that God considered the king illegitimate and had withdrawn his ḥesed, the "grace of kingship," from the king (2 Sam 7:15; see Weiser 1962:214). God's special blessing upon the king was in part a fulfillment of the patriarchal promises of royal descendants (Gen 17:16,20; 35:9). However, God's promise to David of a lasting dynasty in 2 Sam 7, 1 Chr 17 is the most important promise regarding kingship (the chapter only contains brk in a prayer, not in the promise; see under 4.2.2; for instances where the king blessed the people, see 2 Sam 6:18,20 = 1 Chr 16:2,43; 1 Kgs 8:14 = 2 Chr 6:3; 1 Kgs 8:55).

Ps 21 is a royal psalm addressed to Yahweh. Vv 4-7 describe the king's blessings:

> You met him with good blessings,
> you placed a gold crown upon his head.
> He asked you for life; you gave it to him—
> many days, forever and ever.
> Through your salvation his glory is great;
> you have bestowed upon him splendor and majesty.
> You have given him blessing forever,
> you have made him happy with joy before you.

Vv 2-3 (not quoted) state that God has granted the king's request, and so he is happy. The nature of the request is evident in vv 4b-6. V 4 describes God as having met the king with birkôt-ṭôb, blessings that are good, i.e., highly valued (on the attributive genitive, see GKC 128 and Prov 24:25). V 4b specifies the kingship itself as the first blessing. Dahood (1966:132) states concerning "life . . . forever" in v 5: "The king was thought to receive the gift of immortality on the day of his coronation." But the request a king would most likely make would be for the continuance of his dynasty. "2 Sam 7:13,16 agree so perfectly with this thought as to make this interpretation most apropos" (Leupold 1969:192; similarly Wehmeier 1970:78, contra Weiser 1962:213-214 who takes it to signify the "inviolable sanctity of the king's life"). David's dynasty was to be blessed lĕ/ʿad ʿôlām (2 Sam 7:13,16,29; cf. also Ps 45:3; 72:17), and the agreement in thought was probably a strong factor in the ascription of the Psalm to David (v 1).

In v 6, God gives the king splendor (kābôd, hôd, hādār). These words are often used as attributes of God. That the king also possesses them testifies that the king is God's vice regent (Weiser 1962:214). The king possesses them only because of God's *yĕšûʿâ* (v 6a), "through the help of the Lord" (Leupold 1969:192).

There are two possible interpretations of v 7a, *tĕšítēhû bĕrākôt lāʿad*. BDB (139b), Hempel (1961:38), and Weiser (1962:214) take *bĕrākôt* to signify "source of blessings," as the singular form of the noun means in Gen 12:2; Isa 19:24. But the plural is used elsewhere only to denote benefits given as blessings (Wehmeier 1970:78-79), and oral benedictions (Mal 2:2). The second interpretation is therefore to be preferred: the verbal suffix is the indirect object to whom the blessings are given (*GKC* 117 x, so also Dahood 1966:132, Leupold 1969:192), and these blessings make the king rejoice (7b). Three additional benefits follow: God's presence with the king (v 7b, *ʾēt* as in Gen 26:24; 39:2,3), God's *ḥesed* toward the king which is evident in his preservation of the king in his office (v 8), and God's assistance of the king in battle (vv 9-13).

Ps 45 is a royal wedding song. Vv 3-9 describe the king, and vv 10-17 his bride. V 3 extols the king:

> You are the most handsome man,
> > grace is poured upon your lips,
> for God has blessed you forever.[27]

Leupold (1969:355) and Weiser (1962:362) interpret the grace (*ḥēn*) on the king's lips as the gift of gracious speech and of writing poetry, such as David and Solomon possessed. Certainly these qualities are included, but much more important for the king would be the ability to render equitable judgements and administer fairly (cf. vv 5,7,8). In contrast to the verb *ḥnn*, the focus of attention with *ḥēn* is not on the bestower, here implied to be God, but on the recipient and the quality given (Yamauchi 1980:303). The king has received his admirable qualities because God has blessed (*brk*, Piel) him (*ʿal kēn* refers to the preceding—see Dahood 1966:271). Physical attractiveness also distinguished Saul as chosen by God (1 Sam 9:2; 10:23). Beauty as well as splendor (*hôd, hādār*, vv 4-5) and military victory (vv 5-6) are proof that God's blessing rests upon the king. "Forever" means that God will continue to bless the unbroken dynasty (as in

---

[27] The form *yāpyāpîtā* need not be emended to *yāpîtā* (contra *GKC* 55e). Dahood (1966:271) compares the reduplicated form to Ugaritic *dʿdʿ*, "know well," from *ydʿ*, and *ysmst*, "beauty."

2 Sam 7). The king will also forever be remembered as a blessed king who has brought blessing to his people (cf. Ps 72:18; 1 Kgs 2:45).

3.2.2.5   Statements of God's Special Blessing Upon Zion

Three passages in the Psalms discuss how God looks with particular fondness upon Zion and so has made her the special object of his blessings. Zion is a source of blessing for the nation because God's blessings upon her spread to the borders of the nation, and for her sake God preserves the entire nation. These statements are fulfillments of God's promises in Exod 20:24; Ps 132:13-15.

Ps 147 calls for Jerusalem to praise God for restoring her in the second temple period (cf. 3.1.5). Vv 13-14 describe the restoration:

> For he has strengthened the bars of your city gates,
> > he has blessed your children within you.
> He makes your borders peaceful,
> > and fills you with the best wheat.

The suffix on the direct object of *bērak, bānayik*, refers to Jerusalem/Zion (v 12), and so the children are not those of the inhabitants; they are the inhabitants themselves. *bērak* then does not specifically denote the bestowal of the "Nachkommemschaft der nachexilischen Volksgemeinde" (contra Kraus 1961:957); instead, it means "to enable to live the good life," by bestowing such things as children, food, health, and peace.

Ps 133 is a short psalm of ascent describing the beauty of "brothers sitting together" in corporate worship. V 3 likens unity to dew, and stresses that God's election of Zion has made Zion a source of blessing for the nation:

> It is like the dew of Mt. Hermon,
> > descending on Mt. Zion,
> for there Yahweh has stationed blessing,
> > forevermore, life.

Zion is God's resting place, and so it is the place from which he blesses (Ps 128:5; 134:3; 1 Kgs 8). The verb *ṣwh* describes God as dispatching his blessing there (cf. Lev 25:21; Deut 28:8). God has stationed his blessing on Mt. Zion, and from there it spreads to the people. Blessing is only indirectly linked to dew; the thought of dew leads the psalmist to mention blessing. Though dew is a blessing elsewhere (Gen 27:28; Deut 33:13; Zech

8:13), the psalm is not primarily concerned with fertility. *běrākâ* is parallel to *ḥayyîm*. *ḥayyîm* is more than longevity; "All the blessings of God are summed up in "life" in the richest sense of the word" (Leupold 1969:920). *běrākâ* includes all those God-given things which are beneficial for man, not only the physical necessities of life but also peace and happiness, those things which bring contentment and fulfillment to life. Dahood (1970:252-253) argues that *ḥayyîm ʿad hāʿôlām* denotes eternal life as the blessing par excellence, but the phrase *ʿad hāʿôlām* is best understood as adverbial, modifying *ṣiwwâ* (so also Keil and Delitzsch *Psalms:*3.320). Since Zion is Yahweh's eternal dwelling place, it will always be the place from which he dispatches blessing and life.

Ps 84:7 also associates blessing with Zion, but says that those making a pilgrimage to Zion experience God's blessing:

> Those who pass through the valley of Baka
> make it a place of springs;
> also the autumn rain covers it with blessings.

Baka is most likely the name of an arid valley of unknown location with a route to Jerusalem through it (Morton 1962:338). *BHS, RSV,* and *NIV* read *běrēkôt* "pools" for MT *běrākôt*, but this is wholly unnecessary. Just as *brk* Piel can include bestowing rain (Gen 27:27; Deut 28:12; 33:13; Ps 65:11), so the noun can denote rain (Gen 49:25; Mal 3:10), as the collocations *maʿyān* and *môreh* here indicate. Furthermore, though rain is included, the picturesque language primarily denotes plants as the *běrākôt*. Plants spring up after the rains and "cover" or "clothe" the valley. The motif of water in the desert is characteristic of the prophetic apocalypses. The figure here describes how the arid desert seems like a verdant valley to the pilgrims because of their joy in anticipation of entering the temple courts (Weiser 1962:57, Wehmeier 1970:71).

3.2.2.6 Miscellaneous Statements of God's Benefaction

Two passages describe how God's ark brought blessing to Obed-Edom. The passages stress that God's presence, here represented by the ark, brings God's blessing, just as the passages about God's presence in Zion and the passages which state that God was *with* someone (*ʿim*, Gen 26:3,28; 28:15,20; Deut 2:7; 1 Chr 4:10; and *ʾet* Gen 26:24; 39:2,3), picture blessing as a consequence of God's presence. All these passages imply that Yahweh is a God of blessing; it is his nature and desire to bless, and so he blesses those with whom he has contact. In the Obed-Edom narratives, as in the patriarchal promises, God blesses unexpectedly and without a prior display of merit by the recipient (2 Sam 6:11-12; similarly 1 Chr 13:14): "Yahweh's ark stayed in the house of Obed-Edom the Gittite for three months. Yahweh blessed Obed-Edom and his entire household. King David was told, 'Yahweh has blessed the household of Obed-Edom and all that he has on account of God's ark." The Piel of *brk* is used in the general sense of "bestow benefits." As a recipient of blessing, his household would include a wife who had many children and the success of domestic enterprises.

This Obed-Edom is most likely the same person as in 1 Chr 26:4-5, where he appears in a list of temple gatekeepers (on his identity see 1 Chr 15:18-25; 16:5; Corney 1962:579-580, Myers 1965:103,177). 1 Chr 26:4-5 lists the sons of Obed-Edom and concludes abruptly with the explanation *kî běrākô ʾělōhîm*, attributing his eight sons to God's blessing. Comparing this list with the gatekeeper lists in 1 Chr 9 and 16, Ezra 2, and Neh 10-12, Myers (1965:177) notes the growth of the family of Obed-Edom. His family numbered sixty-two, while the families of the other gatekeepers Meshelemiah and Hosah numbered eighteen and thirteen, respectively.

The picture of Job in the prologue and epilogue of his book is an example of the fulfillment of the wisdom aphorisms (3.1.3). Job is blameless and upright, and fears God (1:1). Consequently, he enjoys abundant blessings from God. The adversary describes Job's condition (1:10): "Haven't you made a fence all around him, his house, and everything that he has? You have blessed the work he does with his hands and his animals have spread all over the land." The common Deuteronomic expression *maʿăśēh yādāyw* denotes agriculture (cf. Gen 5:29; Hag 2:14,17). Animal fertility is also a frequent Deuteronomic blessing. God's protection is not explicitly part of the blessing, but it is seen as part of the same beneficent activity of God toward Job as blessing. Job's ideal number of children (1:2) is also indirectly related to God's blessing.

Job 42:12-13 describes Job's restoration: "Yahweh blessed the latter part of Job's life more than the former part." The blessing resulted in exactly twice as many animals as in the prologue. The servants, who are unnumbered in the prologue, are not mentioned in the epilogue. Job's longevity is also a result of God's blessing.[28] Job is also blessed with a

---

[28]MT merely states that he lived (*ḥyh*) one hundred and forty more years after his restoration. The LXX has one hundred and seventy years, and two hundred and forty years for the length of his entire life, making him seventy years old at the time of his affliction. The MT reading of one

second set of children which is of the same number as the first.[29] In the epilogue, it is God's favor toward Job which leads God to bless him and to accept his prayer (nāśā' pānîm, 42:8,9). God also blesses Job so that the friends will realize that Job stands in a favorable relationship to himself and that what Job has said about himself is true (42:7-8).

God blessed Samson in order to enable him to deliver Israel. The chronological order of blessing and deliverance is then the reverse of that in the prophetic apocalypses, where God delivers his people in order to inaugurate an age of blessing. Yet in both cases it is clear that blessing and deliverance are closely related. God's purpose in both blessing and deliverance is to create a state of peace and prosperity among his people which is indicative of his favor toward them. Judg 13:24-25 briefly describes the youth of Samson: "The lad grew, and Yahweh blessed him, and Yahweh's spirit began to impel him at Mahaneh Dan." It can be assumed from Samson's subsequent history that God's blessing included the bestowal of good health and particularly of strength. God's blessing also included the motivating influence of Yahweh's spirit (cf. Isa 44:3).

---

hundred and forty years is therefore exactly twice the length of his previous life implied by the LXX (Driver-Gray 1921:1.375-376).

[29]Several authorities suggest emending šibʿānâ to šibʿâ (BDB 988b, GKC 97c, Bauer-Leander 79i, Driver-Gray 1921:2.350). KB calls it a "forma mixta" combining šibʿâ, "seven", with šibʿān, "fourteen." However, Sarna (1957:17-18) identifies the form as an archaic form of the numeral seven, similar to Ugaritic šbʿny, "seven." It is part of the original epic language dating from the patriarchal age. From the context, the number would be expected to be seven, since the second set of daughters numbers three as in the prologue. The most likely reason that the second set of children was not doubled in number is that the first set was not considered altogether lost for Job (cf. 2 Sam 12:23, Keil and Delitzsch Job:2.390). This is the only passage in the Bible where daughters are specified as the result of God's blessing.

4
Man Blessing Man

Human blessings, like God's blessings, can consist of either a speech act (benediction) or a bestowal of material goods (benefaction). Both types of acts display the favor and goodwill of the blesser. Benedictions can be either declarative or optative, and both types of benedictions are illocutionary utterances.

4.1 Declarative Human Blessings

The declarative blessings spoken by people are illocutionary utterances which describe the relationship between God and the person blessed. The blessings declare that, because of the favorable relationship, the person blessed has been, or will be, the recipient of benefits bestowed by God. Since the blessing is an illocutionary utterance, the pronouncement of the words in itself accomplishes the act of benediction.

However, the effectiveness of the words is not due to a mysterious power within the words, or to the strength of the soul of the person who utters the blessing. The effectiveness of the testamental blessings is based on societal customs and the belief that God will fulfill his promises. The strength of the divination pronouncements is rooted in the belief that divination accurately discerns the relationship between people and the gods, and accurately predicts the future actions of the gods. In both types of blessings, then, it is the divinity who is envisioned as the one who bestows the benefits. The words indicate who the recipient is or will be, but they can accomplish nothing apart from the divinity.

4.1.1 The Testamental Blessing

The distinguishing feature of the blessings in this section is the occasion and purpose of the benediction. The benediction is given by the family or national leader when his death is imminent, and it is given to his sons, or to the tribes of Israel pictured as sons (Gen 49, Deut 33).

Gen 27 shows most clearly how the benediction functioned in its usual and original setting. The blessing has a slightly different meaning in Gen 49 and Deut 33, where it has been developed into a literary genre akin to prophecy.

Archeological discoveries shed some important light on Gen 27 (Speiser 1955 and 1964:212-213, Mendelsohn 1959). Tablets from Nuzi, Mari, and Alalakh have been found which discuss oral testaments given by dying fathers, the status of the firstborn, and the adoption of sons. The tablets make two statements about these social practices during the patriarchal age. The evidence indicates that these statements are valid for Palestine in addition to the Hurrian and Assyrian territories.

First, the oral testament given by a dying father was a legally binding will. It was not simply a wish or a prayer. In a Nuzi tablet (Speiser 1955:252-253), the phrase "I have grown old" is a technical phrase indicating that the following statement is to be regarded as the father's last will and testament. This same phrase appears in Gen 27:2. Gen 48:1 and Deut 33:1 also indicate that the blessings were intended as deathbed testaments (cf. also Josh 23:2). In a Nuzi lawsuit (Speiser 1955:253-254), a father's oral deathbed testament is introduced as evidence. The plaintiff quotes the testament verbatim. Even though the testament was never written down, the judges considered it legally binding. "A final oral disposition by the head of a household had solid legal standing" (Speiser 1955:254).

Second, the status of being the firstborn was not necessarily determined by the order of birth. In several tablets (Mendelsohn 1959, Speiser 1955:255-256), the father decreed that someone other than the first son born was to have the status of the firstborn, which entitled him to a double share of the inheritance. In cases of adoption, an adopted son had the status of the firstborn only as long as no natural sons were born. A natural son, though born later, outranked an adopted son. Gen 15:2-4 indicates that the patriarchs followed this same legal practice regarding adoption.

The importance of all this for Gen 27 is that "in matters of birthright, the father's decree could reverse the natural order . . . the term 'older' was a relative concept from a socio-juridical viewpoint" (Speiser 1955:256). This explains why Jacob made such an effort to obtain Isaac's blessing; if he obtained it, he would be the legal firstborn, even though he was born second. Jacob cannot be faulted for trying to obtain the birthright, since legally it did not belong to Esau automatically; it belonged to whomever the father chose to give it, though ordinarily he would give it to the chronological firstborn.

The proper understanding of the cultural background of Gen 27 makes several popular interpretations look rather ridiculous. The most important issue is the function of the benediction. The benediction itself (vv 28-29) reads:

> May God give you a share in the dew from heaven,
>   in the fertile places of the earth,
>   and much grain and new wine.
> May peoples serve you,
>   may nations bow down to you.
> Be master over your brothers;
>   may your mother's sons bow down to you.
> May those who curse you be cursed,
>   and those who bless you be blessed!

The main point of the benediction is contained in v 29. Jacob is given dominion over his brothers. He is given the status of the firstborn. In addition, the blessing designates Jacob as the heir of the patriarchal promises of fertility and dominion which are part of Isaac's estate (v 29c reflects 12:3a; on v 29c see further under 4.3 and on Num 24:9 under 4.1.2). The blessing has religious as well as legal significance. God will continue his blessing activity through Jacob's line rather than the line of Esau.

In light of the legal and religious function of the benediction, the interpretations of Pedersen, Mowinckel, Hempel, and Wehmeier are untenable. Pedersen (1926:200-201) interprets Gen 27 as a clear illustration of the fact that blessing in the Bible is a transfer of soul-power. The meal Isaac eats before blessing his son is to strengthen his soul so that he can impart a more potent blessing. The power of the animal's soul is added to the power of his own soul (similarly Hempel 1961:56-57). Mowinckel (1961:19-20) has essentially the same interpretation, though he sees the blessing as a family cultic act, and further asserts that the animal eaten embodied divinity, bringing Isaac closer to the divinity. Wehmeier (1970:145,191-193)[1] and Keller (1978:360-361) follow Pedersen.

---

[1] Wehmeier, however, says that the chapter is the only OT passage which pictures blessing as a transfer of soul-power. He correctly states that Pedersen is incorrect in seeing the chapter as representative of the

These interpretations fail to recognize the primary function of the blessing as a legal statement with religious implications. There is no more soul-transfer in Gen 27 than there is in the texts from Mari, Nuzi, and Alalakh. Gen 27:4,19,25,31 provide no evidence whatsoever for blessing being a soul transfer. Isaac's words *baʿăbûr tĕbārekkā napšî* may be translated "so that I may wholeheartedly bless you." Isaac simply wants a delicious meal from Esau so that he will be full and content, in a good mood to give a benediction (cf. Kidner 1967:156). A festive meal would be appropriate for such an important occasion (Leupold 1942:2.737-738). Isaac asks Esau to show his gratitude for obtaining the blessing by once again giving his father pleasure (cf. v 4). If *nepeš* has any nuance of meaning other than standing for Isaac himself (cf. BDB 660a), it would be the nuance of a full and contented appetite (cf. BDB 660b). *nepeš* occurs again with the Piel of *brk* in Ps 103:1,2,22; 104:1,35, all in the phrase *bārăkî napšî ʾet-yhwh*. There is no question there, either, of man transferring some of his soul to God. The psalmodic phrase simply calls for wholehearted praise of God.

The Piel of *brk* occurs in Gen 27:4,7,10,19,23,25,27 (the first occurrence),30,31,33, all referring to Isaac's pronouncement of the benediction over Jacob. The noun *bĕrākâ* occurs in vv 12,35,36 (the first occurrence),38,41, all referring to the benediction itself in vv 28-29. In v 12, *qĕlālâ* stands in opposition to *bĕrākâ*. Jacob expresses apprehension to Rebekah that their wiles may be discovered: "Perhaps my father will feel me, and I will be in his estimation a mocker and will bring a curse upon myself, and not a blessing." The nouns *bĕrākâ* and *qĕlālâ* in v 12, as in Deut 11:26-28; 30:1,19, refer to both a spoken benediction/malediction and its consequences. Jacob is not only concerned with the words spoken by his father, but also with the resulting fortune or misfortune they would bring (cf. Brichto 1963:197-199).

After discovering that Jacob had obtained the blessing by trickery, Esau asked Isaac for an additional benediction in vv 34,38: "Bless me also, my father!" The second occurrence of *bĕrākâ* in v 36 refers to the requested additional benediction. Yet Isaac neither rescinds the first benediction nor gives a comparable one to Esau. When he learns that it was not Esau that he blessed, Isaac asks (v 33), "Who then was it ... whom I blessed? He certainly will be blessed!" Isaac asserts that Jacob

---

biblical concept of blessing. Wehmeier also correctly denies that the kiss, touching, and smelling of Jacob were an important part of the soul transfer—they served merely to identify the son (contra Pedersen and Hempel).

will be *bārûk*, that is, he will retain his status as the firstborn and possessor of the benefits bequeathed him in the testamental blessing.

There has been much debate over the reason that Isaac cannot, or does not, retract the blessing. Hempel (1961:56) and Pedersen (1926:200) argue that the father gives all of his vitality away in the blessing; he has no more to give anyone else, and dies shortly thereafter for lack of it. Hempel also suggests (1961:35) that the blessing is a magical word. Once the blessing is spoken, nobody has control over it. Pedersen explains: "once uttered, then the soul of him who uttered the blessing has really created it, and it must act by the power that has been put into it." Wehmeier (1970:191-192) follows another idea of Hempel (1961:57-58) to some extent. He sees the blessing here as the bestowal of the "positive Kräfte" which dwell in Isaac. After giving away his good powers, Isaac only has a "böse Seele" left to give to Esau.

These explanations are based on a fundamental misunderstanding of the nature and purpose of the blessing. One suspects that the patriarchs and the residents of Nuzi and Mari would have been baffled by these interpretations. Isaac's response to Esau's request (v 37) indicates that Isaac felt that it was impossible for him to rescind the blessing. Since the testamental blessings were normally pronounced shortly before the father's death, it is likely that there was no socially accepted legal procedure for rescinding them (similarly Thiselton 1974:294, Henderson 1977:159-161).

Isaac had also pronounced the testament "before Yahweh" (v 7). This meant not only that Isaac had called upon Yahweh (v 27)/God (v 28) to bestow the blessings upon Jacob, but also that Isaac believed Yahweh approved of Jacob as the beneficiary (so also Speiser 1964:209, Scharbert 1975a:289, Henderson 1977:161-162). The recipient of the testament was to be heir of the patriarchal promises, so God had a vested interest in who it was. The fact that Jacob had received the testament, despite all the precautions taken by Isaac and despite the invocation of God, must have implied to Isaac that God sanctioned the blessing. Isaac may also have remembered the oracle given to Rebekah in 25:23. In any event, the pronouncement Isaac uttered over Esau (vv 39-40) is a shortened, antonymous version of the benediction Jacob received and is a curse rather than a benediction.

In Gen 48, Jacob issues two benedictions over Ephraim and Manasseh. Jacob therefore in effect designates Joseph as his firstborn, since Jacob gives Joseph's two sons a status equal to his other sons for inheritance purposes (vv 5-6). Joseph receives the double portion (but cf. 49:1-12, where Jacob appears to pass over Reuben, Simeon, and Levi and give the status of firstborn to Judah).

Hempel (1961:35,56), Pedersen (1926:201,203), Mowinckel (1961:9) and Harrelson (1962:446) say Jacob's kiss, hug, and laying on of hands on Ephraim and Manasseh (vv 10,14,17) indicate that magical beliefs underlie the blessing custom. Wehmeier, too, (1970:197) says that the reason for laying on hands is the belief that the oral blessing was a transfer of power. Physical contact supposedly facilitated this transfer.

These interpretations are wholly unfounded. Social customs need to be interpreted in light of their social context, rather than in the light of a hypothetical distant magical origin. There is nothing in the words spoken which indicates magical beliefs; God is called upon to bless in both benedictions. The social function of the kiss was to express affection and fellowship; it was given in conjunction with departing blessings between close relatives and friends (Gen 32:1; 2 Sam 19:40). The laying on of hands represents physically the bestowal of the benediction and the patriarchal promises from Jacob onto the sons, just as it symbolizes physically the bestowal of God's spirit, authority, and responsibility in Num 27:18-20 and Deut 34:9. The importance of the right hand is no more an indication of magical beliefs than our preference for it in handshakes today (on physical contact in blessing in Genesis, see further Henderson 1977:170-179).

The Piel of brk in 48:9,15,20 means "to pronounce a testamental blessing formula." The first formula is in vv 15-16. Jacob first invokes the God of his forefathers (v 15). This invocation indicates that Jacob intends to make Joseph's line the special recipients of the patriarchal blessing promises, since he then prays for this God to bless them (v 16):

> May the angel[2] who has delivered me from all harm,
>   bless the youths.
> May they be called by my name,
>   and by the name of my fathers, Abraham and Isaac.
> May they increase greatly in the midst of the land.

The youths are to be associated with the patriarch's names. This means not only that they shall be considered full descendants of the patriarchs despite their Egyptian mother (von Rad 1972:418), but also that God's blessing activity with the patriarchs will be continued with them

---

[2]$hammal^\jmath ak$ stands parallel to $h\bar{a}^\jmath \check{e}l\bar{o}h\hat{\imath}m$ in v 15, and stands for the form in which God has manifested himself to men. He is God's personified help for his people (von Rad 1972:193-194,417; cf. Gen 21:17; 22:11).

(Westermann 1982:214). God's blessing results in numerous descendants.[3] Offspring are the most important of the benefits described in the patriarchal promises. Jacob no doubt also had in mind God bestowing prosperity, dominion, renown, etc., when he called for God to bless (*brk*, Piel) them.

Jacob issues a second benediction over Ephraim and Manasseh in 48:20: "He blessed them on that day, saying,

> Israel will bless invoking you,[4] saying,
> "May God make you like Ephraim and Manasseh!"

Both occurrences of the Piel of *brk* in the verse mean "to pronounce a benediction." Because fertility and prosperity will characterize the tribes of Manasseh and especially of Ephraim (vv 16-19), the tribes will become proverbial examples of people whom God has blessed (see Zech 8:13 where *bĕrākâ* denotes such a proverbial example). Ruth 4:11 contains a similar use of blessed people as examples, though *brk* does not occur in the verse. The people of Bethlehem say to Boaz concerning Ruth, "May Yahweh make the woman coming into your house like Rachel and Leah, the two who built the house of Israel."

Already in Gen 27, the testamental blessing serves another purpose besides designating the legal firstborn. The benediction is a type of prophecy. The deathbed dispositions recorded in the Bible often have strong elements of prediction as well as warnings or instructions (Gen 27; 48:15-49:32; 50:24-25; Deut 33; Josh 23-24; 1 Sam 12; 2 Sam 23:1-7; 1 Kgs 2:1-9; 2 Kgs 13:14-19; however, only Gen 27, 48, 49, and Deut 33 contain *brk*; the closest literary parallel to Gen 49 and Deut 33 is Judg 5:14-18).

While blessing in Gen 27 and 48 serves chiefly to designate the legal

---

[3] The verb *dgh* occurs only here. Westermann (1982:202) suggests a connection with *dāg* and an etymological meaning "das Wimmeln der Fische" (so also von Rad 1972:418), or possibly a connection with *dāgān*. These possibilities, though, are uncertain. *lārōb*, however, clearly indicates the meaning as "increase, multiply."

[4] The preposition in *bĕkā* is the *b* of means or instrument (BDB 889b-890a). With verbs of swearing, prophesying, and blessing, attached to the name of a person, it denotes the invocation of that person in the formula spoken (BDB 890a, *GKC* 119k), as in the frequent priestly blessings pronounced *bĕšēm-yhwh* (see 4.2.1). The *b* used with the Niphal and Genesis Hithpael forms of *brk* is also instrumental, though there it means "through, by means of," rather than "invoking," because those verb forms do not denote speech.

firstborn, Gen 49 and Deut 33 are primarily intended as prophecies. The deathbed occasion and the use of *brk* indicate that Gen 49 and Deut 33 are patterned after the testamental blessing. However, it is more proper to call the chapters testaments, rather than blessings (so also Speiser 1964:370-371, von Rad 1972:421-422). In Gen 49, the first three sons are strongly rebuked, and v 7 even contains an *ʾārûr* formula! Yet Leupold (1942:2.1161-1162) is correct that all tribes are to receive some blessings from God because they are part of Israel; no tribe is cursed outright or denied blessings like Esau was. Even Simeon and Levi, whose anger is cursed in v 7, are to be scattered *within* Israel.

Deut 33:1 pictures Moses more as a prophet—he is a "man of God"—than as a father dividing his estate (cf. Craigie 1976:390-391). In Gen 49:1, Jacob says, "Gather around, and I will tell you what will happen to you in the future." The genre of these chapters taken as wholes is closer to prophecy than to the testamental benediction of Gen 27 or to other types of human blessings. While the individual addresses to each son or tribe are quite diverse, most contain some prediction about their future fate.

The postscript to Gen 49, v 28, states: "These are the twelve tribes of Israel. This is what their father said to them when he blessed them. He blessed each one with its own blessing." The superscript to Deut 33, v 1, states: "This is the blessing with which Moses, the man of God, blessed the children of Israel before he died." The Piel and noun forms of *brk* are used because the chapters are patterned after the testamental benediction, rather than because the addresses are typical human benedictions.

In Gen 49, only Jacob's address to Joseph contains *brk*. The text is difficult. Due to the syntax I will start the translation with 49:24, though the blessings are found in vv 25-26:

> Yet his bow stayed steady,
>> and his arms stayed limber,
> because of the mighty one of Jacob,
>> because of the shepherd, the rock of Israel,
> because of your father's God, who helps you,
>> because of Shaddai, who blesses you, with
> blessings from heaven above,
>> blessings from the deep lying below,
>> blessings from breast and womb.
> Your father's blessings are greater
>> than the blessings of the ancient mountains,
>> than the bounty of the age-old hills.

May they rest on Joseph's head,
on the brow of the prince among his brothers.[5]

---

[5]The preposition *min* in vv 24c and 25a is causal. *miššām* in v 24d and (*mē*)ʾ *ēt* in v 25b both denote the source of help, and so have also been translated by "because." *wĕʾēt* in v 25b is unnecessarily emended by some (O'Connor 1980:177, Cross 1973:9 note 23) to *wĕʾēl*. The phrase *mēʾēt ʾēl šadday* has been broken up into *mēʾēl* in 25a and *wĕʾēt šaddai* in 25b. The breakup of divine names and of stereotyped phrases are common poetic phenomena. On divine names, see the many examples in Dahood 1968:390 under "Breakup of composite divine names," and Dahood 1970:XXXIX-XLI; on stereotyped phrases see Dahood 1970:414-415; however, a few of Dahood's examples of both these phenomena are suspicious.

Speiser (1964:363,369) and Westermann (1982:274), among others, emend *hôray ʿad* to *harrê-ʿad*, based on the expressions *harrê-qedem* in Deut 33:15 and *harrê-ʿad* in Hab 3:6, both of which are parallel to *gibʿôt-ʿolam*, as is the present expression. The parallelism certainly indicates that *ʿad* is to be taken as the noun and not as the preposition, and that it goes with the preceding word, contrary to the Masoretic accents. Yet Thierry (1963:77-82) and Rendsburg (1980:291-293) make a good case for retaining *hôray*. *ô* occasionally stands for *ā* in the MT. Rendsburg (292 note 4) cites examples in Josh 6:13; 20:8; 21:27; 1 Sam 27:4; Jer 9:7 Ezek 34:25 (cf. *GKC* 89 d). Thierry also discusses several examples from extra-biblical Canaanite. The ending *ay* is the uncontracted form of the masculine plural construct (cf. *GKC* 89d). The form is therefore equivalent to *harrê*.

The interpretation of *hôray* as the participle of *hrh* with suffix is difficult to accept because of the meaning of the resulting line. Jacob would be saying that the blessings of Joseph's father, i.e., himself, were greater than the blessings of his progenitors, i.e., Abraham and Isaac. But Jacob's blessings certainly were no greater than those bestowed upon the previous patriarchs. He simply was heir to their blessings. It is doubtful, then, that v 26 is an example of "Janus parallelism" (contra Rendsburg 1980).

brk in v 25b is parallel to *ʿzr* in v 25a. *ʿzr* is used in the general sense of "to aid or help," and the context indicates that this help consists of protection from enemies (vv 23-24). *brk* is used in the general sense of "bestow benefits," and here takes a double accusative (*GKC* 117 ff).

The blessings from heaven would include *ṭal*, as in Gen 27:28,39; Deut 33:13; Zech 8:13; Ps 133:3, and *māṭār*, as in Deut 28:12, as well as sunshine, as in Deut 33:14. *tĕhôm* refers to the primordial waters below, personified somewhat by the participle *rōbeṣet*. The phrase is found again in Deut 33:13. *tĕhôm* denotes the source of ground water. Though "breasts" and "womb" elsewhere occasionally refer to animals, here, as

The blessings are linked with the patriarchal blessings by the reference to "your father's God" in v 25a and to "your father's blessings" in v 26a. The blessings are said to be greater than the blessings found in the fertile hill country.

> The meaning is that the blessings received by Jacob from his ancestors relate to things higher than the merely material products, however choice, of the fertile hills of Ephraim: they include national and political greatness, and also the high religious privileges implied in the "promises" (Driver 1905:393).

Four of the addresses in Deut 33 contain *brk*. All clearly show how God's blessing is related to his favor toward the person blessed. A form of *rṣh* occurs in each address parallel to *brk*. V 11 is addressed to Levi:

> Yahweh, bless (*bārēk*) his capability,
>   be pleased with (*tirṣeh*) what he does with his hands;
> smite the loins of those who rise against him,
>   so his foes will rise no more.[6]

The Piel of *brk* denotes the bestowal of the ability (strength, determination, faithfulness) to carry out his priestly duties outlined in v 10. Here God's blessing enables God to look with favor upon the sacrifices Levi offers up in the proper manner. But God's blessing does not precede his

---

throughout the patriarchal narratives, human fertility is more important than plant or animal fertility.

The final clause includes the element of preeminence. Yet the phrase "prince among his brothers" does not necessarily mean that he has dominion over them, since a similar phrase describes Judah in Gen 49:8, and *nāzîr* does not necessarily connote royalty (Westermann 1982:275, McComiskey 1980:568).

[6] The final *mem* of *motnayim* is probably enclitic, and so the word is in construct (so Cross and Freedman 1948:204). The examples *GKC* 117 11 cites in support of the absolute state all have the second accusative *following* the nearer object. The preposition *min* in the last phrase is privative (*GKC* 119 x,y) and need not be emended (contra Cross and Freedman 1948:204). It is commonly found with infinitives, and this use with an imperfect, though unique, is hardly "quite exceptional" (contra *GKC* 115 b).

favor. God is called upon to bless Levi because of Levi's prior faithfulness to God (vv 8-9).

Deut 33:13-16 describes how Joseph's land will be blessed by Yahweh (mĕbōreket-yhwh) with water and sun so that it is fertile. The final phrase states that these blessings result from "the favor (rāṣôn) of him who dwelt in the thornbush." The Pual participle of brk is in construct with its agent (GKC 116 1), as is the Qal participle in Gen 24:31; 26:29; Isa 65:23.

Wehmeier (1970:107-108,176) distinguishes between the Qal passive participle as denoting one who has bĕrākâ, the emphasis being on the condition of the person, and the Pual participle as denoting the recipient of blessing, with emphasis upon the action of blessing. Here, however, the Pual stresses the blessed condition of the land; the land continually enjoys the blessings of water and sun. By comparison to Gen 49:25-26, it is apparent that mĕbōreket denotes possession of bĕrākôt. While Wehmeier's distinction is often valid, there are cases for both the Qal (as when in construct with yhwh) and the Pual (as here) where it is not.

Naphtali's concise benediction (Deut 33:23) also attributes God's blessing to his favor:

> Naphtali is full of (God's) favor (rāṣôn),
>   filled with Yahweh's blessing (bĕrākâ).
> He will inherit the West and South.[7]

God's blessing here is especially the strength to drive out the Canaanites.
Asher's benediction (Deut 33:24-25) reads:

> May Asher be the most blessed (bārûk) of sons;
>   may he be the most favored (rāṣûy) of his brothers,
>   dipping his foot in oil.
> Your bolts are iron and bronze,
>   your strength equal to your days.

Both bārûk and rāṣûy refer to Asher's relationship to God, not to his family. It is God who looks upon Asher with the most favor and so blesses him with fertility, longevity, and security from attack. Wehmeier

---

[7] The emphatic imperative yĕrāśâ need not be emended to a finite form (contra Cross and Freedman 1948:209, Wehmeier 1970:84, Craigie 1976:401, following the versions); blessings occasionally employ imperatives in this way (Gen 12:3; 27:29; Deut 33:11).

(1970:107-108) claims that the Pual participle of brk in v 13 specifies that the blessings come from Yahweh, whereas bārûk here merely describes Asher as prosperous without specifying the source of his prosperity. However, it is the fact that the participle in v 13 is in construct with Yahweh that stresses the divine origin of the blessings, not the stem. The Qal participle in construct with Yahweh (Gen 24:31; 26:29; Isa 65:23) stresses the divine source just as much as the Pual participle in construct with Yahweh does. Furthermore, the rest of the poem, and the larger context of Deuteronomy, consistently portrays blessings as bestowed or withdrawn by Yahweh, the covenant God. There is no need to emphasize God's agency every time that brk is used. Since brk is so closely tied to God's activity, it is natural to assume that God is the implied agent of the passive forms where this is not expressly stated.

4.1.2   Divination Blessing Pronouncements

The divination blessing pronouncements are declarations which describe the relationship between God and the person(s) blessed. They declare that God is favorably disposed toward certain persons and that God therefore has blessed them and/or will bless them in the future. Divination is employed to determine the will of God regarding the person(s) to be blessed. If divination reveals that God is not favorably disposed, or is angry at the person(s), then a curse predicting their downfall may be uttered in place of a blessing. A striking feature of this type of blessing is that it does not presuppose monotheistic or Yahwistic beliefs for the blesser, and the method of divination employed is quite similar to that used in extra-biblical ancient Near Eastern religions.

Laban used divination to determine that it was because of Jacob that Yahweh had blessed him (nḥš, Piel, Gen 30:27; Balaam's method is called nĕḥāšîm in Num 24:1). However, Laban did not utter a blessing pronouncement; he simply conceded to Jacob that Jacob had been the mediator of God's blessing.

The only true divination pronouncements are in the Balaam narratives. Both in the Balaam narratives and in later references to them, the Piel of brk is declarative, meaning "to declare that someone has been and will continue to be a recipient of blessings from their God." The Piel occurs in Num 22:6; 23:11 twice, 20 twice, 25 twice; 24:1, 10 twice; Josh 24:10 twice. The noun bĕrākâ occurs in Deut 23:6 and Neh 13:2 denoting the four pronouncements Balaam uttered in Num 22-24. The Pual is found in Num 22:6 meaning "to receive benefits from God."

Archeology has shed much light on the Balaam narrative. Balaam is no longer a mysterious character. There is now a great deal of material available illustrating the practice of divination and various related sorts of prophecy in the ancient Near East (see Wilson 1980:89-133 and the extensive literature he cites). Balaam closely resembles a *bārû*, a type of diviner that was quite common, especially in Mesopotamia (so Wilson 1980:150, who cites other authors of the same opinion in note 35; similarly Harrison 1969:630). There is good evidence that the Mesopotamian practices of divination were also common in Canaan in the second millenium (Harrison 1969:630). "The *bārû* played a crucial role in the time of war, determining the sort of military activity that should be undertaken and the propitious times for attack. In some instances the diviner even led the army into battle" (Wilson 1980:98). The *bārû* had several methods of divination that he frequently used. One of the most common was examination of the remains of sacrificed animals, e.g., extispicy and hepatoscopy (Wilson 1980:90-97).

Balaam was hired by Balak because of the threat of war with Israel (Num 22:1-6). He proceded to build seven altars on three separate occasions and make sacrifices in order to obtain a divine oracle (Num 23:1-5,14-17,29-30; cf. 22:40; 24:1). In short, he acted like a typical *bārû*.

Balaam had a reputation as an effective diviner. His widespread fame is now illustrated by an Aramaic text dating from about 700 B.C. from Deir ʿAlla (see Wilson 1980:132-133 for a discussion). The picture of Balaam in this text agrees with the biblical description of him as a professional diviner (*qôsēm*, Josh 13:22; so Wilson 1980:132). Balak summoned Balaam to curse Israel (Num 22:6). He said, "Now, come and curse this people for me because they are stronger than I. Perhaps I will be able to defeat them and drive them from the land, for I know that whomever you bless gets blessed, and whomever you curse gets cursed." *tĕbārēk* and *tāʾōr* are declarative. Based on divination, Balaam declares people to be headed for fortune or misfortune. Balak states that those whom Balaam pronounces blessed/cursed actually meet the fate he predicts. *mĕbōrak* and *yûʾār* do not merely describe the people as having formulas spoken over them (contra BDB 139a), but emphasize the actual reception of fortune/misfortune. There is no agent stated for the passive verbs, implying that the agents are the gods (as in other biblical impersonal constructions with God implied as the agent; see especially 3.1.3).

There is no question, then, about the manner in which Balaam's benedictions or maledictions take effect. Balaam does *not* have an exceptional ability to pronounce powerful formulas which effect what they state (contra Wehmeier 1970:194-195, Scharbert 1975a:296, Brichto 1963:100, and most other interpreters). Neither are the words prayers or wishes for

God to bless/curse. Rather, Balaam is a diviner. His skill lies in his ability to predict the future based on the examination of signs, not in making events occur. Balaam's frequent assertion that he can only speak what Yahweh tells him (22:8,18,35,38; 23:3-5,12,16,26; 24:14) is perfectly consistent with his role. He cannot simply say what he is paid to say (contra Scharbert 1958a:6). When he finds out from the gods what will happen, he cannot change it; he can only relay the information to Balak (23:8,20). Balaam is essentially a prophet, i.e., a spokesman for God. Here his main function is as predictor (so also Wilson 1980:147-150).

Balaam seeks his oracles from Yahweh (see the last cited set of verses). This also is perfectly in keeping with his role. Since Yahweh is Israel's God, Balaam must find out Israel's fate from Yahweh. It would do no good to consult Baal or Ishtar about a people that lies outside of their jurisdiction. The references to Yahweh do not make Balaam a monotheist or a worshipper of Yahweh—when inquiring about another people, Balaam would consult their god.

The curse words used in the narrative are the Qal of $’rr$ (22:6 three times; $yû’ār$ is Qal passive, GKC 53 u; 22:12; 23:7) the Qal of z^cm (23:7, 8 twice), and the Qal of qbb (22:11,17; 23:8 twice, 11,13,25 twice, 27; 24:10). A comparison of the verses shows that $’rr$, qbb, and z^cm are used as complete synonyms. For example, Balak uses $’rr$ in 22:6. Balaam quotes Balak's words in v 11, but uses qbb in place of $’rr$. z^cm is parallel to $’rr$ in 23:7 and parallel to qbb in 23:8.

Brichto (1963:200-202) feels there is insufficient information to define qbb with much assurance, while z^cm has the basic meaning of hostility (202-203). He says $’rr$ clearly has the meaning of "curse" in the sense of "bind with a spell" (100,114-115). Scharbert (1958a:6,14,15) sees all three words in this pericope as having the meaning "verfluchen" with only minor differing nuances, meaning that Balaam puts Israel under a spell or curse which is effective because of the power of the spoken word.

In my estimation, neither author correctly defines the words. All three words mean "curse" in a declarative sense. Balak wants Balaam to declare that Israel is headed for defeat, for he knows that Balaam accurately predicts the future. The strength of Balaam's curse is not in the power of the words, but in the accurate discernment of what the gods have in store.

Yahweh prevents Balaam from cursing. He tells Balaam that Israel is $bārûk$ (22:12). "Blessed" means that Israel stands in a favorable relationship to God; God had blessed and would continue to bless her out of his favor for her (see further on this verse under 3.2 and 6.7 and below). Balaam then asks (23:8,20):

How can I curse (*qbb*) him whom God has not cursed?
How can I curse (*zʿm*) him whom Yahweh has not cursed?
See, I have received a command to bless;
He has blessed, and I cannot change it.

Balaam the prophet must accurately relay what God has told him. After the first two benedictions, Balaam stopped using divination: "When Balaam saw that it was pleasing to Yahweh to bless Israel, he did not employ divination as he had previously" (24:1). Balaam felt that the previous oracles he had received clearly conveyed God's intentions, so that there was no longer any need for divination.

The benedictions spoken by Balaam contain descriptions of typical blessing benefits: fertility (23:10; 24:7), dominion (23:24, 24:8-9,17-19; cf. 24:20-24), prosperity (24:5-7, and royalty (24:7,17). Israel is righteous (22:10,21,23) and Yahweh is with her (*ʿim*, 22:21) and has delivered her from Egypt (23:22; 24:8). The benedictions describe Israel as having been blessed in the past, and destined for future blessing. The strongest element is dominion—Israel will eat other nations as a lion devours its prey (23:24; 24:8-9) and will conquer Edom (24:18). The phrase "those on good terms with you will be blessed, while those hostile to you will be cursed" in 24:9 was apparently a standard formula expressing dominion (cf. Gen 12:3; 26:29; see further under 4.3) Israel's deliverance from Egypt and future dominion are emphasized because of the impending battles of the conquest.

Josh 24 contains a recital of God's saving acts phrased with God speaking in the first person. Vv 9-10 recount the Balaam incident. Balaam was hired to curse (*lĕqallēl*) Israel, but God says, "I was not willing to listen to Balaam, so he emphatically blessed you. I saved you from his hand." Balaam is pictured as wholly subservient to God's command; he exerts no influence over God. Balaam is also pictured as eager to curse Israel. This seems to contradict the Numbers picture, where he firmly states that he would only declare what Yahweh told him. Probably here Balaam and Balak are viewed as united against Israel.

Deut 23:5-6 and Neh 13:2 contain similar recollections. Balaam was hired to curse (*lĕqallēl*) Israel, but God "turned the curse (*haqqĕlālâ*) into a blessing (*bĕrākâ*) for you."

In these three later recollections, the curse word *qll*, Piel, stands as the antonym to *brk*, Piel. *qll* does not actually occur in the Balaam narrative; only *ʾrr*, *zʿm*, and *qbb* do. *qll* is used for two reasons. First, it has the broadest range of meaning of all the curse words and its meaning completely overlaps the meanings of the other words. Second, the Piel of *qll* is the usual antonym to the Piel of brk; the Qals of ʾrr and qbb are much rarer as antonyms to the Piel of brk (cf. Brichto 1963:176).

The same two reasons account for the fact that qĕlālâ, not mĕʾērâ, is used in Deut 23:6 and Neh 13:2 to denote the malediction Balak intended Balaam to pronounce, even though it does not occur in the Balaam narrative. Its range of meaning subsumes that of mĕʾērâ, and it is the regular antonym to bĕrākâ (contra Wehmeier 1970:96, who feels that qĕlālâ cannot denote a curse (mĕʾērâ), and so claims that qĕlālâ refers to Balaam's role in the Baal Peor incident of Num 25). bĕrākâ denotes the four spoken benedictions of Num 23:7-10,18-24; 24:3-9,15-19.

4.1.3   Miscellaneous Declarative Blessings

Solomon declared himself to be blessed before sentencing Shimei to death. Shimei had cursed David as he fled from Absalom (2 Sam 16:5-9), and so Solomon put him on house arrest (1 Kgs 2:42). Because Shimei had left Jerusalem he now had to die. Solomon stated that Yahweh had now repaid Shimei for cursing David, and then declared, "the king Solomon is blessed (bārûk), and David's throne will be established before Yahweh forever" (v 45).

Solomon's declaration asserts that he is the legitimate ruler who has God's approval and protection over his office. The blessing Solomon possesses is the "grace of kingship" (see 3.2.2.4 and on 2 Sam 7 and Ps 72:15,17 under 4.2.2). By his declarative blessing Solomon refutes Shimei's curse of David's dynasty. Shimei's curse (qll, Piel) was also declarative, and stated that Yahweh was repaying David for murder and usurpation. The curse was a pronouncement of Yahweh's judgement upon David (contra Brichto 1963:138-141,178 note 130, who sees it simply as abusive speech, and Blank 1950:86-88, who sees it as a self-fulfilling "spell").

Wehmeier (1970:104) claims that Solomon spoke the bārûk formula in order to protect himself from his own "curse" of Shimei in 1 Kgs 2:44b: "Yahweh has returned your evil onto your head!" Wehmeier asserts that it was common practice to pronounce a blessing over oneself when issuing a curse to prevent the curse from backfiring (similarly Brichto 1963:16 note 12, discussing Judg 17:2).

But nowhere else in the Bible is this practice described (on Judg 17:2 see under 4.2.4). This explanation of the bārûk formula is based on an erroneous conception of how blessings and curses were effected. They are not effected by the power inherent in the words themselves; both Shimei's and Solomon's pronouncements name Yahweh as the agent of judgement. There is no need to fear that a curse could "backfire" since Yahweh is said to have requited David and Shimei because of what they had done, not because of the power of the curse words. Because David in fact had not committed murder, Simei's curse was ineffective. Yahweh instead returned him to the throne.

During Saul's quest for this father's donkeys, he asked some women about Samuel's whereabouts. They told Saul that he could find Samuel as he went up to the high place, since "the people will not eat until he comes. He will bless the sacrifice, and afterward those invited will eat" (1 Sam 9:13).

The meaning of the Piel of *brk* is disputed. The most common explanation is that it denotes the utterance of a table prayer of some sort (Wehmeier 1970:152, Plassman 1913:138, Stoebe 1973:195 following Murtonen 1959:163). Mowinckel (1961:28) argues that the sacrifice represented the divinity, and blessing it increased the blessing power that the sacrifice brought to the community (similarly Hempel 1961:43, Horst 1947:27). Scharbert (1958a:24) surmises that the author reproduced exactly the words of the girls who meant "consecrate" (*qdš*, Piel), but who did not know the correct terminology.

The meaning here is "consecrate, declare to be dedicated to God" (so also McCarter 1980:177). Wehmeier argues that the meaning cannot be "consecrate" since that would require the Piel of *qdš*. However, consecration can be a type of blessing. In Gen 2:3 = Exod 20:11, God blesses (*brk*, Piel) by consecrating (*qdš*, Piel), i.e., declaring the seventh day to be holy. The noun *běrākâ* in Exod 32:29 denotes the consecration which the Levites received because of God's oral declaration (see 3.2.1 on these verses). There is no evidence for the existence of table prayers at the time of Samuel. The examples cited by Wehmeier (1970:152 note 85) are from Qumran and the NT.

4.2   Optative Benedictions

All of the optative blessings are illocutionary utterances. The act of blessing consists of the pronunciation of a formula or phrase. The fact that they are optative wishes means that the speaker is at least partially uncertain whether or not his utterance will be fulfilled. All the types of optative blessings explicitly or implicitly call upon God to fulfill them when a fulfillment is expected.

The types of blessings are quite diverse. Some are spoken as a response to a deed performed by the person blessed, while others presuppose no action meriting the blessing. There are numerous different social settings in which the blessings are uttered. While some are spoken in the cult or court, most are spoken in everyday life situations. The expectations of the speaker also vary. Some types of blessings are mere wishes which the speaker does not expect to be fulfilled, while others approach the certainty of declarations or predictions. Though all are illocutionary utterances, some are uttered primarily because of their perlocutionary force. While most blessings presuppose a favorable relationship between God and the person blessed, and between God and the speaker, others presuppose neither.

4.2.1 The Priestly Blessing

The Priestly blessing (Num 6:24-26) does not simply call for God to bless out of his goodwill. Rather, the blessing calls for God to have an *attitude* of goodwill toward the persons blessed. The benefit which the blessing called upon God to bestow does not consist of fertility, prosperity, or dominion, but God's favor itself:

> May Yahweh bless you,
> and protect you;
> May Yahweh make his face shine on you
> and be gracious to you;
> May Yahweh lift up his face toward you
> and give you peace!

The Piel of *brk* is a general term for God bestowing benefits out of his favor. The emphasis of the word here is almost entirely on God's attitude, rather than on the protection and peace God bestows, as the parallel expressions show.

All three verses commence with a general expression of God's favor and end with a request for a somewhat more concrete benefit. The initial phrase employing *brk* is the most general; it is an "all-inclusive petition" (Miller 1975:243). God making his face shine on someone denotes God displaying his favor (*ḥesed*) toward him by acting on his behalf (Ps 31:17; 80:4,8,20, where God delivers persons from distress). In Ps 44:4, the light of God's face denotes the aid God gives to his people because he is favorably disposed (*rṣh*) toward them. God lifting up his face toward someone is equivalent to making his face shine on someone (cf. Ps 4:7). It denotes God giving attention to someone. It is antonymous to the expression *histîr pānîm*. God hides his face out of anger, signifying that he "withdraws his favour" from them (BDB 711b; on the expressions about God's face, cf. Fishbane 1983:116-117; on *šālôm* in v 26 see under 6.8).

In v 27, God describes the effect that the benediction will have when the priests pronounce it: "They shall place my name on the children of Israel and I shall bless them." The benediction contains three occurrences of *yhwh*, so when the priests recite it, they emphatically invoke Yahweh's blessing upon the people. That is how they place his name on them. God promises to respond to the benediction and bless. The emphatic first person pronoun, like the three-fold repetition of *yhwh*, stresses that the effectiveness of the priestly benediction is due to God's responsiveness to the invocations. It is not due to the power of the priests' souls or their ability to utter self-fulfilling formulas. God is pictured as complying voluntarily with the requests of the benediction.

Yet, to be effective, the benediction must be uttered by the priests, who mediate for God, and in the correct form. The context also implies, and actual practice confirms (see below), that the benediction was to be spoken only on important cultic occasions. When, however, these conditions are met, God promises to respond regardless of the identity or character of the persons blessed.

Besides being an effective blessing, the benediction is important because of its perlocutionary force. The benediction assures the persons blessed that God is indeed favorably disposed toward them and that he definitely will continue to bless them.

The Piel of *brk* is used seven times to denote the pronouncement of the Priestly benediction, and the benediction is called a *bĕrākâ* once. In Num 6:23, God says to Moses, "Tell Aaron and his sons, 'This is how you should bless the children of Israel. Say to them . . .'". The Priestly benediction follows.

None of the other passages quote the Priestly benediction. However, it may be assumed that the Priestly benediction was the benediction spoken because the priests are the ones who pronounce it, and it occurs in a cultic context.

Lev 9 describes the first sacrifices Aaron and his sons made after being consecrated as priests. After offering the sacrifices, "Aaron raised his hands towards the people and blessed them" (v 22). This was the first time that the benediction was actually used. Next, "Moses and Aaron went into the tabernacle, and came out and blessed the people" (v 23). The cultic context suggests that this, too, was the priestly benediction (so also Miller 1975:242). The following theophany is God's stamp of approval on the practice of pronouncing the benediction as well as on the entire cult just founded.

Deut 10:8; 21:5; and 1 Chr 23:13 all describe the privileges of the Levitical priests "to serve him (Yahweh) and to bless using his/Yahweh's name." These verses clearly refer to the priestly benediction which was the exclusive privilege of the priests. The phrase "to bless using Yahweh's name" is not used exclusively for pronouncement of the Priestly benediction (contra Wehmeier 1970:147; see 2 Sam 6:18 = 1 Chr 16:2; Ps 129:8; cf. Ps 118:26). The expression simply denotes pronouncement of a benediction that invokes Yahweh. Yet the Priestly benediction is the model example of a benediction using Yahweh's name.

2 Chr 30:27 tells how the Levitical priests blessed the people at the close of the passover celebration during Hezekiah's reform.

In Mal 2:2, God warns the priests that if they do not start giving him more respect, "I will send the curse against you and curse your blessings. Indeed, I will curse them, because you are not making a conscious effort (to honor me)." Because the blessings belong to the priests, and because of the cultic context of vv 1-9, the blessings are utterances of the Priestly blessing. God would send his curse ($mĕ^{\jmath}ērâ$) and curse ($^{\jmath}rr$) the benedictions. This means that he would no longer honor and respond to them. God does not say that he will take away the priests' status. Rather, God would make their special privilege to bestow blessings worthless—the benedictions would no longer be effective (so also Laetsch 1956:521). Brichto (1963:102-103) and Wehmeier (1970:80-81) understand the blessings as agricultural produce (cf. v 3a and 3:10). The problem with this interpretation is that the Levites were not farmers. Wehmeier suggests then that the verse does not belong in this context—it refers to the people in general, not to the priests. But the preceding verse specifically addresses the priests (cf. also vv 5,7,8). It is better to choose a meaning consistent with the context than to choose a meaning which necessitates removing the verse from its context.

The people who utter the Priestly benediction are always Aaronides (Num 6:23, 1 Chr 23:13) or Levitical priests (Deut 21:5, 2 Chr 30:27). Deut 10:8 names the Levites in general, but this is because the list of duties includes carrying the ark, which is not a priestly function. There is no evidence from the verses in this section that the Aaronic benediction was ever anything but a priestly privilege (contra Wehmeier 1970:147).

4.2.2 Prayers for Blessing

The prayers for blessing occur in diverse circumstances. Some call upon God to honor his promises, while others request benefits from God that he has not explicitly promised to bestow. However, in all cases God is asked to act in accordance with the general principles of retribution described in the blessing promises (3.1.1 - 3.1.5). The person whom the prayer calls for God to bless is always eligible for blessing according to the terms of the promises.

The prayers can have one or both of two purposes. The first type of prayer seeks to cause God to bless when he otherwise would not have done so. Naturally, this type of prayer usually calls for God to bestow a benefit that he had not previously promised to bestow.

The effectiveness of this type of prayer is rooted in the belief that God hears and responds to requests addressed to him (see especially on 1 Sam 2:20 and 1 Kgs 8). Unlike the Priestly blessing, these prayers call for God to bestow specific, observable benefits, so that it will be obvious whether or not God has answered the prayer. Yet because God is asked to act in accordance with the principles of retribution, the power of the prayers is limited. They cannot cause God to bless when the person is ineligible for blessing according to the retribution principles, and the answered prayers show that when God did bless in response to prayers, his blessing activity was much the same as when it was not in response to prayer (as in 3.2.2.1 —3.2.2.6).

The other type of prayer is uttered primarily because of its perlocutionary effect upon man, not because of its effect upon God. These prayers usually ask God to bless in a way that he had previously promised to do, or in a way that he could be expected to act if no prayer was uttered. The prayers usually seek to remind, comfort, or reassure the person for whom the prayer is uttered. I will consider this type of prayer first.

In Gen 28:3-4, Isaac uttered a prayer over Jacob when he sent him to Aramea to acquire a wife:

> May El Shaddai bless you, make you fruitful, and make you numerous, so that you become a group of peoples. May he give you the blessing of Abraham, both to you and to your descendants, so that you inherit the land in which you sojourned, which God gave to Abraham.

The Piel of *brk* in vv 1,6 (twice) denotes the utterance of this prayer. Isaac prays for God to bless (*brk*, Piel) Jacob by giving him Abraham's blessing (*běrākâ*). The context makes clear that Isaac wants Jacob now to be the recipient of the patriarchal blessing promises, which are denoted by *běrākâ*. The prayer is not necessary to cause God to bless Jacob, since he had previously promised to bless Abraham's line, and had sanctioned Isaac's designation of Jacob as his firstborn (see on Gen 27 under 4.1.1). The purpose of the prayer is to remind Jacob of his calling before he starts on his long journey, and to emphasize that his status as heir of the promises makes it inappropriate for him to take a Canaanite wife.

Deut 26:15 instructs the people to utter a prayer after they have distributed their tithe to the Levites and the needy classes in the third year. They are to declare that they have complied with all of God's commandments, and then pray, "Look down from your holy dwelling place, the heavens, and bless your people Israel and the land which you gave to us, as you swore to our fathers, a land flowing with milk and honey." The prayer simply calls upon God to fulfill his covenantal promises.

The purpose of the prayer is primarily to remind the people that they must obey the covenant to obtain blessing, and that the blessings they receive are from Yahweh; the verse actually presupposes that God will have already fulfilled his promises, since the Israelites will have enough to tithe. The prayer does not alter Yahweh's actions.

Moses uttered a prayer in Deut 1:11 to avoid a misunderstanding. While explaining how the Israelites were too numerous for him to deal with, he said, "May Yahweh, the God of your fathers, increase your numbers to a thousand times what they are now, and may he bless you, as he said to you that he would." Moses was not worried that God might not fulfill his promises; he was trying to reassure the people that he did not resent their large numbers, and that he did not appoint assistant leaders in order to avoid contact with them.

Both 2 Sam 7:29 and 1 Chr 17:27 function as an "amen." David expresses confidence that God will fulfill his promises regarding his dynasty, while at the same time he realizes that their fulfillment is a long way off. His precarious position during much of his life must have made him question the security of his dynasty, and so he prays earnestly for fulfillment of what God has already promised to do. In 2 Sam 7 God promises:

1) David's offspring will build the temple, and Yahweh will establish his kingdom (vv 12-13);
2) David's offspring will have a son/father relationship with Yahweh (v 14);
3) Yahweh will not withdraw his ḥesed, "the grace of kingship" (see 3.2.2.4), from David's offspring (v 15);
4) David's kingship and dynasty will be established forever (v 16).

David responds to these promises with a prayer consisting of praise, vv 18-24, and a request that God fulfill his promises, vv 25-29. The last verse (29) reads: "Now, be pleased to bless your servant's dynasty so that

Man Blessing Man 101

it stands before you forever. For you, my Lord Yahweh, have spoken, and because of your blessing your servant's dynasty will be blessed forever."

brk occurs three times. The first is the Piel imperative, which calls for God to actually bestow the benefits he just promised. The chief promise which David singles out is the permanence of his dynasty. *bĕrākâ* here denotes God's verbal promises of blessing, as is made clear by the preceding word: "you have *spoken*, and because of your blessing . . ." The *min* is causal. Wehmeier (1970:83) takes the noun as meaning "Lebenssteigerung im konkreten Sinne," and Scharbert (1975a:299) takes it as the power of God producing fertility and prosperity, but these benefits lie outside the emphasis of this chapter.

The third occurrence is the Pual imperfect. It is the passive of the Piel, and denotes the actual reception of the benefits promised. It expresses David's conviction that God will actually fulfill his promises: "your servant's dynasty *will* be blessed forever." *lĕʿôlam* suggests that again the permanency of his dynasty was the chief benefit in David's mind. Being blessed forever means that his dynasty will always enjoy God's *ḥesed*. God will preserve the dynasty and consider it to be the legitimate dynasty (cf. the promises of royal descendants in Gen 17:16,20; 35:9; and 3.2.2.4).

In the parallel verse 1 Chr 17:27, the Piel infinitive is used in place of the imperative, with no difference in meaning. The Piel perfect is used in place of the noun, and like the noun it refers to the verbal promises: "you have blessed" = "you have promised to bestow benefits." The Pual participle is used in place of the Pual imperfect, with no difference in meaning. The participle lacks a subject noun, but *bêt-ʿabdĕkā* in the first half of the verse is clearly implied as the subject.

I will now discuss the prayers which request from God benefits that he has not already promised. In all but one passage (1 Chr 4:10), the Piel of *brk* occurs meaning "to utter a prayer for blessing." The Piel is normally not delocutive; when the Piel of *brk* denotes the utterance of the prayer, the prayer itself usually does not contain a form of *brk* (Ps 129:8 and Gen 28:3-4 do). Conversely, the utterance of the prayers which do contain a form of *brk* (all the previously discussed prayers and Ps 129:8; 1 Chr 4:10) is not denoted by the Piel of *brk*, except in Gen 28:1,6, referring to vv 3-4, and Ps 129:8.

Jacob refers to the practice of praying for blessing when he says that Ephraim and Manasseh will be proverbial examples of blessed people: "Israel will bless invoking you, saying, 'May God make you like Ephraim and Manasseh'" (Gen 48:20; on the verse see further under 4.1.1 and Zech 8:13 under 3.1.5). "Bless" (*brk*, Piel) means "to pray for God to bless," and the context indicates that fertility and prosperity are the benefits people would pray for.

Examples of such prayers for fertility are found in Gen 24:60 and 1 Sam 2:20. On the occasion of Rebekah's departure to marry Isaac, her relatives "blessed Rebekah, saying to her,

> Our sister, may you become thousands of myriads,
> and may your seed inherit its enemies' gate!

The occasion which prompted the benediction was Rebekah's impending marriage, not just her departure, as seen by the reference to fertility. It may have been customary to pronounce such a benediction upon brides, though the only other example is Ruth 4:11-12. The reason that the benediction of Gen 24:60 was recorded is that its thought and language echoed the patriarchal promises (cf. especially Gen 22:17), and contrary to the likely original expectation, it was fulfilled literally (cf. Leupold 1942:1.682). However, Rebekah's relatives most likely did not realize that they were praying for God to fulfill one of his promises.

A similar benediction is found in 1 Sam 2:20, though the occasion is not a marriage. During Hannah's yearly pilgrimage to the temple to visit her son Samuel, "Eli would bless Elkanah and his wife, saying, 'May Yahweh give you children from this woman in place of the one she asked Yahweh for.'"[8] A major point of the pericope is that such blessings are effective. God responds to the blessing by giving Hannah five children (v 21). The "loan" of Samuel to Yahweh "yields high interest" (Hertzberg 1964:35-36). The preceding account of the birth of Samuel also emphasizes God's fulfillment of prayer (1 Sam 1:11,19-20).

Four passages describe prayers for the king. Ps 72 describes the ideal role of the king. In response to the ideal king's beneficent care of the poor and needy (vv 12-14), the people will wish for the king (v 15):

> Long may he live!
> May gold from Sheba be given to him!
> May people always pray for him,
> and bless him all day long!

---

[8] $šā'al$ should not be emended to $hiš'îlâ$ to conform to 4QSam^a and 1 Sam 1:28 (contra McCarter 1980:80), since the cognate accusative noun $šĕ'ēlâ$ would then have an entirely different meaning than its verb. The wording of MT agrees with 1 Sam 1:17.

The meaning of *brk*, Piel is clear from the parallel *yitpallēl ba'ădô*. The impersonal verbs (*GKC* 144 d) picture the nation praying for God to bless its king. The blessings prayed for would be such things as long life (cf. *wīḥî*), good health, wisdom, the stability of his dynasty, and military victory, which would bring peace and prosperity for the nation (cf. Pss 21 and 72, 2 Sam 7, and 3.2.2.4). The blessing envisioned here is a proper prayer, as opposed to the farewell given to the king by the people in 1 Kgs 8:66, and the congratulations of 2 Sam 8:10 = 1 Chr 18:10.

Ps 72:17 concludes the prayers for the king by calling for God's general blessing upon him and his people:

> May all nations acquire blessing through him,
> may they consider him blessed.

The Hithpael of *brk* with *bô* and *kōl gôyim* is clearly a reference to the patriarchal promise of blessing mediated to others (see Table 2: so also Leupold 1969:521, Weiser 1962:504). The Hithpael therefore has the same middle meaning here as in the patriarchal promises (contra Dahood 1968:185 who takes it as passive, as does the LXX, and Wehmeier 1970:180-181 who translates it as "Mit ihm [als Beispiel] werden sich Segen erbitten"). The middle translation is entirely consistent with the rest of the psalm, which pictures the king as the mediator of blessing for his people. The king justly judges and assists the lower classes (vv 2,4,12-14). During his reign the earth is fertile (vv 3,6,16). The king conquers his enemies, and they bring tribute (vv 8-11,15). Under the king the nation enjoys peace and prosperity (vv 3,7). On the king as mediator of blessing, see further 3.2.2.4 and on 1 Kgs 8:14,55 in this section. The Piel of *'šr* in the second line is declarative. Because possession of blessing is the prerequisite for being *'ašrê*, the Piel is best translated "consider/call blessed" (see Janzen 1965, Hamilton 1980b:80, and 6.8). The people recognize that it is through God's blessing of the king that they acquire blessing.

1 Kgs 1:47 contains a prayer for royal preeminence. Jonathan tells Adonijah about Solomon's recent coronation: "the royal officials came to bless our lord king David, saying, 'May God make Solomon's name more famous than your name, and may he make his throne greater than your throne!'" The blessing is the pronouncement of a prayer for God to bless Solomon's kingship; *lĕbārēk* does not have the nuance "to congratulate" here (contra Wehmeier 1970:157 and Gray 1964:93). Solomon's name (*šēm*) signifies his reputation or fame. As in Gen 12:2, the person's name is made great by God abundantly blessing the person himself (cf. also *zēker* in

Prov 10:7). Though the prayer may reflect the promises in 2 Sam 7, it does not specifically refer to any of them.

After the final plague, Pharaoh told Moses and Aaron, "Take your flocks and herds like you said and go, and bless me too!" (Exod 12:32). Keil and Delitzsch (The Pentateuch: 2.25) interpret brk Piel as denoting a final departing benediction. Mowinckel (1961:24) and Noth (1962:98) suggest that Pharaoh wanted Moses to procure blessing for him from the cultic festival to be held in the desert. However, after several of the previous plagues, Pharaoh had asked Moses to pray to Yahweh for him (haʿtîrû 8:4,24; 9:28; 10:17). The meaning of bless here, then, is to pray for God to bless (so also Childs 1974:183, Wehmeier 1970:158). Pharaoh knew that Moses' prayer could take away the plagues.

An analogous situation occurs in 2 Sam 21:3. God told David that the reason for the three year famine was that Saul had tried to kill off the Gibeonites. David then asked the Gibeonites, "What can I do for you, and how can I make atonement so that you will bless Yahweh's inheritance?"[9] The Israelites had sworn by Yahweh to let the Gibeonites live (Josh 9:15, 18,19). Violation of the oath would bring God's anger on Israel (Josh 9:20). There is no need to assume that the Gibeonites had pronounced a curse because of their mistreatment; the curse was built into the original oath (so also Brichto 1963:89 note 30, contra Wehmeier 1970:155). It is not clear whether David envisioned the Gibeonites praying for Israel, or if the Gibeonites simply needed to declare that they were satisfied with the atonement. In either case, the Gibeonites' words brought about God's blessing in the form of rain which eliminated the drought causing the famine (2 Sam 21:10). There is no evidence that the blessing consisted of the Gibeonites again having friendly relations with Israel, so that brk, Piel means "grüssen" (contra Wehmeier 1970:155), or that the Gibeonites were to resume pronouncing cultic, priestly benedictions over the Israelites at the sanctuary at Gibeon (contra Hertzberg 1964:383).

The Chronicler inserted a short anecdote into a genealogy to show that "God listens to genuine prayer" (Myers 1965:28). In 1 Chr 4:10 Jabez cries out to God: "Oh that you would bless me and enlarge my territory, that your hand would be with me, and that you would keep me from harm so that I might have no pain!" V 10 states that God granted his request.

Ps 129:8 refers to the custom of praying for God's blessing upon those who are harvesting. The psalm likens the wicked to withered grass. Passers-by will not pray for God's blessing upon those harvesting the

---

[9]The imperative bārĕkû is part of a purpose clause (GKC 110 i).

grass: "Those who pass by do not say, 'Yahweh's blessing upon you! We bless you in Yahweh's name!'" The structure of the double benediction is identical to Ps 118:26. The optative wish "Yahweh's blessing upon you" prays for God to grant an abundant harvest. The illocutionary utterance "we bless you" likewise is a prayer for Yahweh to bless (so also Mowinckel 1962:90 and Leupold 1969:900, against Wehmeier 1970:147 and Weiser 1962:772 who take the final line as a Priestly blessing). The context implies that such prayers were customary—it was only under exceptional circumstances that they were not uttered. The only other verse providing evidence for a custom of blessing during harvest-time is Ruth 2:4, though there the blessings, especially the one given to Boaz, seem to be greetings rather than harvest prayers. Yet, as with the marriage benedictions, the practice may have been much more common than the Bible indicates.

There are four passages where the king blesses. David twice blessed after bringing the ark to Jerusalem: "When David finished offering up the burnt offerings and the peace offerings, he blessed the people in the name of Yahweh of hosts" (2 Sam 6:18 = 1 Chr 16:2). David then went home to bless his household (2 Sam 6:20 = 1 Chr 16:43). Solomon twice blessed the congregation during the festival celebrating the finishing of the temple (1 Kgs 8:14 = 2 Chr 6:3; 1 Kgs 8:55).

Wehmeier (1970:147-151) argues that in 2 Sam 6:18 = 1 Chr 16:2 and 1 Kgs 8:14 = 2 Chr 6:3 the kings pronounced the Priestly blessing. David and Solomon were functioning as priests during the ceremonies, offering sacrifices. David was wearing the priestly ephod and performed a cultic dance (2 Sam 6:14,16). David's benediction was in Yahweh's name. However, "in Yahweh's name" only means that Yahweh was invoked. It does not necessarily mean that the Priestly blessing was spoken (see Ps 129:8; cf. Ps 118:26). Though David and Solomon assume some priestly functions, this also does not mean that they had to use the Priestly blessing.

While no benedictions are recorded in 2 Sam 6, the two blessings Solomon spoke are recorded in 1 Kgs 8. "He blessed . . . and he said:" in 1 Kgs 8:14-15 is a frequent formula used for introducing oral blessings. V 14, then, refers to Solomon's doxology and prayer of vv 15-21,23-53. The prayer calls for God to be attentive to his people, to aid them in times of trouble, to forgive them, and to bestow rain. The content of the prayer certainly is appropriate for a blessing prayer (so also Scharbert 1975a:289-290, contra Wehmeier 1970:151).

Solomon's blessing of 1 Kgs 8:55 refers to vv 56-61. Along with a doxology and exhortation to follow the covenantal laws, the prayer calls for Yahweh to be with ($^c im$) his people and not to forsake them (v 56); it prays for the blessing of God's presence.

David's benediction of 2 Sam 6:18 = 1 Chr 16:2 was most likely similar in content (though probably much shorter) to Solomon's benedictions (similarly Scharbert 1975a:289-290). It is likely that David's intended benediction over his household (2 Sam 6:20 = 1 Chr 16:43) was similar to his blessing of the people two verses earlier. David especially desired to have God preserve his household, since the welfare of the nation required God's blessing upon the royal line (see 3.2.2.4; contra Wehmeier 1970:155 and Murtonen 1959:167 who take it as a greeting benediction, and Scharbert 1975a:289 who compares it to the testamental blessings given by dying fathers).

Solomon's blessing prayer of 1 Kgs 8:15-53 describes the temple as having an important function for mediating blessing to the nation. The temple makes God and his grace *accessible*. Previously, God had not designated any of the places where he had made his presence known as *the* place where his name resided (v 16). Now, people could pray toward the temple in Jerusalem and rest assured that God would respond to their prayer.

Although God was not confined to the temple (v 27; vv 30,32,34,36, 43, 49 picture God in heaven), the temple was the visible sign of God's presence. God is pictured as responding to prayers for blessing that are directed toward the temple. God bestows rain and delivers his people from famine, sickness, locusts, national enemies, and exile (vv 33,36-37,47-49). All these benefits are part of the covenantal blessing promises (see 3.1.2 and especially Deut 28).

God will even respond to the prayers of foreigners so that they fear Yahweh just as Israel does (vv 42-43,60); through the temple blessing can be mediated to all nations. In the second temple period, the temple continued to be a source of blessing for the people (see Hag 2:19; Zech 8:13; Mal 3:10 under 3.1.1.5; cf. also Zion as a source of blessing, Pss 128:5; 134:3; and 3.2.2.5, and the ark as a source of blessing, 2 Sam 6:11-12 = 1 Chr 13:14 under 3.2.2.6).

4.2.3 Greetings and Farewells

The Piel of *brk* can be used with the meaning "to greet" or "to say goodbye." The benedictions that are occasionally recorded have the same form as some formal prayers, but they do not request specific benefits from God. Instead, they use general expressions such as "may Yahweh be with you" or "may Yahweh bless (*brk*, Piel) you" (Ruth 2:4). Those who utter the benedictions normally do not expect them to be fulfilled in a striking manner. The greetings and farewells are social customs that usually have little religious value. They are illocutionary utterances whose main importance is the perlocutionary effect. They can express goodwill, friendship, affection, and occasionally, religious fellowship. Because of their social function, they are usually best translated "to greet" or "to say farewell," rather than "to bless," unless they also have a religious function or invoke Yahweh or God.

The greetings and farewells could be uttered in a variety of situations. They could be spoken by those in authority, by subordinates to those over them, and between equals. Ruth 2:4; 2 Kgs 4:29; and Prov 27:14 indicate that they were commonly used in everyday life, probably more frequently than on formal occasions such as in Gen 47:7,10 (contra Wehmeier 1970:154).

It is difficult to generalize about the content of the benedictions, because they are infrequently recorded, but they would naturally be shaped by the situation. A simple *šālôm* would probably suffice for meeting a stranger on the road. Among strangers or those of different religious persuasions, a deity might not be invoked (none is in 1 Sam 25:5-6), but the pious, and those wishing to appear pious, invoked Yahweh (Ruth 2:4; 1 Sam 15:13).

Prov 27:14 says that the social custom of greeting must be performed in the socially accepted manner and context in order for it to have the desired perlocutionary force:

> He who greets his neighbor in a loud voice early in the morning,
>   a curse will be reckoned to him!

The Piel of *brk* means "to greet with a benediction." Because *qĕlālâ* is the antonym of a benediction, it denotes a malediction, not "abusive conduct" (contra Brichto 1963:191, who also denies that the greeting can contain a benediction, i.e., a wish for blessing).

Ruth 2:4 quotes two greeting benedictions: "Just then Boaz came from Bethlehem. He said to the reapers, 'May Yahweh be with you!' They said to him, 'May Yahweh bless you!'" This exchange describes greetings in everyday life among the pious. The reapers respond to Boaz' piety by also invoking Yahweh. Boaz' call for God's presence is no less forceful than the reapers' response using the jussive Piel of *brk* (contra Wehmeier 1970:143). There is no indication that Boaz' words constitute a wish for a plentiful harvest (cf. Ps 129:8). Both expressions are more salutations than prayers. The salutations imply that the two parties are on friendly terms and share a common religious bond.

1 Sam 15:13 also quotes a greeting benediction. After Saul defeated the

Amalekites, "Samuel came to Saul, and Saul said to him, 'May you be blessed by Yahweh. I have fulfilled Yahweh's word.'" The formula *bārûk ʾattâ lyhwh* is a general salutory benediction. Saul is not praying for any specific benefit for Samuel, but is simply wishing him well. Saul wished to appear pious. He had in fact *not* obeyed God's command to exterminate the Amalekites completely. Here, and in 1 Sam 13:10 where Saul offered the sacrifice before Samuel arrived, Saul probably felt guilty because of his disobedience and sought to forestall Samuel's anger by greeting him piously. Saul's words of greeting are not recorded in 13:10, but they probably were similar to the salutation of 15:13.

2 Kgs 4:29 indicates that it was common practice to salute others along the road. Elisha tells Gehazi to return to the Shunamite woman: "Tuck your cloak into your belt, take your staff, and go! When you meet someone, do not greet him, and if someone greets you, do not answer him." The Piel of *brk* here simply denotes a friendly greeting. Because the two parties are strangers, the salutation is not intended to establish a lasting relationship or to express a common religious bond, as with Saul and Samuel, and Jehu and Jonadab in 2 Kgs 10:15. The prohibition is merely intended to keep Gehazi from spending time conversing with people along the way. He is to hurry to heal the son of the Shunamite. There is no indication that Gehazi would transfer blessing power to others by greeting them and so lessen his ability to heal the boy (contra Pedersen 1926:201, Mowinckel 1961:9).

In 2 Kgs 10:15, Jehu greets (*brk*, Piel) Jonadab with a view toward establishing a common religious bond. Jehu has been killing Baal worshippers. When Jonadab affirms that he is of a similar mind with Jehu, Jehu takes him into his chariot and continues his purge (vv 16-17).

In 1 Sam 25:14, one of Nabal's servants tells Abigail, "David sent messengers from the desert to greet our master, but he shrieked at them." The meaning of *brk*, Piel is clarified by vv 5-6, where David tells his messengers, "Ask him in my name if he is well. Say to him, 'Long life to you! Peace to you! Peace to your house! Peace to all that you have!'" David expressed the desire for friendship and good relations by his salutation. His purpose was not so much to establish a lasting relationship, but to make Nabal more inclined to grant his request for food (v 8).

Jacob spoke greeting and farewell benedictions to Pharaoh (Gen 47:7,10). By doing so, he expressed respect and thanks for preservation from the famine, as well as deference to the sovereign (cf. Ruth 2:4b; 1 Kgs 8:66).

In Gen 32:1 and 2 Sam 19:40, a kiss (*nšq*, Piel) is given in conjunction with a farewell benediction. The kiss was simply a sign of affection given before departing (cf. Gen 31:28; 1 Kgs 19:20; Ruth 1:9,14). It was not necessary to kiss or have another type of physical contact to transmit blessing (contra Pedersen 1926:203). There is no physical contact mentioned with most departing benedictions. The kiss was only given when the people shared close emotional ties. In Gen 32:1, Laban kissed his daughters and grandchildren goodbye, and in 2 Sam 19:40 David kissed his dear friend Barzillai goodbye.

The only other instance where physical contact occurred with a departing benediction is in Gen 32:25-32, when Jacob struggled with the mysterious wrestler. The contact, however, had nothing to do with the benediction. When the wrestler asked Jacob to let him go, Jacob replied, "I will not let you go until you bless me" (v 27). V 30 states simply "he blessed him there." Jacob desired a departing benediction from the wrestler because such a benediction would express friendship and signify that he was no longer hostile, but an ally. Jacob identified the wrestler as divine (v 31; cf. v 29), and desired his assistance and protection during the imminent conflict with Esau. The blessing which the wrestler gave answered Jacob's prayer for protection in 32:11-13 (cf. von Rad 1972:323). The renaming is also a type of blessing because the new name denotes conferral of a new status. Jacob will no longer be known as ya'ăqōb, "cheater" (Gen 25:26; 27:36), but as Israel, "he who has struggled with God" and with men and has prevailed (v 28; on renaming see further on Gen 17:5,15,19 under 3.1.1). Jacob has not cheated here, but has legitimately won divine blessing. The narrative confirms Jacob's stolen blessing as legitimately his.

On two occasions the national leader utters a departing benediction. In Josh 22:6-7, Joshua blessed the tribes of Reuben, Gad, and half the tribe of Manasseh as he sent them to their allotted territory to the east of the Jordan. The passage twice states that Joshua blessed them, emphasizing that they have Joshua's approval to settle in their separate territory. As the national leader, Joshua's approval represents God's approval. The blessing emphasizes that they share in the fellowship of the other Israelites despite their location. Joshua's benediction is recorded in v 8: "Return to your tents with great riches, an extremely large amount of animals, silver, gold, bronze, iron, and clothes. You get to share in the plunder from your enemies with your brothers."

On a more mundane occasion, David gave Absalom his blessing after declining his invitation to attend a feast (2 Sam 13:25). David gave his blessing in lieu of going himself (cf. Scharbert 1958a:20 note 1). By giving his blessing, David said that he wished he could go, and gave his approval of the venture.

The people blessed King Solomon at the end of the fourteen-day celebration of the dedication of the temple (1 Kgs 8:66): Solomon "sent the people away, and they blessed the king." The only other cases of subjects blessing their king are Gen 47:7,10; Exod 12:32; Ps 72:15. The people here respond to the King's blessing upon his reign and express their gratitude for all the good God had done through him (v 66).

4.2.4   Thanksgiving Benedictions

The Thanksgiving benedictions are optative wishes for God to reward the person thanked for performing a beneficent act. They are wishes, rather than prayers, because they do not call upon God to bestow specific benefits, nor does the speaker expect the utterance to be fulfilled in a striking manner. Instead, they are general wishes that God will make things go well for the person thanked.

Whereas the prayers are based on the belief that God hears and responds to individual pleas, these wishes are based on a belief in God's general retribution (so also E. Campbell 1975:112-113; cf. Scharbert 1975a:286). This belief is evident especially in the covenantal blessing promises and the wisdom aphorisms (3.1.2 and 3.1.3), which assert that God normally blesses the pious who do good to others. The thanksgiving benedictions apply this belief to individuals. The speaker says that God should bless the life of the person thanked because of his piety, as evidenced by his good deed.

Yet the formulas do not dogmatically claim that God will automatically reward people. Campbell's explanation of the process (1975:113) is worth quoting in full:

> In terms of the now well-known covenant formulations of the OT, God first favors his people on his own initiative, then requires that they live in accord with their status as his people, and then responds with blessing or curse to their obedient or disobedient living . . . . God's people do acts of ḥesed not in order to deserve God's grace, but in order to respond to his grace. God's blessing is then a response to the response, one of which his people may be confident but of which they cannot be mechanically sure.

The thanksgiving benedictions are uttered in gratitude for special, important acts of kindness, often called ḥesed (2 Sam 2:5-6; Ruth 2:20; 3:10). All of the benedictions are uttered in everyday life situations, rather than in the court or cult. Ruth 2:19-20; 3:10, in particular, emphasize that the kindness (ḥeseḏ) shown by people to each other is a response to the kindness God has shown his people. In 2:20, Naomi gives thanks for the kindness God has shown her and Ruth, and then Ruth shows kindness toward Boaz (3:10). Boaz invokes God's blessing upon Ruth, only to become the agency for the fulfillment of that blessing (3:10; 4:10). "ḥesed in the human scene is evidence of God's ḥesed, his faithful magnanimity" (E. Campbell 1975:113).

Scharbert (1958b, 1975a:284-288) rightly stresses the solidarity and fellowship expressed by the bārûk formula. Even when the person thanked is unknown (Ruth 2:19), the formula expresses a strong sentiment of goodwill and friendship.

The benedictions are primarily directed toward the person thanked, rather than toward God, since they are general wishes, not prayers. The speaker expresses appreciation and praise by the benediction. The utterance of the benediction is intended to repay the person thanked. Yet the perlocutionary force is more than an effort to make the person thanked realize that the *speaker* appreciates his deed. The speaker intends to convey the notion that *God* is pleased with his behavior (cf. the wisdom aphorisms such as Prov 11:26 which stress that in addition to human praise, God's approval rests on the pious).

Most of the thanksgiving benedictions contain a bārûk formula. The most common form of the formula is bārûk-person-lyhwh (Judg 17:2; 1 Sam 23:21; 2 Sam 2:5; Ruth 2:20; 3:10). The formula means "may the person be blessed by Yahweh." The preposition *l* introduces the agent of the passive participle, and the nominal sentence has an optative mood (*GKC* 116 r note 1, 121 f, 141 f, Davidson 1901:sections 81,133, Schottroff 1969:168-169, Williams 1976:sections 280,551,580; cf. Brockelmann 1913:2.25-27). Although the formula is optative, the utterance of the formula accomplishes the act of blessing because it is an illocutionary utterance.

Wehmeier (1970:108-111) and Keller (1978:356-357) argue that the lamed is the lamed of relation, based on Aramaic parallels which use qodām, and the ʾārûr formulas of Josh 6:26; 1 Sam 26:19 which use lipnê (similarly Scharbert 1958a:21-22 and 1973:26). They also argue that the participle is stative in meaning, not passive, and so describes the person as possessing blessing, rather than as being the recipient of blessing (Keller 1978:355, Wehmeier 1970:117). They also view the formula as an indicative statement, rather than an optative wish (so also Scharbert 1975a:286). They therefore confuse the optative mood with the illocutionary force of the pronunciation of the formula.

The meaning of the Hebrew formula must be determined by its usage in context, not by analogies to ʾārûr or Aramaic formulas. Difficulties immediately arise when these views of Wehmeier and Keller are applied to the verses in context. In 2 Sam 2:5, for example, David tells the men of Jabesh-Gilead, "May you be blessed by Yahweh, you who did this kindness to your lord Saul, namely, that you buried him. Now may Yahweh do kindness and faithfulness to you." David is not stating that they already possess blessings; he wishes for God to reward them by blessing them. The bārûk formula is therefore optative, not indicative. V 6 confirms the optative interpretation: "Now may Yahweh do kindness and faithfulness to you." The form yaʿaś is jussive, not indicative. Because the men had shown ḥesed toward Saul in burying him (v 5), David wishes that God will show ḥesed to them in return (v 6).

The interpretation of the force of the lamed is dependent upon the interpretation of the voice of the participle. In all five verses, the bārûk formula expresses the wish that the person thanked would receive benefits from Yahweh. The participle is therefore passive. It is not stative; the person does not already possess benefits, but would be made to possess benefits by Yahweh.

Wehmeier (1970:111) and Keller (1978:356) both recognize God's agency in the bestowal of benefits. They translate lyhwh as "bei Jahwe" and "dank Jahwe," respectively. God is responsible for the prosperous condition of the person who is bārûk. It is really not accurate, then, to call the preposition the lamed of relation, since it introduces the person responsible for the condition of the subject. Even by Wehmeier's and Keller's own explanation of bārûk the lamed amounts to the lamed of agent.

Keller (1978:256) translates bārûk in the five thanksgiving bārûk person lyhwh passages as "ein Wohltäter, d.h. von Jahwe mit wohltuender Kraft ausgestattet." But this confuses the reason for the utterance of the formula with the purpose of the formula. The formula is pronounced over a benefactor because of his benefaction. The purpose of the formula is not simply to describe the benefactor as a benefactor; it is obvious from the benefactor's good deed that he is a benefactor. The point of the response is to wish that the benefactor will be rewarded for his benefaction.

The simple formula bārûk person lyhwh, with no appended phrases, is found in Judg 17:2 and 1 Sam 26:25. In Judg 17:2, Micaiah's mother said "May my son be blessed by Yahweh" when he returned the money he stole from her. In addition to thanks, the formula expresses the mother's desire to nullify the curse she had pronounced over the person who stole her money (cf. Exod 12:32; 2 Sam 21:3, where prayers for blessing remove national disasters). The verb ʾlh used in Judg 17:2a denotes the utterance of a curse or malediction (Brichto 1963:44-45,70-71). Brichto (44-45) suggests that the mother suspected her son and pronounced the curse to force him to confess in order to escape the curse. However, there is no indication of this. Because the deed was already committed, and the perpetrator was unknown, the imprecation was "a prayer form, addressed to the deity . . . asking for punishment of a malefactor whose guilt cannot be proved"—a common use of *ʾlh* (Brichto 1963:70).

The function of the *bārûk* formula is antonymous to the function of the curse. It calls for God to reward her son, and replaces her earlier call for God to punish (similarly Murtonen 1959:170, Keller 1978:356, and Brichto 1963:45). Yahweh is clearly stated as the source of blessing (cf. Scharbert 1975a:286).

The other short form occurs in 1 Sam 26:25. After Saul learned that David had crept into his camp and taken his spear and water jug without harming him, he exclaimed, "May you be blessed, my son David. You certainly will do great things and triumph!" *bārûk* does not describe David as possessing abilities that would enable him to be successful in the future—David was not at that time full of blessing, but was living the life of a fugitive (contra Wehmeier 1970:113). David had expressed the hope that God would value his life and aid him in future situations (v 24). Saul responded by uttering the *bārûk* formula which expressed his conviction that God would indeed aid him because his deed revealed his righteous and faithful character (v 23).

In four verses the good deed of the person thanked follows the *bārûk* formula. 2 Sam 2:5 (discussed above) introduces the deed with an *ʾăšer* clause.

The *ʾăšer* clause in 1 Sam 25:33 likewise describes the deed which evoked thanks. David thanks Abigail for preventing him from murdering Nabal: "May your shrewdness be praised, and may you be blessed, you who prevented me today from committing murder to avenge myself with my own hands."

The *bārûk* formula with *ṭaʿmēk* as the subject is a formula of praise, since such an abstract entity can hardly be thanked. The phrase really functions as praise of Abigail, since it is *her* shrewdness that is praised (on the *bārûk* formulas of praise, see 5.2). Again, *bārûk* can hardly mean that Abigail at that time possessed blessings. Rather, David hoped that God would reward her for her deed.

1 Sam 23:21 introduces the deed with a *kî* clause. Saul thanks the Ziphites for telling him the location of David: "May Yahweh bless you because you have had compassion on me."

In Ruth 3:10, the deed is introduced asyndetically. Boaz thanks Ruth for offering herself to him as a wife (on v 9 see E. Campbell 1975:123,131): "May you be blessed by Yahweh, my daughter. You made your latter deed of kindness better than the former one by not chasing after the young men, whether rich or poor." In Ruth 2:20, an *ăšer* clause is appended which refers to Yahweh rather than to the subject of the formula (E. Campbell 1975:106, Gerleman 1965:28; cf. Gen 24:27). After Ruth tells Naomi that it was in Boaz' field that she had gleaned so much, Naomi says, "May he be blessed by Yahweh, who has not forsaken his kindness with the living and with the dead." While the formula itself expresses gratitude toward Boaz, the appended phrase makes it clear that Naomi is primarily grateful toward God.

Ruth 2:19 contains a *bārûk* formula of a different form. Before Naomi heard that Ruth gleaned in Boaz' field, she asked Ruth: "Where did you glean today? Where did you work? May he who recognized you be blessed!" This form, *yĕhî* person *bārûk*, occurs four times elsewhere (1 Kgs 10:9 = 2 Chr 9:8; Jer 20:14; Prov 5:18). *yĕhî* clearly identifies this form as an optative wish (so also Scharbert 1975a:286). The fact that it is parallel to the *bārûk* person *lyhwh* form in v 20 further confirms the optative force of the latter form. Though unnamed, God is clearly implied as the agent of *bārûk* because the *bārûk* formulas frequently name him as the source of blessing. Naomi wishes for God to reward whomever it was that had shown such kindness (contra Wehmeier 1970:115, who denies that blessing is a reward from God). There is no real difference in meaning between this form and the usual form with *lyhwh*.

There are four passages where the Piel of *brk* means "to pronounce a benediction in thanks." In addition, one verse contains *bĕrākâ* denoting a benediction pronounced in gratitude. None of the passages quote the benedictions, but it is probable that the benedictions were similar to the *bārûk* formulas discussed earlier in this section (so also Scharbert 1975a:289-291, Wehmeier 1970:170-171). They occur in situations similar to those of the *bārûk* formulas. The Piel of *brk* in these verses then is delocutive, meaning "to utter a *bārûk* formula in thanks."

The first three verses are concerned with social justice. Deut 24:13 states that a garment taken in pledge from a poor person must be returned by nightfall, "so that he can sleep in his garment, and bless you, and you will have righteousness before Yahweh, your God." *ṣĕdāqâ* is covenantal righteousness; by following the commandments, a person is considered as living in accord with the covenant, and so entitled to God's blessings. God can be expected to respond to the wish.

Job 31:20 is similar. In his negative confession, Job asserts that whenever he saw a poor person without a garment,

His loins certainly blessed me,
and he warmed himself by the wool of my sheep.

The wool of Job's sheep represents Job's own garment, which he would give to the poor man. In response, the man's loins bless Job. This is the only verse in the Bible where something besides God or man blesses, but clearly the term is a metaphor for the man himself.

Again describing his former days, Job says in 29:12-13:

For I would save the poor person crying out,
the fatherless who had nobody to help him.
The blessing of the perishing man would come upon me,
and I would make the widow's heart cry for joy.

From the context it is clear that *běrākâ* denotes a benediction for Job spoken by the poor whom he helped. *'amīn* in 13b emphasizes that the blessing is spoken out of joyful gratitude.

In 2 Sam 14:22, Joab blessed King David for agreeing to bring back Absalom, who had fled after raping Tamar three years previously. The depth of Joab's gratitude is shown by the parallel expressions "he fell on his face to the ground" and "he bowed down."

Moses in Exod 39:43 blessed the workers who had constructed the tabernacle and its equipment. It is particularly appropriate that Moses should commend them to God for a blessing since they did the work for God.

4.2.5 Benedictions of Praise and Congratulations

The benedictions in this section differ from the thanksgiving benedictions in that the speaker does not thank the person blessed for a deed done for the sake of the speaker, though the speaker may indirectly benefit from the deed. Instead, the speaker expresses praise, admiration, and/or congratulations to a person for performing a deed for the sake of others, or simply out of piety. The benediction asserts not only that the speaker admires the deed, but that *God* approves of it. However, only Gen 14:19 explicitly names God; in most of the benedictions, as in most of the Wisdom aphorisms, God's approval is simply implied by the use of *brk*, since it is the usual word in prayers and wishes for *God* to bless.

The benedictions of congratulations are similar to those of praise in that the speaker expresses admiration, approval, and at times a sort of positive envy, saying in effect, "I wish I had done that."

There are two passages which employ *bārûk* formulas. The first also contains the Piel, meaning "to utter a benediction of praise and congratulations." In Gen 14:19-20, Melchizedek congratulates Abraham after his victory over the kings from the East (cf. 2 Sam 8:10 = 1 Chr 18:10): "He blessed him, saying,

> May Abram be blessed by El Elyon,
>   creator of heaven and earth,
> And may El Elyon be praised,
>   who delivered your enemies into your hand.

Wehmeier (1970:110) argues against most commentators that the formula is indicative and describes Abraham as "segensreich" or "voll Segen" in that God had enabled Abraham to achieve victory. But then the formula would serve no purpose; Melchizedek would tell victorious Abraham only that his victory was due to God's help, something of which Abraham was doubtless aware already. The *bārûk* formula is much better understood in its usual sense as an optative wish (see 4.2.4). As a priest, Melchizedek's blessing does more than thank Abraham for expelling their common enemies. As the representative of El Elyon, he declares that his God is on Abraham's side. The *bārûk* formula affirms that God will continue to bless Abraham.

By giving a tithe (v 20) Abraham accepts Melchizedek as a legitimate priest, and accepts his blessing as authoritative (similarly von Rad 1972:180-181, Westermann 1981:239-240, Driver 1905:166; on *bārûk* in v 20 see 5.4).

In Jer 20:14, a *bārûk* formula of praise is negated:

> Cursed be the day on which I was born,
>   the day when my mother bore me!
> May it not be blessed!

The formula is the negative of the *bārûk* formula found elsewhere only in 1 Kgs 10:9 = 2 Chr 9:8; Prov 5:18; Ruth 2:19. *yĕhî* clearly indicates that the formula is optative. Yet the illocutionary force of the formula is the same as if he had said, "I hereby declare that I consider my birthday a terrible day." *bārûk* is the regular antonym to *ʾārûr* (see on Deut 28 in 3.1.2). Here, the meaning of the formula repeats and thereby strengthens the thought of the *ʾārûr* formula. "Not blessed" means "cursed." A birthday would be considered blessed (*bārûk*) because on it a blessing—a child—was received. As in Prov 5:18 and Deut 28:5, *bārûk* itself has both a passive and an active meaning. The day is blessed by God, and so is a source of blessing for man. The day of stillbirth would be considered ᵓārûr, cursed, because a tragedy occurred on it.

Jeremiah pronounces a reversal of status. He wishes that he had been stillborn (v 17), and pronounces his birthday a cursed day, meaning that he considers his birth a terrible thing, because his life is a waste of time (cf. v 18). The passage is quite similar to Job 3:3-12. Jeremiah curses his birthday because he cannot curse God or his parents (Lev 20:9; 24:10-16). Yet in doing so he in effect curses God for calling him from birth as a prophet (Thompson 1980:464).

In Judg 5:24 the Pual imperfect calls for praise:

> May Jael be the most praised of women,
>   the wife of Heber the Kenite,
> the most praised of women in tents.

The following verses (25-27) recount her courageous deed. There is no ᵓăšer or kî clause. The form of the first phrase is strikingly similar to the bārûk formula of Deut 33:24: bārûk mibbānîm ᵓāšēr, v.s. tĕbōrak minnāšîm yāʿēl. This comparison shows that there is little difference in meaning between the Pual and Qal passive participle (contra Wehmeier 1970:176). Here both are passive in meaning and optative in mood. The only difference here is that the Pual is addressed to other people, while the Qal participle is addressed to God. But this difference in use is not characteristic of the different stems. The Pual can be used in optative calls for God's blessing (Deut 33:13; 2 Sam 7:29 = 1 Chr 17:27), and the Qal participle is often used in optative calls for praise of God (see 5.4).

Three verses in addition to Gen 14:19 employ the Piel meaning "to utter a benediction of praise or congratulations." In Josh 14:13, Joshua blessed Caleb when he gave him the territory around Hebron as an inheritance. Though Caleb was going to depart, the unrecorded benediction was probably not a departing blessing patterned after the testamental blessings (contra Wehmeier 1970:145). Vv 12 and 14 suggest that the benediction would have praised Joshua for having wholeheartedly followed God, and would have asked for God's help in driving out the Amalekites (so also Woudstra 1981:230).

In 2 Sam 8:10 = 1 Chr 18:10, "Toi sent his son Joram to King David to greet him and congratulate him (brk, Piel) for fighting against Hadadezer and defeating him." Toi was also an enemy of Hadadezer (v 10). The reason for the congratulations is the same as in Gen 14:19.

Neh 11:1-2 discusses how post-exilic Jerusalem was repopulated. Lots

were cast, and one out of ten people were to resettle in Jerusalem with the leaders, while the others stayed in the surrounding cities. "The people commended (*brk*, Piel) all those who were willing to live in Jerusalem" (v 2). The people commended those that accepted the lots as the will of God and so were willing to move (so also Fensham 1982:242-243). The meaning is not "congratulate" (contra Wehmeier 1970:157) since the necessity of the lots and the term *mitnaddĕbîm* imply some reluctance on their part to resettle. Rather, the people praised them and perhaps said something like "May God bless you for your willingness to move."
Prov 10:7 contains a difficult use of *bĕrākâ:*

> The memory of a righteous man is blessed,
> but the name of the wicked will rot away.

The phrase *libĕrākâ* could mean that the righteous person will be used as a proverbial example of a blessed person (so Wehmeier 1970:100, cf. Scharbert 1975a:299-300), but in that case the person himself, not his memory, would have been said to be a *bĕrākâ*, as in Zech 8:13. McKane (1970:422-423) understands the verse as saying that the good done by the righteous man continues to have a beneficial effect upon the community after he dies. The verse could also mean that the righteous man is an inspiration, causing others to follow his example and so be blessed by God (cf. BDB 139b, "source of blessing").

The best explanation is that the noun means "object of blessing," as it does in Ezek 34:26 and Ps 37:26. Here, the "blessing" that the memory receives consists of respect, thankfulness and admiration. People remember the righteous man fondly, and speak of him fondly (similarly Scott 1965:81). In contrast, the name or reputation of the wicked rots away, meaning that they are remembered with disgust for the short time that they are remembered at all.

Jewish tradition has used the abbreviation *z"ṣl* for the first half of the verse after the name of those deceased who are particularly beloved. The tradition, then, has understood *bĕrākâ* as meaning "object of blessing, i.e., respect and admiration."

Ps 37:26 and Prov 10:7 extend the usual doctrine of retribution to include the period after death. Not only do the righteous receive blessings while alive, but their children after them are blessed as well (Ps 37:26), and their memory receives the respect of those still alive (Prov 10:7).

4.2.6 Psalmodic Concluding Benedictions

Many psalms conclude with a benediction. There are two types of benedictions which employ brk. The first type is a prayer. Pss 3 and 28 are individual laments that turn to praise after the petitions. The praise signifies that the psalmist is confident that God has heard his prayer and will come to his aid (Westermann 1965:79-81). In the concluding benedictions the psalmist then prays that the entire nation would experience God's blessing just as he will:

> Salvation belongs to Yahweh;
> > may your blessing be on your people (3:9),

> Save your people,
> > bless your inheritance;
> tend them and carry them forever! (28:9).

The reason for these prayers is that the psalmists recognize that they are part of a community (cf. Weiser 1962:258). It is not enough for them personally to experience God's blessing. They desire their community also to experience God's blessing because they feel united to the nation in their common faith in Yahweh. In both verses blessing consists of deliverance from enemies. In 3:9 bĕrākâ is parallel to yĕšû'â, and in 28:9 bārēk is parallel to hôšî'â. Westermann's (1978) distinction between blessing and deliverance certainly is not valid here.

The other prayers are similar, though they do not occur in individual laments. Psalm 128 is a wisdom psalm which describes the blessings that the pious possess. The psalm concludes (vv 5-6):

> May Yahweh bless you from Zion,
> > and may you see Jerusalem prosperous,
> > all the days of your life.
> May you see your children's children;
> > Peace upon Israel!

The prayer calls for the nation to experience the same blessing of prosperity (ṭûb, v 5) that the pious individual enjoys (ṭôb, v 2). The welfare of the nation depends on the piety of its individual members (Weiser 1962:769).

Both Pss 115:15 and 134:3 refer to God's activity in creation. The reference identifies Yahweh as the one who has previously shown himself to be a God of blessing by bestowing life, fertility, and his favor upon the creation (Gen 1:22,28; 2:3; 5:2; cf. Gen 14:19; Ps 124:8). Based on his previous record, the psalmist believes that Yahweh can be expected to continue to bless. Ps 115:15 uses the optative *bārûk* formula (on which see 4.2.4):

> May you be blessed by Yahweh,
>   the maker of heaven and earth.

Ps 134:3 uses the jussive Piel (so also Kraus 1961:893 and Weiser 1962:787, contra Wehmeier 1970:139 note 34 who follows Mowinckel 1961:47 in seeing the verse as an indicative hymn):

> May Yahweh bless you from Zion,
>   he who made heaven and earth.

This verse also refers to Zion as the source of Yahweh's blessing for the nation (see 3.2.2.5 and on 1 Kgs 8 under 4.2.2).

The second type of concluding benediction is the indicative statement of faith, "Yahweh will bless us." At first glance the statement might appear to be a promise. However, the psalmists are not speaking for God, but for Israel. They assert that they have confidence that just as God has blessed Israel in the past, so he will continue to bless them. Like the optative concluding benedictions, they seek to instill faith in God's future blessing in the people, but their perlocutionary effect is stronger since they are indicative. They are also like the optative benedictions in that they express the people's yearning for God's blessing.[10]

Ps 67:7-8 describes how Yahweh blesses by providing the necessities of life through the natural processes:

> The land gives its produce,
>   God, our God, blesses us.
> God will bless us,
>   so all the ends of the earth will fear him.

The imperfect Piel in v 7b refers to God's past, present, and future blessing activity, while the imperfect in v 8a refers primarily to God's future

---

[10] They have been included here for this reason and because of their similarity to the optative benedictions, even though they are not optative.

activity, as seen by the following purpose clause (contra Weiser 1962:472, Kraus 1961:461; cf. Wehmeier 1970:138). The blessing of the natural produce is indicative of the greater benefits of God's mercy and favor which co-occur with brk in v 2 (Weiser 1962:476-477; on v 2 see under 4.2.7). The purpose of God blessing Israel is that all peoples will recognize the power and graciousness of Israel's God and so reverence (yrʾ) him (see also vv 3-4; the idea is the same as in the patriarchal promises).

Ps 115 contrasts the pagan idols with Israel's God. After an exhortation to trust in Yahweh, an assurance of blessing is given (vv 12-13):

> Yahweh remembers us, and will bless,
> > he will bless the house of Israel,
> > he will bless the house of Aaron.
> He will bless those who fear Yahweh,
> > the small as well as the great.

The Piel imperfects are indicative, not jussive, since they follow the perfect of zkr which has a durative present meaning (so also Weiser 1962:717, contra Wehmeier 1970:138 note 30). The passage asserts that Yahweh, unlike the idols, is a God of blessing.

Ps 29 describes a storm as an epiphany of God. In the genre of the epiphany, the purpose of God's appearance is to aid his people (see Westermann 1965:93-101). This purpose is seen in v 11:

> Yahweh will give strength to his people,
> > Yahweh will bless his people with peace.

Strength and peace denote national security. The psalmist is confident that Yahweh will use his awesome power to this end.

Ps 109 is an imprecatory psalm. After calling for God to punish his adversaries, the psalmist confidently states (v 28):

> Though they abuse me,
> > you will bless me;
> They attack but are put to shame,
> > while your servant rejoices.

The Piel of qll does not just denote hostile speech, but hostile action (see on vv 17-18 under 4.3, and Brichto 1963:127). God's blessing consists of deliverance from the psalmist's adversaries (cf. vv 26,31). Brichto (1963:127) and Leupold (1969:769) take the verse as a prayer for God to bless, as are the imperatives in vv 26-27. But the imperfects imply that the verse goes with the following three verses where the lament has turned into a confession of trust and praise. The use of the waw adversative attached to the subject at the beginning of the clause, translated "but," supports this view, since it indicates "a transition from lamentation to another mode of speech, the confession of trust or the assurance of being heard" (Westermann 1965:72; see 70-75).

4.2.7 Miscellaneous Wishes

Ps 67:2 draws upon the Priestly benediction:

> May God be gracious to us and bless us,
> may he make his face shine on us.

Ps 67 is not a benediction, but a liturgical prayer that God may bless Israel so that all nations may come to praise God (so also Fishbane 1983:116-117, Leupold 1969:485-488, Wehmeier 1970:142,221). God's blessing consists of him being gracious and showing his favor. The result of God's favor toward Israel is that God's salvation will be known among all nations (v 3). All nations will then praise God (vv 4-6).

The idea is the same as that found in Gen 12:2-3 and Isa 19:24-25. God blesses Israel, who in turn becomes a source of blessing for the rest of the world. The language of the Priestly benediction is used in v 2 to denote the essence of God's blessing activity toward Israel. All of God's historical dealings with Israel stem from his favor (or anger) toward her, and the Priestly benediction is one of the clearest statements that God's blessing is a result of his favor.

Jer 31:23 refers to what was apparently a common wish in pre-exilic Israel, and predicts that the wish will once again become common: "This is what Yahweh of hosts, the God of Israel, says: 'They will again speak this saying in the land of Judah and its cities when I bring them back from captivity: "May Yahweh bless you, O righteous dwelling, O sacred mountain."'" The vocatives refer to Zion. The point of the passage is that Yahweh will once again dwell in Zion and so bless her and the surrounding nation (vv 24-25; so also Bright 1965:282, Thompson 1980:577). Zion is again the source of blessing for the nation. The content of God's blessing is implied in vv 24-25 as crops and flocks, as well as refreshment for the weary.

In Ps 62, the psalmist finds hope in God (vv 2-3), while people assault him (vv 4-5). He describes his adversaries as plotting against him (v 5), and says:

> With their mouth they bless,
> but in their hearts they curse.

The collocation of *peh* (the singular suffix is distributive) makes it clear that the blessing consists of speech. The adversaries speak well about the psalmist and wish him well (so also Wehmeier 1970:154), while at the same time plotting evil against him in their hearts. The antonym *yĕqalĕlû* has the common meaning "they wish him evil" (Brichto 1963:126), rather than denoting formal curse formulas or imprecations.

The meaning of Ps 118:26 is disputed. The psalm is a liturgical temple psalm. The immediate context does not help clarify the verse. Most likely the verse describes the priests as blessing the worshippers as they enter the temple (so Leupold 1969:819-820, Wehmeier 1970:104; similarly Murtonen 1959:167):

> Blessed is he who comes in Yahweh's name;
> we bless you from Yahweh's temple.

The verse quotes a double benediction, as does Ps 129:8. The Piel of *brk* in the second line means to pronounce the benediction of the first line; it does not denote pronouncement of the Priestly benediction (contra Wehmeier 1970:147).

The chief question is whether "in Yahweh's name" goes with *bārûk* or *habbāʾ*. *bārûk* occurs only here with "Yahweh's name," though the Piel often occurs with it, meaning "to bless in Yahweh's name."

The expression "to come (*bôʾ*) in Yahweh's name" occurs twice. In 1 Sam 17:45 David comes against Goliath "in the name of Yahweh of hosts," and in 2 Chr 14:10, King Asa says that he has entered battle against the Cushites in Yahweh's name. In both passages the expression primarily denotes reliance upon Yahweh for help (so also Blank 1961:76-77). The phrase also means that the people represent Yahweh in the conflicts—they are Yahweh's people. The verb *hlk* is used with *bĕšēm yhwh* in Micah 4:5 denoting loyalty and dedication to Yahweh (cf. also Isa 2:5).

Biblical use, then, requires taking *bĕšēm yhwh* with *habbāʾ* (so also Leupold 1969:821, Wehmeier 1970:104, contra Blank 1961:75-79). The expression describes those entering the temple as trusting in Yahweh. The priests pronounce them *bārûk*. *bārûk* means that God's favor rests upon them. They can expect to receive help, strength and the necessities of life from Yahweh, the one in whom they trust.

Prov 5:18 contains another difficult use of *bārûk:*

> May your fountain be a source of blessing (*bārûk*);
> rejoice because of the wife of your youth.

The context (vv 15-20) discusses why one should drink only from his own "well" = wife, rather than commit adultery. The difficulty shows up in commentators who insist on giving the passive participle a passive meaning. McKane (1970:319) interprets *bārûk* as meaning that the wife has many children, but there is no mention of children in the context. Marital relations are being discussed. Scott (1965:55,58) interprets the phrase as the wife being blessed or praised by the husband, and translates "Be grateful for your own fountain." This interpretation only catches half of the meaning of *bārûk*. The participle has both an active and a passive meaning, as in Deut 28:4-5; Jer 20:14. The wife who is blessed by God becomes a source of joy for her husband. Wehmeier (1970:59,115) compares the verse to an Aramaic inscription from Palmyra which describes a well as an '*yn' brykt'*, that is, a well that has been blessed by God and so provides the blessing of water. He accurately paraphrases the line as "der Umgang mit deiner eigenen Frau bringe dir Erfüllung und Glück." This interpretation is fully in keeping with the next verse which urges satisfaction from sexual relations with one's wife.

The last three verses treated in this section discuss instances where people wish or hope for blessings for themselves.

Deut 29:18 and Isa 65:16 use the Hithpael of *brk* with a reflexive meaning. The word in Deut 29:18 has a bad connotation. The context (vv 16-28) warns against turning from the covenant God to idols. V 18 describes an apostate person: "When he hears the words of this curse he considers himself blessed, saying 'I will have prosperity, although I will walk according to my stubborn heart.'" *'ālâ* here denotes the curse sanctions or imprecations of the Sinai covenant (cf. Brichto 1963:70). It has the same meaning as *qĕlālâ* in Deut 30:1,19. When the stubborn apostate hears the covenantal curses, he ignores them, thinking that he is still under the covenantal blessings simply because he is an Israelite. *hitbārēk* means that he considers himself *bārûk*, a person whom God will bless (similarly Brichto 1963:29 and Scharbert 1975a:296, contra Wehmeier 1970:183 who translates "für sich eine Segensformel sprechen").

There is no indication that *hitbārēk* means "bless himself . . . = immunize himself" against the curses (contra Brichto 1963:29 note 14, followed by Wehmeier 1970:183 note 30). The apostate takes no measures to "immunize himself" against the covenantal curses; he simply thinks that he can escape God's retribution. The final clause "so that the moist is destroyed along with the dry" is best understood as a result clause. The merism indicates that the apostate will bring judgement upon the whole community, upon good and bad alike (so also Craigie 1976:359). It is hard to see how the clause could be a purpose clause describing the apostate as nullifying the curse (contra Brichto).

The reflexive meaning of the Hithpael has a good connotation in Isa 65:16. The context envisions a future time when God's servants will prosper, but his enemies will suffer and be destroyed (vv 13-16). "He who invokes blessing for himself will do so by the God of truth, and he who swears will swear by the God of truth." The Niphal of $šbʽ$ is parallel to the Hithpael of brk. "To swear" means "to pronounce a conditional curse upon oneself" (Brichto 1963:25-40,70). $hitbārēk$ here is used as the antonym. It means to invoke God's blessing upon oneself (so also Wehmeier 1970:183-184, Westermann 1969:403, Young 1972:512, contra Scharbert 1975a:296 and Murtonen 1959:172 who give the Hithpael the same meaning as it has in Deut 29:18).

The point of the verse is that God will be recognized as fulfilling his promises. The "God of truth" is the God who truly does what he promises (so also Young 1972:512, Pieper 1979:673-74). This is why people will invoke God's blessing or curse—God can be counted upon to act.

These two Hithpael verses raise the question of whether people ever did pronounce blessing formulas over themselves. The closest thing to an example is 1 Kgs 2:45, where Solomon declares "the King Solomon is blessed," but this is an assertion, not an invocation (see under 4.1.3). There is a parallel to Deut 29:18, however. Ps 49:19-20 describes the fate of a wealthy man who cannot take his wealth past death:

> Though he considered himself blessed during his life,
> and people praise you when you do well,
> you will go to the generation of his fathers,
> who will never again see light.

$yĕbārēk$ with $napšô$ as object has the same reflexive meaning as $hitbārēk$ in Deut 29:18. The wealthy man "blesses himself" in that he considers himself to be blessed, i.e., wealthy. He has acquired the blessing of prosperity (contra Wehmeier 1970:164 who translates "seine Seele preisen," and Dahood 1966:302 who translates "worships his appetite" based on the supposition that $yĕbārēk$ is denominative from $berek$). Others agree with the wealthy man's assessment of himself; they praise *(hôdâ)* him as a fortunate and prosperous person.

4.3   Human Benefaction

brk is used only a few times to denote human benefaction. The Piel means "to treat with respect, treat well, be on good terms with." The noun can mean either "benefaction," or "a gift."

There is a close similarity between the meaning "gift" and the meaning of the noun when it denotes benefits given by God. The gifts which people give to others consist of the same types of goods as the blessings God gives. Yet it is more important that the human gifts are bestowed for the same reasons as God's blessings. This similarity is probably why the human gifts are denoted by *bĕrākâ*, and not by a more common word for gifts (contra Wehmeier 1970:92 who, like Pedersen, (1926:201) argues that the bestowal of a gift increases the vitality (*Lebenskraft*) of the recipient just as God's blessing does).

bĕrākâ denotes a gift which is given freely, not because of obligation or coersion. It is often given out of thanks for something the recipient has done for the donor, and often on a special occasion such as a marriage or military victory. The purpose of the gift can be to express thanks, to express friendship, or to appease an angry person. The desired perlocutionary effect is to make the recipient favorably disposed toward the donor.

In Gen 33:11 and 1 Sam 25:27, the gift is intended to appease an irate foe. When Jacob returned from Aramea he assumed Esau was still angry with him for stealing his blessing (Gen 27). Esau was reluctant to accept the gift, but Jacob insisted: "Please take my gift which was brought to you, because God has been gracious to me and I have everything."

It is significant that Jacob attributes his ability to bestow the gift to the fact that God had bestowed upon him the goods he wanted to give. This is the only verse where the human gift is expressly attributed to God's blessing. The verb *ḥnn* actually describes God's favorable disposition toward Jacob, rather than his bestowal of benefits, but the latter is clearly implied as a result of the former. The gift is fully described in 32:15-16 as consisting of male and female goats, sheep, cattle, and donkeys, and female camels with their young. These are typical of the blessings bestowed by God in the realm of animal fertility.

The gift is previously called a *minḥâ* five times (Gen 32:14,19,21,22; 33:10). *minḥâ* here as often simply denotes a gift, rather than an offering to God, though Jacob likens Esau to God (33:10). Like an offering, it is intended to appease the recipient, and in fact it does. Jacob describes Esau's favorable reaction using *rṣh* (33:10), a term often used for God's favorable response to offerings. *běrākâ* and *minḥâ* in this passage are synonymous. They have the idential referent and there is no difference in their connotation. In their use in other passages and their other meanings, however, they are substantially different (so also Henderson 1977:55).

1 Sam 25 describes David's encounter with Nabal and Abigail. When Abigail hears that David, enraged by Nabal's rebuff, is coming to attack her family, she prepares a gift and goes out to meet him. She pleads for David's pardon and says (v 27): "Now may this gift which your handmaid has brought to my lord be given to the men who follow my lord."

The *běrākâ* consisted of bread, wine, dressed sheep, roasted grain, raisins, and figs (v 18). As with Jacob's gift, it clearly is intended as an appeasement gift. It fulfills David's request (v 8) for food for his men. Like Jacob, Abigail is anxious about the outcome of the encounter, but the gift is still not obligatory. The bestower wishes the gift to be received as a freely given expression of goodwill.

In 1 Sam 30:26 and 2 Kgs 5:15, the gift is an expression of thanks. 1 Sam 30 narrates the plunder of the town of Ziklag by the Amalekites and recovery of the plunder. When David returned to Ziklag, "he sent some of the plunder to the elders of Judah who were his friends, saying 'Here is a gift for you from the spoil of Yahweh's enemies.'" Vv 27-31 list the people to whom he sent the gifts. V 31 describes them as places where David had stayed during his travels. The location of several of the places is uncertain, and several are not mentioned elsewhere as places where David stayed (on the problem see McCarter 1980:434,436; Stoebe 1973:517-519). At any rate, the purpose is clear. The *běrākâ* is a freewill gift given to thank the friends for their hospitality. The gifts also strengthened good relations with the towns and these towns are important later in David's transition into the role of king.

2 Kgs 5 describes the cure of Naaman the Syrian from his leprosy at the hands of Elisha. After washing in the Jordan seven times, the healthy Naaman returns to Elisha and says (v 15): "Now please accept a gift from your servant." Elisha, unlike Esau, firmly refuses. The nature of the *běrākâ* is clarified by vv 22-23 where Naaman gives Gehazi two talents of silver in two bags and two sets of clothing. These articles are not called a *běrākâ*, but they show the type of thanksgiving gift Naaman had in mind. He also had previously offered gold, silver, and clothes to the King of Israel for his cure (v 5).

The meaning of *běrākâ* in Josh 15:19 = Judg 1:15 is disputed. Caleb gave his daughter Acsah to his brother Othniel as a wife after Othniel captured Kiriath-Sepher. Acsah convinced Othniel that they should ask Caleb for a field. Acsah then asked Caleb, "Give me a gift. Because you have given me land in the Negeb, you should give me springs of water." Because the request was for a field (v 18 = Judg 1:14), the bĕrākâ denoted a tract of land with springs on it as a gift (so also Wehmeier 1970:93). Murtonen (1959:164) and Plassman (1913:98-99) say bĕrākâ refers to the springs alone. Murtonen compares bĕrākâ to bĕrēkâ (without explaining how he thinks they are related). Though it is true that springs and water can be blessings given by God, that does not mean that bĕrākâ by itself can denote springs. bĕrākâ is a general term for a freely given gift, and only here does a human gift include springs.

Wehmeier (1970:193) defines bĕrākâ here as an "Abschiedsgeschenk," and compares the present passage to Josh 14:12-14, where Joshua blesses Caleb (i.e., utters a blessing formula) and gives him the area of Hebron. However, there is no indication in either passage of an impending departure. The reason that the term bĕrākâ is used here is because Caleb has already given his daughter to Othniel and given the city to the couple; he is certainly not obligated to give the couple anything more. The gift is a "special favor" (NIV). It may here also be a marriage gift (so Woudstra 1981:241).

The Piel of brk denotes human benefaction in four passages. Three of these passages use brk in the stereotyped blessing formula, "May those who treat you well (mĕbārăkeykā) be blessed, and may those who maltreat you be cursed" (Gen 27:29; Num 24:9; Gen 12:3 has been modified somewhat (see under 3.1.1), but contains the same participle with the same meaning). The Piel of brk is used in a general sense to denote a favorable relationship which is evidenced by both benediction and benefaction. Brichto (1963:157 note 92) and Wehmeier (1970:160) emphasize benefaction and translate "treat with favor" and "freundlich begegen," respectively. Scharbert (1975a:291) emphasizes benediction and describes a possible origin of this meaning of brk: "This participle refers to persons or tribes who are on friendly terms with the patriarchs and their descendants, and who demonstrate a solidarity and appreciation for them by uttering the bārûk formula in their behalf or by wishing them well." Yet the meaning includes both benediction and benefaction, and may be rather loosely translated as "those on good terms with you." The meaning may also have arisen from the use of the Piel to denote benefaction by God, rather than from its use to denote benediction.

The antonym in Gen 27:29; Num 24:9 is ʾōrăreykā. It denotes those who are hostile and so engage in both malediction and malefaction (Wehmeier 1970:153 overemphasizes malediction). The malediction can consist of threatening or abusive speech, and need not consist only of formal imprecations (contra Scharbert 1958a:6). Anyone, not just God or representatives of God, can be the subject of ʾrr when it has this meaning (cf. Brichto 1963:110-112).

The antonym in Gen 12:3 is *měqallelkā*. It also includes both speech and action. Contrary to most translations and commentators, *qll* usually does not correspond to English "curse" (Brichto 1963:118-117; Scharbert 1958a:8-14 to some extent overemphasizes the element of speech). Brichto (1963:119) states that "in no instance will the verb be seen to have the force of 'curse' = 'imprecation'," though he later modifies this statement (pp 172-176), allowing for five passages where *qll* denotes a malediction (in all five of these passages, Deut 23:4-5, quoted in Neh 13:1-2; Josh 24:9-10; 1 Sam 17:43; 2 Kgs 2:24, *qll* in my opinion means "to curse or imprecate"). Nevertheless, *qll* is the most general of the "curse" terms, and seldom involves an imprecation. It denotes abusive or disrespectful action more frequently than abusive speech.

> The interpretation of *qillēl* as 'to curse', as old as the Septuagint translation, is the result of understanding *qillēl* as primarily the antonym of *bērēk*, the latter term understood in the sense of an utterance expressing a favorable wish. The limitation of either of these terms to a spoken phenomenon is as misleading as it is without foundation. (Brichto 1963:177)

Prov 30:11-14 contains four statements commencing with *dôr*. Wehmeier (1970:159) argues that an introduction of the type "Drei oder vier Geschlechter hasst Jahwe:" has dropped out, based on analogy to 6:16-19 and 30:15-31 (so also Scott 1965:181). This assumption, however, misunderstands the form and function of the statements. They are "observations in so far as they have the form of wisdom sentences, but it must be recognized that their formulation in the third person barely conceals their character as denunciatory preaching directed at contemporaries" (McKane 1970:650; cf. Jer 2:31; 7:29).

V 11 reads:

> Some people curse their father,
> and do not bless their mother.

brk, Piel is used as the antonym of *qll*, Piel (cf. Ps 109:17). The Piel of *qll* denotes disrespectful and abusive behavior and, as in Gen 12:3, does not refer to speech alone (so also Brichto 1963:136, Wehmeier 1970:159). Both verbal and physical abuse of parents were punishable by death (Exod 21:15-17; Lev 20:9; Deut 21:18-21; 27:16). The Piel of *brk* denotes respectful, obedient conduct, including speech. It is synonymous with *kabbēd* in Exod 20:12.

The noun *bĕrākâ* occurs twice denoting human benefaction. Prov 11:25 reads:

> A generous person is made fat,
> and he who gives drinks to others is himself rained upon.[11]

nepeš-bĕrākâ means a generous person who habitually engages in benefaction. The unnamed agent of retribution is implied by the reference to rain and the impersonal constructions (as often in 3.1.3) to be God.

Ps 109 is one of the strongest imprecatory psalms of the entire psalter. As v 20 clearly states, vv 6-19 are a series of imprecations by the psalmist directed at his adversaries. However, due to the harshness of the imprecations, some commentators (Wehmeier 1970:95, Weiser 1962:688-691) construe the imprecations as a quote of the adversaries accusing the psalmist. Weiser even goes so far as to interpret vv 16-19 as an accusation that the psalmist killed a poor man by means of magically effective curses (against which see Brichto 1963:127).

There is no need to ascribe the imprecations to the adversaries, contrary to v 20. The imprecations are consistent with the biblical concept of retribution and with the stated piety of the psalmist (so also Leupold 1969:763-765, Brichto 1963:120-127). In vv 17-18 the psalmist says:

> He loved malefaction (*qĕlālâ*); may it overtake him!
> He did not delight in benefaction (*bĕrākâ*);
> may it be far from him!
> He wore malefaction like his garment;
> may it enter him like water,
> into his bones like oil![12]

The meaning of *bĕrākâ* is determined by its opposition to *qĕlālâ*. *qĕlālâ*

---

[11] On *yôre'* see *GKC* 69 w and BDB 432a-b.
[12] The second and third imperfect consecutives in vv 17 and 18 should probably be emended to jussives with conjunctive waws, unless the imperfect consecutive can function as a jussive (cf *GKC* 111 w). The LXX understands them as jussives.

denotes actual material misfortune more frequently that the invocation of misfortune (Brichto 1963:197). Here it denotes malefaction or "abuse" (Brichto 1963:198), rather than verbal cursing (contra Leupold 1969:767-768, Weiser 1962:689). The psalmist's adversaries had delighted in abusing him, and so he prays according to the *lex talionis* for them to receive the same sort of abuse. The reference to water entering them is perhaps an allusion to the ingested "waters of curse" of Num 5:22 (so Weiser 1962:691). As the antonym to qĕlālâ, bĕrākâ denotes deeds, i.e., benefaction, rather than words.

5
The Use of *BRK* in the Praise of God

Praise occupied a central place in the religion of Israel. Praise is pictured in the Bible as the expected response of man to God's benefaction. Praise was first uttered spontaneously by individuals in response to specific deeds of God. It is found sporadically throughout the historical writings and rarely in the prophets. In the cult, however, praise became a dominant theme. Spontaneous thanks was developed into doxological praise of God for who he was, regardless—or in spite of—what he did. Praise became just as important in cultic worship as sacrificing. The psalms describe the proper attitude toward God of pious individuals as well as of the nation as praise. By praising God man fulfills his obligation to repay God for his benefaction.

Though doxological praise was not an immediate, spontaneous response to God's deeds, it was not totally divorced from history. Westermann (1965:155) rightly concludes,

> the praise of God in Israel never became a cultic happening, separated from the rest of existence . . . that had become independent of the history of the people and of the individual. Rather it occupied a central place in the total life of the individual and the people before God . . . the clearest expression of the relationship to God was the act of praising God.

But Westermann goes too far when he claims that "the praise of God occupied for Israel actually the place where 'faith in God' stands for us" (155). Praise expressed Israel's faith in God's goodness and trust in his future benefaction (as in the vow of praise), but it did not encompass all of Israel's faith. The petitions in the laments, the long recitals of God's saving acts, and the exhortations to follow the law are just as important as praise in expressing Israel's faith.

5.1 brk, Piel in Indicative Statements

The Piel of brk with God as object usually means "to praise," though occasionally the meaning is "to thank" or "to worship." The synonymous collocations clearly indicate that these are the meanings of the Piel (see especially 5.2 and 5.3).

As with the Piel in 4.1 and 4.2, the Piel with God as the object can be delocutive, though it is not always so. The Piel in Gen 24:48; 1 Chr 29:10 denotes the utterance of a bārûk yhwh formula. The Aramaic Pael in Dan 2:19 denotes the utterance of a formula with the Pael passive participle of brk. However, the Pael in Dan 4:31 denotes the utterance of a doxology that does not contain brk. Most of the passages which contain the Piel in indicative statements do not quote the words of praise uttered. The Piel imperative rarely evokes a formula of praise containing brk; most responses to the imperative consist of praise employing other common words for praise (see 5.3). The Piel then simply means "to praise," and not specifically "to utter a bārûk formula of praise."

It is possible that the Piel with God as object was first used meaning "to pronounce a bārûk formula of praise," after the development of the meaning of bārûk, and that subsequently brk, Piel became a more general word meaning "to praise" (on the development of the meaning of bārûk, see 5.4). It is also possible that the Piel started taking God as the object after it was used with man as the object meaning "thank, praise" (see 4.2.4 and 4.2.5), and that the bārûk formula had nothing to do with the extension of its range of application to include God. Since the meaning "praise" was an inner-biblical development, and the biblical texts provide no clear answer to this question, it must remain open (cf. Scharbert 1973:22-25, 1975a:305, Murtonen 1959:175).

Yet it is clear that the meanings "to praise" for the Piel and "praised" for bārûk became frequently used about the same time and in the same traditions. Both are found primarily in the cultic, liturgical texts of the Psalms and the books of the Chronicler, though isolated instances occur throughout the Bible (see also 1.3).

Most of the indicative statements express praise to God for benefaction done to the speaker. Thanks is also included in the meaning of brk. However, because God generally is considered to be rather distant, praise is the dominant element. When people are thanked, the thanks turns to praise when the person to be thanked is remote or unknown, since a person to whom one is not directly speaking cannot be thanked, but only praised (see Ruth 2:19; Judg 5:24). God is usually praised as the remote, ultimate source of the benefaction, although the benefaction is often actually performed by another person (see especially 2 Chr 31:8 below and Ruth 2:20 under 4.2.4). The bārûk formulas almost always speak of God in the third person because he was considered to be remote, while the bārûk formulas with human subjects often speak of the person thanked or praised in the second person (4.2.4 and 4.2.5).

The reasons for praise are quite diverse. They range from God aiding individuals in everyday life settings to God aiding the nation in national conflicts. The praise ranges from relief at averted conflicts and simple contentment from full stomachs, to heartfelt religious praise extolling God's power and goodness, praise that constitutes an act of worship. In most of the passages, praise is a part of worship.

In the first three verses, individuals praise God in non-cultic situations. The praise is an acknowledgment of God's sovereignty and power as well as his benefaction, and is tantamount to an act of worship. In Gen 24:48, Abraham's servant reported how he praised God for making his mission successful. He rejoiced both that he was able to accomplish his assignment, and that his master's son Isaac now had a wife. The praise is stronger than simple thanks; it is part of an act of homage and worship. He said, "I bowed down (qdd) and worshipped (ḥwh) Yahweh, and praised (brk Piel) Yahweh." An ʾăšer clause describing Yahweh follows which is quite similar to the ʾăšer clause in the bārûk formula of v 27. wayyĕbārek person ʾăšer here narrates the fact that he spoke a formula of the form bārûk person ʾăšer.

Daniel praised God in Dan 2:19 for revealing the interpretation of Nebuchadnezzar's dream to him: "Then Daniel praised the God of heaven:

> May God's name be praised forever and ever,
> to whom belong wisdom and might.

Here the Pael denotes the utterance of a formula employing the Pael passive participle of brk. The formulaic use of the D passive participle is synonymous in meaning with the G passive participle (see on Ps 113:2 and Job 1:21 under 5.4). Daniel describes his action of praising (brk Pael) using the synonyms ydʾ and šbḥ in v 23.

Nebuchadnezzar reports in Dan 4:31 how he praised God for restoring his sanity: "I praised (brk Pael) the most high one, and lauded (šbḥ) and glorified (hdr) he who lives forever." The doxology that follows ascribes eternal dominion and omnipotence to God, and does not contain brk. The context again indicates that the praise was an act of worship.

In contrast, the three non-cultic verses where the nation praises God simply express contentment and relief. The context of Deut 8:10 warns against becoming complacent and ignoring God's commands when the people take up residence in the promised land: "You will eat and be full and praise Yahweh your God for the good land he gave to you." The conditions which occasion the praise here will lead to apostasy, not to worship, if the people forget God's benefaction (vv 17-18).

The tribes west of the Jordan praised God in Josh 22:33 when they learned that the transjordanian tribes had built their altar as a memorial rather than for cultic purposes. The praise was more a sigh of relief than thanks for benefaction; now they did not need to wage war against their brothers or fear punishment from God (vv 31-33).

King Jehosaphat and Judah praised God in 2 Chr 20:26 for a similar reason. Moab, Ammon, and some Edomites came to make war on Judah. God caused them to slay each other, and so all Judah had to do was plunder the dead for three days. The verse contains two of the three occurrences of *běrākâ* meaning "praise," and the context leaves no doubt about the meaning and its derivation: "On the fourth day they gathered at the Valley of Praise (*běrākâ*), for there they praised (*běrăkû*) Yahweh. That is why they called that place the Valley of Praise, as it is called to this day." (The other occurrence of the noun is in Neh 9:5b; see under 5.3). The Piel of *brk* does not denote utterance of a liturgical or cultic type of prayer (contra Wehmeier 1970:161 and Scharbert 1975a:299). The context is military, not cultic. The Piel of *brk* is a general term for the expression of thanks to God, and nothing definite can be said about the precise form of speech used.

In all three cultic verses where praise is a response to a specific act of God, the reason is the donation of goods for cultic use. David praised Yahweh in 1 Chr 29:10 before the congregation for all the materials that people gave for the construction of the temple. He employed a *bārûk 'attâ yhwh* formula (on which see under 5.4). The praise is a product of joy on the part of David as well as the people (v 9). The following doxology is similar to the non-cultic doxologies in Dan 2:20-23; 4:31-32. David then exhorted the people to praise God too (v 20; on the imperative see 5.3). The people praised God as part of their worship; they also bowed down and worshipped God (v 20).

Hezekiah and his officials responded to the donation of heaps and heaps of tithes by the people (2 Chr 31:8): "Hezekiah and the officials came and saw the heaps and praised Yahweh and his people Israel." Here the meaning of *brk*, Piel includes both "to thank" and "to praise." The verb takes both God and man as the direct objects.

There is, however, a difference in the meaning of the verb with each direct object (contra Wehmeier 1970:162; Scharbert 1975a:290). As the immediate donors, the people are thanked, and the element of praise is secondary. God is ultimately responsible for the donations, but as a more remote party, he is primarily praised (cf. 1 Sam 25:32-33 which addresses second person bārûk formulas to a person but a third person formula to God; Gen 14:19-20, however, uses third person formulas for both God and man). The difference in the identity of the two objects is enough to indicate that a different nuance of the verb is intended, as in 1 Chr 29:20 where "they bowed down and worshipped Yahweh and the king" uses identical syntactical constructions for both objects. The writer felt that the difference in the objects themselves was enough to indicate to the reader that the people worshipped Yahweh, but only showed reverence and respect to the king. A change in the meaning of a word because of a change in the referent is a common linguistic phenomenon (see 5.4, and Heestermans 1980:288).

Neh 8:6 differs from the previous passages in that the praise is doxological, rather than a spontaneous response to God's benefaction. The occasion for the praise is the public reading of the Torah: "Ezra praised the great God Yahweh, and all the people answered 'Amen! Amen!' with raised hands. They bowed down and worshipped Yahweh with their faces to the ground." By saying "Amen," the people affirmed that Ezra's praise expressed their own sentiments (as also in 1 Chr 16:36). As in most passages, the praise is an act of worship.

Isa 66:3 contains a unique use of the Piel of brk. The participle denotes someone engaged in worship:

> He who burns memorial incense,
>   is like someone who worships (mĕbārēk) an idol.
> They have chosen their ways,
>   and delight in their detestable idols.

The context (vv 1-4) discusses the inadequacy of corrupt cultic worship without true piety. Most of the unquoted parallel verbs in v 3 are cultic technical terms for sacrifices used in worship. The last line makes clear that mĕbārēk ʾāwen refers to idolatrous worship. Though the meaning "worship" is unique for the Piel of brk, it is easy to see how it could acquire this transferred meaning because of the use of praise in worship.

5.2 The Vow of Praise

The vow of praise characteristically is found at the beginning of psalms of declarative praise (also called psalms of thanks), and at the end of individual laments. The vow of praise shows how praise is an essential element of Israelite religion as described in the psalms. The Psalms stress that it is man's duty to praise God while he is alive (see especially on 115:17-18 below). Westermann's (1965:155-161) conclusions regarding the theme of the living, not the dead, praising God rightly describe the importance of praise. He concludes that praise is an essential part of all life. It is only in death that there is no praise. Man will always praise something--if not God, then an institution, another man, or an idea. But lasting, happy life, true life, requires the praise of God, since "there cannot be such a thing as true life without praise" (155).

It is clear from the synonymous collocations that the Piel of *brk* means "to praise." The praise never entails *bārûk* formulas or other forms of *brk*. Instead, the praise consists of descriptions of God's virtues and deeds. The form of *brk* in the vow of praise is the voluntative imperfect. Most vows of praise in the psalms actually do not contain *brk*, and those that do frequently are in psalms of mixed literary genre, indicating that *brk* was not originally used in the standard vow of praise. Individual lament psalms usually use *hôdâ*, *šîr*, and *zimmēr*, while the psalms of declarative praise commonly use *hôdâ*, *hillēl*, *zimmēr*, *sippēr*, *rômēm*, and *šîr* (Westermann 1965:102,103,107). The use of these verbs and of the Piel of *brk* indicates that within the vow of praise they are all general words for praise and they differ very little in meaning from each other (similarly Wehmeier 1970:167, who lists several other synonyms).

I will discuss the psalms of individual lament first, since they shed light on the psalms of declarative praise. The vow of praise is present in practically all individual lament psalms, and is almost always found at the end of the psalm (Westermann 1965:75). It is an essential element of this type of psalm. There are four instances where the Piel of *brk* occurs, Ps 26:12:

> My feet stand on level ground;
> in the great congregation I will praise Yahweh!

Ps 63:5:

> So I will praise you while I am alive,
> I will lift up my hands in your name.

Ps 16:7:

> I will praise Yahweh who counsels me;
> even at night my heart instructs me.

The Use of *brk* in the Praise of God   139

and Ps 115:18:

> But we will praise (*nĕbārēk*) Yah,
> from now forevermore.
> Praise (*halĕlû*) Yah!

Ps 26 is a typical individual lament. However, it lacks that feature which explains the vow of praise. After the lament and petition, these psalms normally contain a statement of assurance that the petition has been heard (Westermann 1965:75-81). The vow of praise arises from the psalmist's conviction that God will respond to his prayer. Often the reason given for the praise employs a prophetic perfect, as in Ps 16:7, but this only expresses the psalmist's belief in God's responsiveness to prayer; it does not mean that God has already acted. The psalmist feels that he owes something to God, and so he gives God praise. He does not praise God to elicit a response from God, but because he feels that praise is necessary to maintain a proper relationship to God. He wishes to give in response to God's giving.

Pss 63 and 115 are of mixed literary genre. This is probably why *brk* is used instead of the usual vow of praise verbs. Ps 63 in some respects resembles a psalm of lament, but it also resembles a psalm of trust, a related genre (Kraus 1961:441). The vow of praise in v 5 has the same cause and meaning as in the psalms of individual lament—God came to the aid of the psalmist (vv 4,8,9) while he was being persecuted (v 10). God's aid is a response to the psalmist's longing for God (vv 2,9). The phrase "I will lift up my hands in your name" denotes calling upon God's name in prayer (cf. Weiser 1962:455, Kraus 1961:442-443). The psalmist vows to praise and pray to God in the future because of the kindness (*ḥesed*, v 4) God has shown him.

Ps 16 is a psalm of trust (Kraus 1961:119, Weiser 1962:172-173). The genre is a more optimistic form of the genre of individual lament. It contains a short petition for God to aid the psalmist (v 1), followed by a description of how God responded to his petition and helped him (vv 2,6), and statements of the psalmist's trust in God's future help (vv 7-11). The genre differs from the individual lament in that the petition is short and the statement of assurance that God will help in the future is expanded to become the dominant theme of the psalm. But the vow of praise is again the psalmist's response to the help he anticipates that he will receive from God.

Ps 115 contains a mixture of several literary genres (Westermann 1965:59, Kraus 1961:785). The vague, catch-all label "liturgy" is about the most precise label possible (so also Kraus and Weiser 1962:714). The psalm closes with a vow of praise in the first person plural. This part of the psalm most closely resembles a lament of the people. The lament of the people genre does not always conclude with a vow of praise, and the form of the vow, when it occurs, is not as standardized as in the lament of the individual (Westermann 1965:59-61).

The vow of praise in Ps 115:17-18 is a response to God's aid as described in vv 9-13, and a recognition of God's superiority over other gods, as described in vv 2-8. The vow implies that it is man's duty to praise God while still alive:

> The dead do not praise (*yĕhalĕlû*) Yah,
>   not those who go down to the place of silence.
> But we will praise (*nĕbārēk*) Yah,
>   from now forevermore!

The vow of praise is also found characteristically at the beginning of psalms of declarative praise (also called psalms of thanks; Westermann 1965:102-108). The psalm of individual declarative praise begins where the individual lament concludes. Many of the individual laments have a sentence of declarative praise immediately following the vow of praise. The psalms of declarative praise commence with the vow of praise and the declarative praise following the vow is developed into the main theme of the psalm.

As in the individual lament, the vow and the praise arise from the psalmist's conviction that his prayer has been heard and that God will or has already responded. The main concern of the psalms of declarative praise is not to tell others about the psalmist's experiences, but to call others to praise God with the psalmist.

There are two verses which use the Piel of *brk*, Ps 34:2:

> I will praise (*ʾăbārĕkâ*) Yahweh at all times,
>   praise of him (*tĕhillātô*) is always in my mouth,

and Ps 145:1-2:

> I will exalt you (*ʾărômimkā*), my God, my king,
>   I will praise (*ʾăbārĕkâ*) your name forever and ever,
> Every day I will praise you (*ʾăbārĕkekkā*),
>   I will praise (*ʾăhalĕlâ*) your name forever and ever.

While Ps 34 is a typical psalm of declarative praise, Westermann (1965:131-132) considers Ps 145 to be an imperative psalm, and Kraus (1961:947-948) considers it to be a somewhat distorted hymn (Westermann calls hymns "psalms of descriptive praise"). The acrostic structure interrupts the flow of thought to some extent.

In any event, the vow of praise is still based on God's aid given to those who call to him in times of need (vv 18-19), and like a typical psalm of declarative praise, the praise of God's deeds is the main theme of the psalm.

5.3 The Imperative Call for Praise

The imperative call for praise occurs almost exclusively in psalms of praise. It usually calls for doxological praise of God because of his qualities or past acts, rather than spontaneous thanks and praise for a recent act. It urges those hearing or reciting the song to join the speaker/author in enthusiastically praising God. The purpose of the imperative is not to elicit a spoken response, but an emotional response. It urges those listening to the song to have an attitude of praise as the song describes God's goodness. The imperative reflects the psalmist's concern that without the exhortation, God might not be praised as he should be.

The imperative obviously has a perlocutionary force, since it seeks to affect the attitude of others. However, it also has an illocutionary force. Uttering the imperative is in itself an expression of praise by the speaker, because he calls for others to praise God *along with himself*. This is seen clearly in Ps 34:4:

> Magnify (*gaddĕlû*) Yahweh with me;
> let us exalt (*nĕrômĕmâ*) his name together!

The imperative can be delocutive. In Ps 135:19-21, a *bārûk* formula answers several imperatives, and in Neh 9:5 a jussive Piel of *brk* answers an imperative. However, the imperative normally does not evoke any standard response. The imperative is intended to evoke an *attitude* of praise, rather than a *bārûk* or other formula.

The synonymous collocations of the imperative, like those of the Piel in the vow of praise, indicate that the Piel imperative has the general meaning "to praise." The synonyms are also used as general expressions for praise, and differ very little in meaning from each other and from the imperative of *brk* (so also Wehmeier 1970:168-169). These words occur as synonyms both next to the imperatives of *brk*, and in imperative calls to praise at the beginning of descriptive psalms of praise which do not contain brk. The most frequent synonym is halĕlû (Pss 104:35; 106:48; 113:1; 117:1; 135:1,3; 148:1-4; 150:1-6). Other synonyms are baśśĕrû (96:2), gaddĕlû (34:4), zammĕrû (33:2; 66:2; 105:2; 135:3), hôdû (33:2; 105:1; 106:1; 107:1; 118:1; 136:1-3), sappĕrû (96:3), harî'û (47:2; 66:1; 81:2; 100:1), rannĕnû (33:1), harnînû (81:2), šabbĕḥû (117:1), and šîrû (33:3; 96:1-2; 98:1; 105:2; 149:1).

In addition to these single word synonyms, there are a large number of synonymous phrases, such as "say to God, 'How awesome are your deeds!'" (Ps 66:3), "Proclaim the sound of his praise" (66:8), "make known his deeds among the nations" (105:1), and "enter his gates with praise" (100:4). Such phrases are too numerous and diverse to list. These phrases are more specific expressions of praise than the single word synonyms, but they still differ very little in meaning from the imperative of brk.

The usual form of the imperative is the masculine plural. The phrase bārăkî napšî with a reflexive meaning also occurs in Pss 103 and 104. In Ps 145:10, 21, jussives are used as imperatives.

Westermann (1965:123 note 74, 132 note 85) suggests that the imperative call to praise originally stood as an introduction separate from the psalms themselves, as in Neh 9:5, but in time became a part of the psalms. The imperative was then added to the end of some psalms to form an inclusio. Wehmeier (1970:168) goes one step further and claims that the imperatives found in the body of the psalms were patterned after the opening call for praise.

Westermann's hypothesis is based entirely upon Neh 9:5, the only instance where the imperative of brk is separate from the psalm (in 1 Chr 29:20, an unrecorded psalm or bārûk formula may have followed the imperative). In Neh 9:5, some Levites exhort the people who are confessing and mourning for their sins, "Arise! Praise (bārăkû) Yahweh your God forever and ever!" The congregation then responds with a psalm (vv 5b-37) which begins:

> May your glorious name be praised (wîbārĕkû),
> may it be exalted above all praise and glory.[1]

---

[1] The two occurrences of the Piel of brk meaning "to praise" earlier in the verse and the following synonym tĕhillâ leave no doubt that bĕrākâ here, as in 2 Chr 20:26, means "praise." The phrase means that God is even more wonderful than the expressions of praise indicate.

The syntax of the verse has occasioned suggestions for emendation. But good sense is obtained if all of 5a is part of the call to praise, and 5b is

The Use of brk in the Praise of God   143

Westermann's hypothesis explains the function of the imperatives in Ps 96:1-3 and Ps 134:1-2, which clearly serve the same function as in Neh 9:5. They set the stage for the following psalm of praise by instilling a praising frame of mind in the people.

Though no psalm of praise follows the imperatives in Ps 134, vv 1-2 still serve to get the people in a praising frame of mind for worship. The psalm is a miniature liturgy consisting of a call to worship (vv 1-2) and a closing benediction (v 3) (so also Kraus 1961:892-893):

> Praise (bārăkû) Yahweh, all you servants of Yahweh,
>   who stand in Yahweh's temple in the evenings!
> Lift up your hands in the sanctuary,
>   and praise (bārăkû) Yahweh!
> May Yahweh, maker of heaven and earth,
>   bless you from Zion!

There is no indication whatsoever that the people are called to praise God in order to increase God's power, so that God can bless the people more effectively (contra Mowinckel 1961:47, Weiser 1962:786-787). This hypothesis is based on the erroneous assumption that human praise of God and God's blessing of man are both transfers of power (see further under 6.3; on v 3 see under 4.2.6).

Though Ps 100:4 is not part of the psalm's introduction, it does serve as the introduction to v 5, the last verse of the psalm, which consists of descriptive praise:

> Come into his gates with praise,
>   into his courts with thanksgiving!
> Laud (hôdû) him! Praise (bārăkû) his name!
> For Yahweh is good,
>   and his love (ḥesed) lasts forever,
>   his faithfulness lasts for all generations.

---

taken as the beginning of the psalm. wîbārĕkû in 5b then should be taken as an impersonal jussive used as a passive (GKC 144 g), since it is parallel to a Polal; it need not be emended to a Pual (contra Fensham 1982:223, Myers 1965:164). Neither is there any warrant for inserting a bārûk formula (contra BHS, Wehmeier 1970:161 note 116). The impersonal Piel phrase "may your glorious name be praised" is synonymous in meaning to a bārûk formula.

Though the context is somewhat unclear, Ps 68:27 appears to be a call to liturgical or psalmodic praise:

> Praise (*bārăkû*) God from the great assembly,
> (praise) Yahweh from the congregation of Israel![2]

The context (vv 25-28) seems to describe a cultic procession or festival in the temple (so Weiser 1962:489, Kraus 1961:476). Though the type of praise called for is not described, the cultic context indicates that some form of doxological descriptive praise is intended.

The phrase *bārăkî napšî ʾet yhwh* functions as a reflexive form of *bārăkû*. The speaker exhorts himself to praise God. But speaking the phrase also invites others to join in praising God. The phrase, then, has the same force as *bārăkû*: it is both an expression of the speaker's own praise, and an invitation for others to join in praising God, though the first element is more prominent in the reflexive phrase, while the second element is more prominent with *bārăkû*.

The reflexive phrase is used as an introduction to Pss 103 and 104, both of which are descriptive psalms of praise. Ps 103 has a two verse introduction:

> Praise Yahweh, O my soul,
>   all that is within me, (praise) his holy name!
> Praise Yahweh, O my soul,
>   do not forget all that he has done!

The introduction to Ps 104 consists of the single phrase "Praise Yahweh, O my soul!" In both psalms the descriptive praise follows. The reflexive phrase functions just like *bārăkû*. It is quite unlikely that the reflexive phrase could ever have stood by itself. In Ps 103 the descriptive praise commences with participial phrases which require the introduction to supply the antecedent *yhwh*.

Westermann is correct that the imperatives are in some cases added to the end of the psalm to form an *inclusio*. The imperative is only found at

---

[2] The meaning of *māqôr* here is uncertain. Its usual meaning, "spring" or "fountain," would be peculiar as a designation for the temple or Zion, despite Isa 48:1; 51:1 (so also Kraus 1961:467 who reads *mimmiqrāʾê*). Dahood (1968:148) derives the word from a root *qwr* meaning "to call," but the Ugaritic and biblical evidence for the root is somewhat shaky. In any event, the context demands that the word designate the place of worship.

The Use of brk in the Praise of God   145

the end of psalms that begin with an imperative call for praise which includes bārăkû, bārăkî, or (Ps 135) halĕlû, so the final imperatives are clearly a secondary stylistic development. Ps 103, which begins with four reflexive imperatives, concludes (vv 20-22) with three bārăkû phrases followed by one reflexive phrase. Ps 104, which begins with one reflexive phrase, concludes (v 35) with a reflexive phrase followed by halĕlû yah. Ps 135 begins with four halĕlû imperatives, and concludes with four bārăkû imperatives in vv 19-20, and a bārûk formula followed by halĕlû yāh in v 21. Ps 66:8, though in the middle of the psalm, forms an inclusio with the calls to praise of vv 1-3 (which do not use brk) and also introduces the descriptive praise which follows.

The occurrences of the imperative call to praise in Judg 5:2,9, however, cannot be explained as introductions to descriptive praise that have been incorporated into the body of the song (contra Wehmeier 1970:168). Wehmeier's hypothesis, then, is valid only for the imperatives found within the psalms of the Psalter. The praise in Judg 5:2,9 is a spontaneous response to the military victory, rather than doxological praise. In both verses, the immediate reason given for the praise is that the people volunteered to fight, but in the larger context of the song, God is praised for the victory over Sisera and Jabin (4:23):

> Because princes in Israel took the lead,
>   because the people volunteered,
> praise Yahweh! (v 2)

> My heart goes out to Israel's rulers,
>   who volunteered to lead the people;
> praise Yahweh! (v 9).

Such spontaneous expressions of praise were probably the older basis for the later use of the imperative in doxological praise (cf. Westermann 1965:84-89 discussing the bārûk formula).

In Ps 145:10,21, jussives are used for calls to praise:

> May all that you have made praise (yôdû) you, Yahweh,
>   may your pious ones praise (yĕbārăkû) you!
> My mouth will declare praise of Yahweh,
>   and may all flesh praise (wîbārēk) his holy
>   name forever and ever!

The function of the jussives is identical to that of the imperative calls to praise (so also Westermann 1965:131,132).

5.4 bārûk and mĕbōrak Formulas with God as Subject

The bārûk and mĕbōrak formulas with God as subject are optative calls for God to be praised. bārûk yhwh means "may Yahweh be praised." The formulas can be spoken either as a spontaneous expression of thanks for a deed done by God, or as an expression of doxological praise.

The perlocutionary force is of secondary importance; the speaker's purpose in uttering the formula is to express his own praise and thanks, rather than to move others to praise (contra Wehmeier 1970:121,174).

The illocutionary force of the formula is the same as if the person said "I hereby praise (brk, Piel) Yahweh." However, this expression does not occur; the bārûk formula was the normal means for expressing one's praise toward God in the Bible. It is normally in the third person rather than the second person, both because that was the usual form for deferentially referring to a superior, and because God was viewed as transcendent and somewhat remote, as compared to the formulas addressed to people which frequently are in the second person (see 4.2.3 and 4.2.4).

The meanings of bārûk and the bārûk formula have been disputed. Some authors have attempted to find a single meaning for bārûk that is valid both when God and when men are the subject of the formula. However, the meanings that these authors have proposed are not accurate for either case. This study has shown that when the subject is human, bārûk means "one whom God has, does, or will bless" (see especially 4.2.4 and 4.2.5). When God is the subject, bārûk must have a different meaning, since it would be pointless to speak of God blessing himself, i.e., bestowing some benefit upon himself. Also, man cannot bless God by bestowing the benefits (children, prosperity, etc.) that God does when he blesses man.

Practically all scholars and Bible translations have recognized that regardless of the lexical meaning of bārûk, the bārûk formula with God as subject expresses praise toward God, just as the formula with human subjects can express praise and thanks (4.2.4 and 4.2.5). This has led some scholars to conclude that bārûk must mean "praised" when God is the subject. This conclusion is entirely correct.

One of the most common causes of meaning change is a change in the referent of a word (Heestermans 1980:288, Jeffers and Lehiste 1979:127). The bārûk formula was used first with human subjects (see 1.2 and 1.3; so also Scharbert 1973:21-25). When the bārûk formula was later used to express praise toward God, the meaning of bārûk changed because the earlier meaning was unsuitable. The new meaning, however, was related. Instead of calling for God to be blessed, i.e., to receive prosperity, fertility, etc., bārûk called for the praise of God. Praise was what man could give to God in lieu of material benefits as an expression of appreciation for God's benefaction. The fact that the formula itself was already an expression of thanks and praise, and that the Piel of brk occurred frequently in the same texts with the meaning "to praise" (see 5.1, 5.2, and 5.3), probably facilitated the change in meaning of bārûk.

1 Sam 25:33 and Jer 20:14 illuminate how the meaning of bārûk changed from "blessed" to "praised." In both verses, bārûk refers to non-human entities which could not be blessed. In 1 Sam 25:33, David praises Abigail's shrewdness with the formula bārûk ṭaʿmēk, "May your shrewdness be praised." Because her shrewdness is an abstract quality, it cannot be rewarded by receiving prosperity or fertility; it can only be praised. bārûk cannot mean "blessed"; it must mean "praised."

In Jer 20:14, Jeremiah utters a negative formula about his birthday: ʾal yĕhî bārûk, "May it not be praised!" If it was not negated, bārûk would mean that people considered the day to have been a day on which God bestowed a blessing. It was blessed by God, and so was esteemed by men. However, Jeremiah has already been born; the only way that his birthday now could not be bārûk is if people did not extol the day as a good day. Again, bārûk must mean "praised," rather than "blessed."

Scharbert (1973:26, 1975a:284-288, especially 287) views the formula as indicative, except in the few cases where it is preceded by yĕhî (1 Kgs 10:9; Jer 20:14; Prov 5:18; Ruth 2:19; 2 Chr 9:8) or the subject precedes bārûk (Gen 27:29; Num 24:9; 1 Kgs 2:45).

However, the subject normally follows the predicate in Hebrew nominal sentences, including nominal sentences that function as optatives (Williams 1976: sections 551, 580, Davidson 1901:133, *GKC* 116 r note 1, 141 f). Word order, then, is a poor criterion for determining the mood; there is no reason why the usual form of the formula, with the subject following the predicate, cannot be optative. The mood must be determined by the *context* (so also *GKC* 141 f).

The context repeatedly forces Scharbert himself to include or use optative translations when he defines the meaning of bārûk (1973:26-28, 1975a:284-287). Scharbert defines the meaning of bārûk as "gerühmt, gepriesen ist/sei N.N. oder zu rühmen, zu preisen ist/sei N.N." (1973:27), regardless of whether the subject is God or man. But then when he further explains this meaning, he says that the basic meaning of bārûk is not "blessed," or "in possession of blessing" (against Wehmeier 1970; see below), but "würdig, Lobpreis von Seiten der Menschen und Segen von Seiten Gottes zu empfangen" (1973:28). Two distinct meanings are present in Scharbert's own explanation. These two meanings cannot be combined. When men are *bārûk*, they are to be blessed by God. But when God is *bārûk*, he is to be praised by men.

Scharbert argues that the fact that the *bārûk* formula is of the same form whether God or man is the subject shows that *bārûk* has the same meaning (1973:26). But identical syntactical constructions do not necessarily imply identical meanings. The Piel of *brk* is often used in identical syntactical constructions meaning "bless, bestow benefits" when God is the subject and man is the object; meaning "pronounce a benediction" with human subjects and objects; and meaning "praise" when man is the subject and God is the object. In each case the *context*, not the syntactical construction or the grammatical form, is the surest guide to the meaning.

Wehmeier (1970:107-108,117-119,130-131) follows Pedersen (1926:199) and Plassmann (1913:110-125) in seeing *bārûk* as primarily a verbal adjective with a stative, not a passive, meaning. It means "voll Segen, segenreich" (118). Wehmeier allows only the Pual to have a passive meaning, except for an occasional verse which uses *bārûk* in an imprecise way (131; Keller 1978:355-357 gives a similar definition for *bārûk*).

The inadequacy of the stative interpretation, when the subject is a person, was shown in 4.2.4 and 4.2.5 (see also on Gen 24:31; 26:29; Isa 65:23), where the context demands a passive meaning. However, greater problems are caused when the stative meaning is applied to God.

Wehmeier combines three quite different meanings when he says God is "als Besitzer und Spender der *bĕrākâ* gepriesen" by *bārûk*. There are no verses which describe God simply as the possessor of blessing (*bĕrākâ*). Blessings are always benefits which are *bestowed*; if God simply possessed beneficent powers and material goods but did not bestow them, they would not be blessings. Not even the doxological *bārûk* formulas praise God for possessing blessing; they praise God for his character as revealed by the blessings he *bestows* and his acts of deliverance.

If *bārûk* described God as the bestower of blessing, then one would expect to find synonymous formulas using the Piel, *mĕbārēk*. But such formulas never occur; the synonymous formulas use the Pual *mĕbōrak* with the *passive* meaning "praised" (Ps 113:2; Job 1:21; Dan 2:20 has the Aramaic Pael *passive* participle).

The *bārûk* formula frequently has a *kî* or *ʾăšer* clause appended which describes the act for which God is praised. It is this appended phrase, not *bārûk*, that describes God as a benefactor. *bārûk* expresses praise toward God *because* he is a benefactor; it does not *designate* him as a benefactor (contra also Keller 1978:357). The *kî* and *ʾăšer* clauses appended to the formulas in 4.2.4 and 4.2.5 have the same function; they describe the *reason* God should bless the person who is the subject of the formula.

Concerning Wehmeier's argument that *bārûk* denotes a timeless quality of God, see on 1 Kgs 5:21 = 2 Chr 2:11 under 5.4.3.

Westermann (1965:84-89) has proposed a general history of the *bārûk* formula that is probably correct. The developments proposed by Towner (1968:388-390) and Scharbert (1973:23-24) are similar. Westermann postulates that when the formula was first applied to God, it was an immediate, spontaneous expression of joyful praise in response to a deed of Yahweh. The original form of the formula was short (usually one sentence), and contained the reason for the praise. The formula was later adopted by the cult and developed into a liturgical formula. The reason for the praise was extended to include God's actions over a longer period of time. The formulas became less of a response to specific acts of God, and more doxologies. In the final stage, the formula became purely doxological, with no historical reason whatever given for the praise, as in the doxologies concluding the books of the Psalter.

However, Westermann's contention that the form of spontaneous praise is shorter and simpler is not correct. David's spontaneous thanks in 1 Sam 25:32-33 is rather long, while some doxologies are quite short (Ezek 3:12; Job 1:21; Pss 89:53; 119:12; 124:6). The best criterion for determining whether the praise is closer to spontaneous thanks or to a doxology is the *content* (or absence) of the *reason* for the praise, which is appended to the formula.

There are four major types of *bārûk* formulas:

1) *bārûk yhwh ʾăšer/kî*; the relative clause describes the beneficent act of God for which he is praised;
2) *bārûk yhwh*, with a clause describing God's beneficent action following in apposition to *yhwh* or asyndetically;
3) *bārûk* followed by a title of God as the subject; the title gives the reason for the praise; and
4) *bārûk yhwh* with no reason following; a clause modifying *bārûk* such as "forever and ever" may follow.

The first three types of formulas usually are spontaneous expressions of thanks and praise. The last type is primarily doxological. If any reason for the praise is given, it is God's past benefaction to the nation, rather than to an individual, and the benefaction is usually described as a series of mighty acts, rather than as a single historical event. Doxological praise often praises God for his *character*, rather than for his actions (see especially on Job 1:21 under 5.4.4).

The difference in form between the first three types of formulas does not denote a difference in the meaning of bārûk. The reason for the praise can be expressed in any of the three forms. I have therefore organized these verses according to the reason for the praise, rather than the form. However, the fourth form does denote a distinct meaning. The general reason, or the lack of a reason in the fourth form, signifies that the praise is general, doxological praise, and not thanks.

The first type of formula is the most common. It is spoken usually in response to protection, deliverance, fulfillment of a request, or some similar act of kindness by God. It is usually spoken by individuals. Surprisingly, only about half of the occurrences are spoken by the person directly benefitted; the rest are spoken by people only indirectly involved, such as friends, relatives, or servants. The second and third types are not very common. There does not appear to be any historical development between the first three forms. The fourth form is almost as common as the first. It is especially frequent in the later psalms, and rarely occurs in other books.

5.4.1 bārûk Formulas Expressing Praise for Protection and Deliverance

There are three verses in psalms of lament where the bārûk formula signifies a transition from petition to praise. God is praised for having heard the petition and delivering the psalmist, and the rest of the psalm consists of declarative praise (see further Westermann 1965:64-75,102).

Pss 28:6 and 31:22 contain the only bārûk praise formulas with kî introducing the relative clause (kî also occurs in a formula with a human subject expressing thanks, 1 Sam 23:21). There is no difference in meaning, however, between the kî clauses and the ʾăšer clause of the third verse, Ps 66:20.

In Ps 28, the psalmist calls for God to hear his prayer and punish the wicked. V 6 makes the abrupt change from imprecation to praise:

> May Yahweh be praised,
>   because he has heard my supplications.

The rest of the psalm praises God for delivering the psalmist from his enemies. It is not necessary to assume that the psalm was composed after

God had actually acted (so also Westermann 1965:73-74, contra Wehmeier 1970:124); the psalmist is expressing his confidence in God's retribution and responsiveness to prayer by praising God proleptically, as also in Ps 31:20-25.

Ps 31 is quite similar. The transition from imprecation to praise occurs in v 20. The *bārûk* formula occurs in v 22:

> May Yahweh be praised,
>   because he showed amazing kindness to me in a besieged city.

The reference to a besieged city is figurative for the distress the psalmist suffered at the hands of his adversaries. God is praised in a general way for his responsiveness to prayer. Yet this is quite distinct from doxological praise; God has aided an individual in a specific conflict situation.

Ps 66 is a psalm of praise. Vv 17-20, however, form a miniature psalm of lament that turns into praise. The psalmist relates how he called to God when he was in distress, and how God heard his prayer. The psalm concludes with a *bārûk* formula (v 20):

> May God be praised,
>   who did not reject my prayer or withhold his kindness from me.

The reason for praise combines the two elements of answered prayer, present in Ps 28:6, and of God doing kindness (*ḥesed*), as in 31:22. Because of the covenant relationship between God and his people, God responds to both national and (as here) individual needs (see further Westermann 1965:120-122).

David uttered four *bārûk* formulas in the course of his conflict with Nabal (1 Sam 25). V 33 contains two formulas expressing thanks to Abigail (see under 4.2.4). Vv 32 and 39 contain type 1) formulas praising God for sending Abigail to prevent him from committing an act that would have hurt him later in his role as king (cf. v 31), and for executing retribution on his behalf by killing Nabal.

Daniel praised God for revealing the secret of Nebuchadnezzar's dream to him so that he was not put to death (2:20):

> May God's name be praised forever and ever,
>   to whom wisdom and might belong!

The *dī* clause is equivalent to the Hebrew *ʾăšer* clauses. The ascription of wisdom to God refers to his revelation of the dream, so the praise is not doxological. *lehĕwē*ʾ functions as the jussive *yĕhî* in the *bārûk* formulas of 1 Kgs 10:9; Jer 20:14; Prov 5:18; Ruth 2:19; 2 Chr 9:8, and in the *mĕbōrak* formulas of Job 1:21; Ps 113:2. Formally, the verse is identical to the two Hebrew *mĕbōrak* formulas (see under 5.4.4).

2 Sam 22:47 = Ps 18:47 uses a *bārûk* formula of the third type:

> Yahweh lives! Praised be my rock!
> May the God who gives me salvation be exalted!

The psalm was uttered in response to God delivering David from his enemies (v 1). In the formula, the title *ṣûrî* contains the reason for the praise, making a relative clause superfluous.

Wehmeier (1970:119) draws attention to the previous clause *ḥay-yhwh* in support of his contention that the *bārûk* formula is indicative. However, *ḥay-yhwh* is not a simple assertion; it is an acclamation contrasting Yahweh with the Canaanite gods who periodically die and are impotent to help their adherents (Kraus 1961:149, Weiser 1962:196; cf. Dahood 1966:118 who translates it as an optative). Wehmeier follows Dahood (1966:118) in taking *yārum* (Psalm 18:47 *yārûm*) as a Qal passive participle of *yrm*, but Dahood's evidence for the biform *yrm* is questionable. It is much better to take *bārûk* as optative, as is the parallel jussive *yārum*. "May be praised" and "may be exalted" certainly are good semantic parallels.

Ps 144:1 is quite similar to 2 Sam 22:47 = Ps 18:47:

> May Yahweh, my rock, be praised,
>   who teaches my hands for war,
>   my fingers for battle.

The verse combines types 1) and 2), with both a title and a participial phrase in apposition to *yhwh*.

There are only two verses where the nation collectively praises God for deliverance; all previous formulas have been spoken by individuals. Ps 68:20 uses a type 2) asyndetic formula:

> May the Lord be praised!
>   Day by day, God, our salvation, bears our burdens.
> God is a God of salvation for us;
>   to Yahweh, the Lord, belongs escape from death.

Vv 22-24 describe God aiding the nation against her enemies. Ps 124:6 uses a type 1) formula with še in place of the usual ʾăšer:

> May Yahweh be praised,
> who has not made us prey for their teeth.

These two collective praise formulas are patterned after the statements of individuals, but they have been generalized in two ways. First, the nation stands in place of the individual. Second, no specific historical deliverance is referred to; God is praised for repeatedly delivering the nation from various unspecified enemies. Yet the formulas are not as general as the doxologies because the reason for the praise includes God's contemporary activity.

5.4.2 bārûk Formulas Expressing Praise for Acts of Kindness

In the first six passages, people praise God for benefits they themselves have received.

God is praised in three passages for fulfilling his promises. In 1 Kgs 1:48, David says, "Praised be Yahweh, the God of Israel, who today has provided someone to sit on my throne while my own eyes see," in response to the enthronement of Solomon which fulfills God's promise of 2 Sam 7:12-16. The verse declares David's approval of Solomon as his successor. In 1 Kgs 8:15 = 2 Chr 6:4, Solomon praises God for fulfilling his promise to David that his son would build the temple. Solomon again praises God in 1 Kgs 8:56 for fulfilling his promise to give rest to his people. "Rest" refers to the establishment of the monarchy and cult.

The kings not only thank God for receiving personal benefits, but as representatives of the nation, they thank God on behalf of the nation for giving national benefits. The monarchy and cult are essential for maintaining the health of the nation. God is not only thanked for bestowing the benefits, but also praised for faithfully executing his promises.

There are three verses where God is praised for various acts of kindness. Noah pronounced a curse and two benedictions over his sons for their treatment of him while he was asleep. An ʾārûr formula is addressed to Canaan (Gen 9:25): "Cursed be Canaan! He will be the lowest slave to his brothers." The bārûk formula addressed to Shem has God as the subject (Gen 9:26): "May Yahweh, the God of Shem, be praised!"

ʾārûr and bārûk here are not precise antonyms. The bārûk formula praises Shem's God, rather than directly praising Shem. But praising someone's God does serve to praise the person himself (Gen 14:19-20;

Deut 33:20; 1 Sam 25:32-33; 1 Kgs 5:21 = 2 Chr 2:11, 1 Kgs 10:8-9 = 2 Chr 9:8). There is no need, then, to emend the *bārûk* formula so that it directly praises Shem (contra Brichto 1963:87, "Blessed of YHWH, my God, be Shem"). The *bārûk* formula also declares that Yahweh is Shem's God. Noah states that Shem has acted in accordance with the Yahwistic religion, and can expect to receive the benefits associated with being a follower of Yahweh (similarly Kidner 1967:104, Leupold 1942:1.351).

In Ezra 7:27, Ezra praises God for moving Artaxerxes to let him go to Jerusalem and to provide funds and goods for the restoration. He uses the standard *bārûk* formula, "Praised be Yahweh, the God of our fathers," with an *ʾăšer* clause describing the reasons. The formula is a spontaneous expression of gratitude.

Zech 11:5 is a diatribe against evil leaders in Israel. The leaders are pictured as abusing the sheep, i.e., the people. They say, "Praised be Yahweh! I am rich." By using the *bārûk* formula, the leaders assume that God sanctions their activities. They attribute their wealth to God's beneficent activity, or at least to the lack of his interference. The irony is that God does not approve, as the prophet makes clear.

There are eleven verses where a *bārûk* formula is spoken by someone who has not benefitted directly from God's beneficent activity. In the first four verses, the person speaking has benefitted indirectly, while in the other verses, the person speaking has not benefitted at all. In all verses the formulas and the reasons are similar to those uttered by individuals directly benefitted.

Moses' benediction over the tribe of Gad begins (Deut 33:20): "May he who enlarges Gad be praised!" The reason for the praise is contained in the title of God. *bārûk* modifies a participle only here and Ps 118:26, but there is no warrant for emending the participle to *merḥab*, "blessed be the broad lands of Gad" (so also Scharbert 1973:16 note 45, contra Cross and Freedman 1948:195, Craigie 1976:400). The praise of God really serves as a benediction over the person to whom the formula is addressed (see above on Gen 9:26). The purpose of the phrase is not so much to praise God, but to predict that God will aid Gad in acquiring territory. Moses himself will not benefit from Gad's success, but as Israel's leader he rejoices in her future good fortune.

Melchizedek praised God for Abraham's victory over the kings from the East (Gen 14:20): "May El Elyon be praised, who delivered your enemies into your hand." The formula was not intended to depreciate Abraham's role in the victory, but to declare that God is on Abraham's side (see further on v 19 under 4.2.5).

After Abraham's servant succeeded in finding a wife for Isaac, he praised God (Gen 24:27): "May Yahweh, the God of my master Abraham, be praised, who has not stopped showing his kindness and faithfulness to my master. I am on the road on which Yahweh has led me, to the household of my master's brothers." The formula shows no cultic influence (contra Wehmeier 1970:121); the praise is not doxological, and the activity of bowing down can occur outside the cult. The statement is a spontaneous expression of thanks both for the success of the servant's own sworn mission, and out of joy for his master's good fortune.

Ahimaaz used a bārûk formula to report the death of Absalom to David (2 Sam 18:28): "May Yahweh your God be praised, who delivered up the men who raised their hand against my lord the king." Ahimaaz rejoiced both because of his master's victory and because he was a member of the victorious army. As in Gen 14:20, the bārûk formula attributes the victory ultimately to God. The formula also has a juridical function; because the formula attributes victory to God's retribution, it declares David to be in the right, and Absalom as the guilty party.

5.4.3   bārûk Formulas Expressing Wonder and Admiration

In the following seven verses, the bārûk formula is uttered spontaneously out of wonder and admiration. There is always a specific, immediate reason for the praise, so the praise is not doxological. The person speaking has not benefitted from God's activity, but praises God for what he has done to others. The speaker usually stands in some close relationship to the person benefitted; the speaker can be a relative, fellow townsman, or fellow king. The joy which causes the praise is vicarious.

Foreign monarchs praise Yahweh in three passages. Hiram, the king of Tyre, praised Yahweh in 1 Kgs 5:21 = 2 Chr 2:11 for installing Solomon as king over Israel: "May Yahweh be praised today, who has put a wise son of David over this great people!" Hiram had been very close to David, and is happy because of the prospect of continued good commercial relations with Solomon. Hiram also admired Solomon's dedication to fulfilling David's plan for the temple.

Wehmeier (1970:127-128) sees hayyôm as a secondary liturgical addition. He claims that the addition changes the meaning of bārûk from "reich an Segen" to a call for praise of God, because "reich an Segen" is a timeless quality of God which cannot be limited to a single day. However, the fact that Wehmeier needs to change his definition underlines the implausability of his usual translation of bārûk. The addition of "today" merely spells out what is clear from the context of the other occurrences of the non-doxological bārûk formula, namely, that the formula praises

God on a specific occasion, for a specific act of God. It is *not* a description of a timeless quality of God (cf. *hayyôm* in the formula of Ruth 4:14).

The form of Hiram's formula in 2 Chr 2:11 is identical, but the *ʾăšer* clause referring to God is expanded and an *ʾăšer* clause referring to David is appended. Yahweh is described as the one "who made the heavens and the earth," an epithet of God used in *bārûk* formulas with human subjects in Gen 14:19; Ps 115:15, and as an epithet of God in general descriptions of, or wishes for, God aiding man in Pss 121:2; 124:8; 134:3. The *ʾăšer* clause referring to David simply states that he intends to build the temple and a palace for himself; this is the reason Hiram considers him wise.

The Queen of Sheba uttered a similar *bārûk* formula in 1 Kgs 10:9 = 2 Chr 9:8. She was awed by Solomon's wisdom and the splendor of his court, and exclaimed, "May Yahweh your God be praised, who desired to put you on Israel's throne out of his eternal love for Israel." The form *yĕhî* person *bārûk* occurs only here and Ruth 2:19; Prov 5:18; Jer 20:14. The jussive *yĕhî* leaves no doubt that the form is optative and calls for praise (see also Scharbert 1973:16-17, Wehmeier 1970:128,130). But this is not an imprecise use of *bārûk* in place of *mĕbōrak* (contra Wehmeier 1970:131); *yĕhî* simply spells out the mood which is the same mood as in forms without *yĕhî* (on *ʾašrê* in the preceding verse, see under 6.8).

Nebuchadnezzar praised the God of Israel when he delivered Shadrach, Meshach, and Abednego (Dan 3:28): "May the God of Shadrach, Meshach, and Abednego be praised, who sent his angel and delivered his servants who trusted in him." Nebuchadnezzar certainly did not benefit from God's action. He praised God purely out of wonder and marvel. He was impressed by the men's refusal to obey his orders and willingness to die for their faith. Nebuchadnezzar realized the uniqueness of Israel's God (v 29), but did not personally worship him.

The *bārûk* formulas spoken by the Queen of Sheba and Hiram likewise are not statements of personal faith or trust in Yahweh, but simply expressions of admiration and praise. The *bārûk* formula does become a statement of faith or trust in God when it is accompanied by acts of worship (Gen 24:26-27; Exod 18:10-12), or when the speaker declares his faith in God's continued deliverance in the reason for the praise. The doxological use of *bārûk* and the Piel with God as object do express faith in God (see 5.1, 5.2, 5.3, and 5.4.4).

Jethro praised Yahweh after learning from Moses how he had delivered Israel from Egypt (Exod 18:10): "May Yahweh be praised, who delivered you from the hand of Egypt and Pharaoh, who delivered the people out from under the hand of Egypt." Childs (1974:328) explains that "to bless God . . . acknowledges in thanksgiving that one's trust in God's care (ḥeseḍ) has been fully vindicated." While often true, Child's explanation is not applicable here. Jethro, unlike Moses, was not anticipating deliverance, and in fact experienced no deliverance himself. Instead, he rejoiced vicariously with Israel (v 9). The fact that he subsequently engaged in cultic worship of Israel's God (v 12) shows that he considered himself united with Israel in worshipping Yahweh.

The women of Bethlehem vicariously rejoiced with Naomi when her daughter-in-law Ruth bore a son (Ruth 4:14): "May Yahweh be praised, who has not left you without a redeemer today. May he become famous in Israel!" Naomi will now have someone to take care of her in her old age (v 15; on the grammatical subject of v 14 b (the child) see Campbell 1975:163-164). The women of the town can sympathize with her position, and so praise God on her behalf.

5.4.4 Doxological *bārûk* and *mĕbōrak* Formulas

The doxological *bārûk* formulas represent the final biblical stage in the evolution of the *bārûk* formula (similarly Scharbert 1973:23-24, Towner 1968:388-390, Westermann 1965:84-89). The formula is occasionally found with recitals of God's great acts of deliverance and past care of Israel. There it still functions to call for praise of God in response to his benefaction. But the formula also occurs without mention of God's acts. It is frequently used as a call for praise and adoration of God simply because of God's majesty, power, goodness, faithfulness, etc. Since God's character is revealed only by his actions, we must assume that the doxological praise stems from a general belief in God's grace as demonstrated by his acts of salvation.

Because the *bārûk* formula is one of the most general expressions of praise, it is frequently used as an introduction or conclusion to psalms and prayers (cf. the use of *halĕlû*). In Ps 68:36, the simple phrase *bārûk ʾĕlōhîm*, "May God be praised!", concludes the calls for extolling God in vv 33-35 ("sing to God," "ascribe might to God," etc.). The psalm describes various beneficent acts of God on behalf of his people, and how various peoples will serve God. The *bārûk* formula is a summary of man's response in praise.

Ps 135 is a liturgical recital of God's great deeds, such as the Exodus and Conquest, along with general statements of God's care of the nation. It ends with a call for various peoples to praise (*bārăkû*) God. The psalm closes with a statement of praise (v 21):

> May Yahweh, he who dwells in Jerusalem,
> be praised from Zion.
> Praise (*halělû*) Yah!³

Like *halělû-yāh*, the *bārûk* formula calls for general praise of God for all that he is and does. It summarizes the contents of the psalms of declarative and descriptive praise (on which see Westermann 1965:52-151). The *bārûk* formula in 1 Chr 16:36 likewise serves as a concluding expression of praise. The psalm of vv 8-36 is quite similar to many psalms of descriptive praise (hymns).

The final stage in the doxological use of the *bārûk* formula appears in the four doxologies concluding the books of the Psalter (so also Westermann 1965:88-89):

> May Yahweh, the God of Israel, be praised,
> forever and ever!
> Amen and Amen! (41:14);

> May Yahweh, God, the God of Israel, be praised,
> who alone does wonders!
> May his glorious name be praised forever,
> and may all the earth be full of his glory!
> Amen and Amen! (72:18-19);

> May Yahweh be praised forever!
> Amen and Amen! (89:53);

> May Yahweh, the God of Israel, be praised,
> forever and ever!
> May all the people say "Amen! Praise (*halělû*)
> Yah!" (106:48).

---

³The *min* on *miṣṣiyyôn* is difficult. Kraus (1961:895), among others, suggests reading *b* for *min*, while Dahood (1970:263) suggests that the *mem* is enclitic. However, similar phrases occur in Ezek 3:12 and Ps 68:36a. Just as Yahweh blesses from (*min*) Zion (Pss 128:5; 134:3), so the congregation gathered on Zion is exhorted to praise him from there (similarly Weiser 1962:788,790, Keil and Delitzsch Psalms:3.327), as in Ps 68:27: "In the congregation, praise (*bārăkû*) God, (praise) Yahweh, from (*min*) the spring of Israel."

These doxologies are intended to summarize the message of the books of the Psalter. They are not responses to any specific deed of God, or even to any psalmodic list of God's deeds or catalogue of his attributes, but simply responses to the entirety of God's personality as depicted in the Psalter. The doxologies are not spontaneous, but fully developed, stylized liturgical formulas in solemn language, "like the heavy golden implements of an altar" (Westermann 1965:89).

There are two psalms which begin with a *bārûk* formula, Ps 144, discussed under 5.4.1, and 1 Chr 29:10-19, which is a descriptive psalm of praise with a prayer at the end. The *bārûk* formula is one of the most general expressions of praise, and so is suitable for use as an introduction. More specific praise statements follow, such as "To you belong greatness, power, glory, etc."

1 Chr 29:10 and Ps 119:12 are the only two *bārûk ʾattâ yhwh* formulas, though the second person form occurs with human subjects in Ruth 3:10, 1 Sam 15:13; 23:21; 25:33; 26:25; 2 Sam 2:5. The addition of *ʾattâ* transforms the doxology into a prayer form. The formula in 1 Chr 29:10 was probably harmonized to the second person form employed throughout the rest of the prayer. Thus the third person formula, usually used as a stylistic introduction and conclusion to psalms and prayers, was made part of the prayer itself.

Ps 119:12 occurs in an acrostic poem extolling Torah piety:

> May you be praised, Yahweh;
> teach me your statutes.

The surrounding verses all address God in the second person, and so the usual third person formula was again changed to the second person prayer form to make it an integral part of the prayer.

Though biblical prayers normally use the third person *bārûk* formula, the second person form became the dominant type in the Apocrypha, the sectarian Qumran writings, and post-biblical Jewish prayers and liturgies (for a survey of the literature see Towner 1968:393-399, Wehmeier 1970:129-130).

Towner quite plausibly suggests that the post-biblical Jewish use of the second person formula does not derive from the two biblical occurrences, but from the actual Jewish liturgical practice during the late biblical period, since it is improbable that such a rare biblical form would be adopted as the normative form by so many groups if it was not commonly employed outside the Bible. But less probable is his further assertion that the temple liturgy was responsible for the emergence of the form in the

Bible. 1 Chr 29:10 certainly occurs in a cultic context, but Ps 119, as Towner (393) admits, derives from the wisdom tradition. It is more likely that both instances of the form are due to harmonization to the second person contexts.

The MT of Ezek 3:12 contains a *bārûk* formula, though the text is not free from suspicion. Many commentators (*BHS*, Zimmerli 1979:1.12, Eichrodt 1970:60, Cooke 1936:41) read *bĕrûm* for *bārûk*. Though the emendation is quite attractive, it is without textual support.

In the MT, the formula "May the glory of Yahweh be blessed from his place" is best understood as a doxology exclaimed by the creatures supporting God; this doxology is the "great rushing sound" Ezekiel hears behind him (so also Scharbert 1973:23 note 72, Murtonen 1959:169). "His place" probably refers to Zion—cf. Pss 68:27,36; 135:21, which use *min* in a similar way in similar formulas. "The glory of Yahweh" is priestly periphrasis for Yahweh himself (cf. Ps 72:19 for a similar use of *kābôd* in a *bārûk* formula). It is less likely that the prophet himself pronounced the doxology, since the context is describing the sounds Ezekiel heard the creatures make (contra Wehmeier 1970:127). Like the Seraphim's praise in Isa 6:2-3, the praise is purely doxological. The attending creatures praise God simply for who he is, not because of anything he has done.

The Pual formula *yĕhî šēm-yhwh mĕbōrak* occurs in Ps 113:2 and Job 1:21. The analogous Aramaic formula occurs in Dan 2:20, discussed above under 5.4.1. Ps 113 is a descriptive psalm of praise. The theme of such psalms is God's *ḥesed*, that is, that God displays his benevolence by caring for the lowly and downtrodden. Yet unlike the declarative psalms of praise, the descriptive psalms of praise are doxological, i.e., not concerned with reporting specific acts of deliverance by God (Westermann 1965:118-121). The *mĕbōrak* formula is synonymous with the *bārûk* formulas in the other descriptive psalms of praise.

The function of the formula in Job 1:21 is similar to its function in Ps 113:2, though the praise is even further removed from any benevolent act of God. Job assumes that God is ultimately responsible for all that has happened to him. By praising God, Job affirms that he still believes in God's innate goodness.

Doxological praise is a response to the entirety of God's character, rather than a spontaneous response to a recent, specific act of God. God reveals his character by his actions. However, doxological praise can be uttered even when a certain act of God does not directly benefit, or in the case of Job, adversely affects, man. This is due to a belief in God's ultimate goodness and grace, notwithstanding human inability to comprehend the reason for some of God's actions (cf. Job 38-42, and 5.4.3).

5.5 Euphemism: "Praise/Worship" for "Blaspheme"

The Piel of *brk* is used seven times euphemistically with God as the object. The meaning is "to blaspheme" (see below). This meaning is the direct antonym of the meaning "to worship" for the Piel in Isa 66:3; the meaning of *brk*, Piel includes both praise and worship in many of the verses discussed under 5.1, 5.2, and 5.3.

The euphemistic Piel of *brk* stands for the Piel of *qll* (so also Brichto 1963:170-172, Scharbert 1975a:295, Wehmeier 1970:165-166). The Piel of *qll* means "to blaspheme" with God as the object in Exod 22:27; 1 Sam 3:13 (Tiq. Soph. *lāhem* for *ʾĕlōhîm*); Isa 8:21. Exod 22:27 expresses in commandment form the Israelite belief that blasphemy should be avoided, the same belief that caused the euphemism to be employed: "You shall not blaspheme (*tĕqallēl*) God, nor shall you curse (*tāʾōr*) the leader of your people."

The Qal of *ʾrr* is much less common than the Piel of *qll* as an antonym of *brk*, Piel. It is quite unlikely that the euphemistic use of *brk* stands for *ʾrr* (contra Blank 1950:83), because *ʾrr* denotes pronouncement of an imprecation or spell to be effected by God, and God could hardly be invoked against himself. The curse terms *ʾrr*, *ʾlh*, and *zʿm* never have God as their object because "man Jahwe weder verfluchen, noch mit magischen Formeln bannen, noch ihn ernstlich bedrohen kann. Man kann ihn höchstens "lästern" aber nicht beseitigen und ausschalten" (Scharbert 1958a:16).

The verb *nqb/qbb* occurs with God as the object meaning "to blaspheme" in Lev 24:11,16, where it is parallel to the Piel of *qll*. It is possible that *nqb/qbb* could be the verb which the euphemistic Piel of *brk* stands for, since its meaning is suitable, but because *qbb* is much rarer than *qll* (fifteen occurrences, primarily in the Balaam narrative, versus forty-seven occurrences), this is unlikely.

It is improbable that the euphemism is due to scribal emendation, because of the verses where God is the object of *qll*, Piel and *nqb/qbb*, Qal. Authors apparently were free to choose whether or not to use the euphemism. Yaron (1959) convincingly argues for the antiquity of euphemisms to avoid references to blasphemy from an euphemism in an eighteenth century B.C. Egyptian text which is analogous to 2 Sam 12:14, where the Piel of *nʾṣ* with Yahweh as object is avoided.

BDB suggests that the Piel is actually not euphemistic, but has developed the meaning "to curse" from the use of the Piel and *bārûk* in farewells (on which see 4.2.3). However, the farewells are always spoken as a sincere expression of affection and respect between persons on good terms. It is difficult to imagine how such an expression could naturally develop into a curse. BDB also suggests that the Piel could denote "a blessing overdone and so really a curse." It is true that if spoken in an improper way, a blessing can be misunderstood (Prov 27:14):

> If a person blesses his neighbor in a loud voice
>   too early in the morning,
> a curse (*qĕlālâ*) will be credited to him!

But there is no indication in the euphemistic verses that a blessing has been "overdone" or spoken in an improper manner or context. As Yaron (1959) points out, euphemisms to avoid blasphemy were an accepted part of language in the ancient Near East, and so the best explanation for this use of *brk* remains that it is an euphemism. A similar euphemism with *n'ṣ* occurs in 2 Sam 12:14. The qere *ʾădōnāy* for *yhwh* and the later Jewish use of *haššēm* for *yhwh* are also attempts to avoid blasphemy.

Because the words of blasphemy are never quoted, it is difficult to define precisely what biblical blasphemy consisted of. Presumably, it included verbally denigrating or expressing contempt for God, denying God's goodness and other attributes, and defiance of God's authority. Though the Piel of *qll* can denote mere contemptuous speech or action when humans are the object, the contempt or abuse denoted by the euphemism was perhaps more extreme than the protests found in books such as Jeremiah, Job, and the Psalms, since these protests did not merit capital punishment.

The meaning of the euphemism is "to blaspheme," rather than "to curse" in the sense of uttering an imprecation against God. There are no biblical examples of imprecations against God (cf. Blank 1950:83, Brichto 1963:170). Since Yahweh was considered supreme over other gods and over magic, there was nothing that could be invoked to effect such an imprecation. In extra-biblical texts, imprecations against gods are extremely rare (Wehmeier 1970:165 note 133; the conditional curse in the Egyptian text in *ANET* 327a relies on magic). The translation "to curse" is viable only if "curse" is understood in the sense of blasphemy, rather than an imprecation (so also Brichto 1963:164-165,170, although he calls the utterance of an imprecation against God "blasphemy," and defines "curse" as I have defined "blaspheme").

Naboth was stoned for blasphemy in 1 Kgs 21. The accusation against him was "Naboth blasphemed (*bērak*) God and the king" (v 13; the accusation is in the second person in v 10). Blasphemy of God had a legal precedent requiring the death penalty (Lev 24:11-16; cf. Exod 20:7 = Deut 5:11).

In reference to the king, the verb denotes disrespect for and defiance of the king in his office as God's representative ruler. Reviling the king alone does appear to be a capital offence (2 Sam 16:5-12; 19:21-23; 1 Kgs 2:8-9, 44-46), though it never requires an euphemism.

Job's wife envisions death as the result of blasphemy in Job 2:9. She tells Job, "Blaspheme God and die!" Although Pope (1973:22) sees the wife as simply suggesting that Job vent his feelings since he was going to die anyway, it is more likely that she, like the "friends," saw Job's sickness as proof of God's hostility. If Job would completely repudiate God, then God would quickly finish Job off, and such a death would be better than a protracted painful illness (cf. Horst 1968:28).

Job's wife suggests that Job fulfill exactly the satan's prediction: "he certainly will blaspheme you to your face!" (1:11; 2:5). In doing so, Job would give up his religious integrity (*tummâ*, 2:3,9) and cease fearing God (*yĕrê* - *ʾĕlōhîm*, 1:1,8,9; 2:3). Not only would he express his frustration, but he would openly renounce his belief that God was good.

Job had been concerned that his sons might offend God: "Perhaps my sons have sinned and blasphemed God in their hearts" (1:5). The feared sin of the children is less serious than open blasphemy; it only occurs "in their hearts," not to God's face (unlike 1:11; 2:5), and Job supposes that he can atone for it with sacrifices (1:5). It probably refers to disdain for God or simply to evil thoughts, but in keeping with the pious picture of Job in the prologue, Job considers such thoughts blasphemy.

The second line of Ps 10:3 is difficult:

> The wicked man boasts about what his heart craves,
>   and the greedy man blasphemes and despises Yahweh.

The line reads *ûbōṣēaʿ bērēk niʾēṣ yhwh*. If *bērēk* is not taken as an euphemism, then the only way to make sense of the verse as it stands is to take *bōṣēaʿ* as the direct object: "he (the wicked man) blesses the greedy man and despises Yahweh" (so *NIV*). But the word order argues against this interpretation. Plassmann (1913:141) translates "the covetous has blessed (but inwardly) despised Yahweh"; Brichto (1963:170) translates "when the rapacious blesses he is holding Yahweh in contempt"; neither translation makes much sense.

Many commentators (Weiser 1962:147, Kraus 1961:75-76, Wehmeier 1970:163-164) emend *bōṣēaʿ* to *beṣaʿ*, "he praises profit and despises Yahweh," but the emendation is without textual support and is unnecessary.

The best solution is to take *bērēk* as euphemistic (so also BDB 139a). It is synonymous with *ni'ēṣ*, which itself requires an euphemism in 2 Sam 12:14. Wehmeier (1970:166) argues that *brk* is not euphemistic in other passages where it is parallel to *hillēl*, but in those verses both verbs denote praise of God. *hillēl* here denotes insolent boasting, and the Piel of *brk* meaning "to bless" never occurs parallel to *hillēl* when *hillēl* has this meaning.

6
Conclusions

The use of speech-act semantics and archeological research has enabled this study to resolve several fundamental issues concerning the concept of blessing which previously have been poorly understood. This study has clarified what blessing consists of, how blessing operates, and why God and men bless. In addition to these conceptual issues, this study has improved the understanding of the lexical meaning of the *brk* derivatives in many passages.

6.1   God Blessing Man

All the major authors who have written on blessing lay heavy emphasis on the supposition that the basic, original meaning of blessing in the Bible is the bestowal of fertility. This emphasis upon fertility is at least partially a result of concentrating on the content of blessing rather than on the connotations and purposes of blessing.

The main thesis of this study, however, is that fertility, as well as the other benefits such as prosperity and dominion, are really not essential elements of blessing at all. The factor that makes a blessing a blessing is the relationship between God and the person blessed. God blesses because of his favorable attitude toward a person or group of people. A blessing is any benefit or utterance which God freely bestows in order to make known to the recipient and to others that he is favorably disposed toward the recipient. The type of benefit God actually bestows when he blesses is of secondary importance.

Certainly it is true that fertility is the most common benefit God bestows. However, the reason God blessed by bestowing fertility, dominion, prosperity, etc., is that these were the most valued benefits during the biblical period. These were the benefits that people needed to thrive in their culture. By bestowing these benefits God loudly proclaimed his relationship to his people.

God's blessing is a visible sign of his favor that attracts the attention of others and makes them desire God's blessing too. Because of God's blessing, "everyone who sees them (Israel) will recognize that they are the people whom Yahweh has blessed" (Isa 61:9); "all nations will consider you (Israel) blessed because you are a desirable land" (Mal 3:12: cf. v 10). With regard to individuals, others say, "we have seen quite clearly that Yahweh is with you" because God had blessed them (Gen 26:28; see also Gen 39:2-6).

Blessing connotes a favorable relationship between God and the person blessed. God blessed Job (42:12) to make evident to the "friends" his gracious disposition toward Job. The declarative *bārûk* formulas (see 3.2.1) are clearly based on God's relationship to the person(s) declared *bārûk*. God tells Balaam, "Do not curse the people because they are blessed" (Num 22:12); God's favor toward Israel is made clear by his blesser/blessed relationship with her. Balaam cannot predict that God will abandon or be angry with his people and so let them be defeated. In Isa 19:25, God calls Egypt and Assyria, as well as Israel, *bārûk*. The context makes clear that "blessed" means that the two countries will have a covenantal relationship with God just as Israel does.

The covenantal blessing promises (3.1.2) emphasize that the blessing relationship is a two-way street. God promises to maintain his role as blesser as long as Israel abides by the terms of the covenant. Israel's role in the relationship is not simply as a passive recipient of blessing; she must pursue God's standards in everyday life as well as engage in the specified cultic worship to satisfy God. The later historical books and psalms of praise emphasize that it is the duty of man to give doxological praise to God in response to his blessings.

The wisdom literature uses *brk* as a term of retribution, as it is in the Sinai covenant, but in the wisdom literature it is used primarily for individual retribution (see 3.1.3). The prerequisite for blessing is at times one's relationship to God (Pss 112:1-2; 128:4; Prov 28:20), and at other times one's relationship to other people (Prov 11:26; 22:9; 24:25). Yet these are not two distinct criteria; because the pious fear God, they follow his laws and so treat others well. Their relationship to God determines their conduct toward others. Prov 3:33 summarizes the entire message of the wisdom literature concerning blessing:

> Yahweh's curse is on the house of the wicked,
> but he blesses the home of the righteous.

Conclusions

The Priestly benediction shows more clearly than any other passage how God's blessing is intimately connected to his favorable attitude. The benediction asks for God to be favorably disposed toward his people. The request for God to bless (*brk*, Piel) is parallel to requests for God to lift up his face and make his face shine upon his people, and to be merciful (*ḥnn*) to them (see further 4.2.1).

brk is most frequently used when God blesses those who are already in a close relationship to him. However, it is also used when God calls people *into* a close relationship with himself. In the creation narrative, God calls the life forms into being and blesses them with fertility and vitality. In the patriarchal narratives, God, on his own initiative, makes numerous unconditional blessing promises to Abraham and his descendants, promising to be their God and to make them into his people. He also repeatedly promises that all nations will eventually acquire blessing (see further 3.1.1).

This theme is repeated at the opposite end of the spectrum of God's blessing activity. God promises through the prophets to restore the nation to a new blessed state, and even to bring other nations to share in Israel's blessings (see 3.1.4, especially on Isa 19:24-25). *brk*, then, can have the connotation of God reaching out, desiring to bring people to himself.

Wehmeier's verdict (1970:229-230) that "Nach allen Schichten des AT besteht der Segen Gottes in konkreten irdischen Gütern . . . "Geistliche" Gaben werden nirgendwo also "Segen" bezeichnet" is hardly justified in light of the connotations of *brk*, not to mention verses such as Isa 44:3 where God's *rûaḥ* is parallel to his *bĕrākâ* as a benefit bestowed (similarly Judg 13:24-25). Many verses explicitly tie God's blessing activity to his love for or favor toward man using words such as *ʾāhab* (Deut 7:13; 23:6), *ḥanan* (Num 6:25; Ps 67:2), *ḥesed* (Deut 7:12), *rāṣâ* (Deut 33:11,24), and *rāṣôn* (Deut 33:16 (cf. v 13),23; Ps 5:13) to describe God's attitude toward the person(s) blessed. In Pss 24:5; 112:3b (cf. v 2b; cf. also Deut 24:13), God's blessing is equated with *ṣĕdāqâ*, covenantal righteousness; God's blessing includes God's legal verdict of "righteous" pronounced upon the person blessed.

6.2   Man Blessing Man

Most human blessings in the OT are based upon the relationship between God and the person blessed. The declarative benedictions (4.1.1-4.1.3) are always declarations that God has blessed and/or will bless the person to whom the benediction is addressed. They never have a magical or self-fulfilling power (see further under 6.4 and 6.5).

The majority of human blessings are optative. The optative blessings are always wishes or prayers for God to bless. The optative blessings are an expression of the speaker's sentiments. They may be spoken out of thanks or praise to a benefactor, as a greeting or farewell to express friendship or fellowship, or as a prayer for someone the speaker cares about. They too never have a magical or self-fulfilling power, although they can influence God and cause him to bless (see further under 6.4 and especially 6.5).

Most greetings and farewells, and many of the thanksgiving and praise benedictions, are primarily expressions of the speaker's sentiments. The speaker rarely expects these benedictions to be fulfilled literally. The benedictions imply little or nothing about the relationship between God and the addressee, who may be a perfect stranger (see, for example, Gen 47:7,10; 1 Sam 25:14; 2 Kgs 4:29). They do express the fact that the speaker is favorably disposed toward the addressee.

Some greetings, many thanksgiving and praise benedictions, and especially the prayers, do imply something about God's relationship to the addressee and/or the speaker. A greeting invoking Yahweh may be used by the pious (Ruth 2:4a) or those wishing to appear pious (1 Sam 15:13). The thanksgiving and praise benedictions usually are spoken to a benefactor who by his actions has shown that he merits blessing according to the principles of retribution outlined in the covenantal promises (3.1.2) and wisdom aphorisms (3.1.3). The speaker usually does not expect the benediction to be fulfilled in a striking manner, though unlike in the greetings he often does expect some fulfillment. The benediction in effect says, "I hereby acknowledge that you merit blessing. God generally blesses persons such as yourself" (see further under 4.2.4).

The prayers often do seek a visible, striking response from God. Unlike greetings, thanksgivings, and praise benedictions, prayers often seek to cause God to do something which he may not have done if the prayer had not been uttered. Prayers, then, are not simply based on a belief in God's general retribution, i.e., that he generally blesses the pious. They are based on the belief that God hears and often responds to individual and collective requests (see further under 4.2.2).

The *bārûk* formulas have been a problem area for scholars because the usual form is a nominal sentence with no explicit indication that it is anything but indicative, while the contexts demand an optative translation. Wehmeier (1970:102-131), Scharbert (1973:26) and Keller (1978:355-358) interpret the *bārûk* formulas as indicative except for a few cases where *yĕhî* is prefixed to the formula or (for Scharbert) where the subject precedes *bārûk*. These authors confuse the illocutionary force of the formula with an indicative mood. The illocutionary force is the same as that in the indicative statement, "I hereby declare that God should bless you," but the usual formula is still optative (see further 4.2.4). The *bārûk* formulas which occur in narrative statements, declarations, and promises are indicative. However, the majority of the formulas occur in optative wishes. The indicative interpretation of these wishes is also based upon a misunderstanding of the normal Semitic form of nominal wishes. Brockelmann (1913:2.26) recognized that "Nominale Wunschsätze werden nun aber in den meisten sem. Sprachen schon mit Vorliebe dem Bau der normalen Aussagesätze angepasst" (see also *GKC* 116r note 1, 141 f). Both *GKC* and Brockelmann (p 27) recognize the optative mood of the usual forms of the *bārûk* formula in Hebrew and (Brockelmann) biblical Aramaic (see further under 4.2.4).

The stative interpretation of *bārûk* advocated by Wehmeier (1970) and Keller (1978), following Plassman (1913) and Pedersen (1926), simply is not appropriate for most of the contexts (see 4.2.4). Blessing is not a power given by God or another person which a person can keep and distribute as he wishes; it is not something that man can possess apart from God. *bārûk* used in human optative benedictions calls for *God* to bless the person, not simply for the person to possess benefits. God is pictured as the ultimate source of blessing throughout the Bible because blessing is a result of a favorable relationship to God. It is therefore impossible for someone to have the stative quality of being "full of blessing" unless he has been blessed by God.

Two comparisons clearly show both the optative mood and passive voice of the usual *bārûk* formula. The psalmodic formula "May you be blessed (*bĕrûkîm*) by Yahweh, maker of heaven and earth" (Ps 115:15, similarly Gen 14:19) is equivalent to "May Yahweh bless you (*yĕbārekkā*) from Zion, maker of heaven and earth" (Ps 134:3, similarly Ps 128:5). The greeting "May you be blessed (*bārûk*) by Yahweh" (1 Sam 15:13) is equivalent to the greeting "May Yahweh bless you (*yĕbārekkā*)" (Ruth 2:4b, and the farewell benediction of Gen 28:3). Two verses in Isaiah also clearly show the passive voice of *bārûk* (*bārûk* is not in the standard formula, and is indicative here). Isaiah describes the people in the future golden age as *hēm zeraʿ bērak yhwh* (61:9) and *zeraʿ bĕrûkê-yhwh hēmmâ* (65:23). Compare also Deut 33:24 to Judg 5:24.

6.3 Man Praising God

The praise of God is portrayed in the OT as man's natural

response to God's benefaction. Many of the passages employing brk contain spontaneous expressions of praise uttered by people in response to a specific act of God in the course of everyday life. Such praise could be part of an act of worship (Gen 24:26-27,48; Exod 18:10-12). The cult made praise just as much an integral part of corporate worship as sacrifice. The psalms encourage the praise of God both because of his saving acts and because of his character. They emphasize that it is man's duty to praise God. Praise is what man should give to God in lieu of material goods to repay God for his benefaction (see further under 5.1-5.4).

Praising God has both an illocutionary and a perlocutionary force. Both forces are present in all forms of praise employing brk. The bārûk formulas and the vow of praise spoken by a person whom God has benefitted primarily have an illocutionary force. By saying, "May Yahweh be praised," or "I will praise Yahweh," the person in effect says, "I hereby praise Yahweh for doing such-and-such." Both forms also have a perlocutionary force as well; they invite and urge others to join the speaker in praising God. Although the utterances are not addressed to anybody in particular, the speaker intends the hearers to acknowledge God's goodness as evidenced by God's deed or trait described, and so join him in praise. The praise also is intended to serve as a model of how people should respond to God.

The imperative calls for praise, as well as the jussives and cohortatives, primarily have a perlocutionary force. The speaker exhorts his audience to praise God. By using the verbs, he intends to instill an attitude of praise into his listeners. Yet the verbs also have an illocutionary force; the speaker himself declares his own praise of God. It is as if he says, "Look what God has done. You should praise God too!" (see further 5.3).

The synonymous collocations of the Piel of brk with God as object indicate that it means "to praise" and not "to bless" (see 5.2 and 5.3). The bārûk formula with God as subject, like the formula with human subjects, is optative. bārûk in the formula means "praised." The attempts of Wehmeier (1970), Scharbert (1973, 1975a) and Keller (1978) to find a single (indicative) meaning for bārûk regardless of whether God or man is the subject are unconvincing and motivated by etymology, not contextual evidence (see further 5.4).

The use of the bārûk formula to praise God evolved from the uses of the formula as an expression of thanks and praise of men which asked God to bless the person thanked or praised, and the change in the meaning of bārûk from "blessed" to "praised" was caused by the change in the referent, a common phenomenon (see further 5.4).

Conclusions

Mowinckel (1961:27-30) and Blank (1961:87-90) contend that to praise God really means to bless God when *brk* is used, because *brk* is also used when God blesses man and men bless other men. They further contend that "blessing" God must give something to God that benefits him, just as God blessing man benefits man (similarly Horst 1947:31 discussing the pre-biblical meaning of blessing). Mowinckel claims that pronouncing the formula *bārûk yhwh* had the same purpose as an old Norwegian cultic formula: "man segnet die Gottheit, damit diese wieder mit grösser Wirkung segnen könne" (29).

Mowinckel and Blank base their interpretations on etymology, not on the contextual meaning of *brk* or on explicit biblical statements. They seem oblivious to the existence of polysemy. It is unwarranted to assume that a verb must retain the same meaning when the subject and object are interchanged.

Practically all contexts where God is praised using *brk* describe the reason for the praise as a prior beneficent act by God, or, if the praise is doxological, as a trait of God. Mowinckel's cultic hypothesis, then, is incorrect. God is not praised in order to *elicit* greater blessing from God; he is praised because he has *already* blessed the people.

It is true that man praising God is the counterpart to God blessing man. It is man's duty to praise God in return for what God has done for man. But man gives praise to God *in lieu of* materially benefitting God. It is hardly possible for man to increase God's power. Man can only give God the worship, praise, and thanks he deserves and desires.

6.4   Magic and Blessing

There is no evidence in the Bible for a magical view of blessing, i.e., the idea that blessing can be acquired from sources other than God, or that there exist means by which blessing can be coerced from God. The biblical evidence indicates that God always bestows blessing of his own free will. God always blesses in order to display his favor toward the person blessed. Often he bestows blessing in accordance with the biblical principles of retribution, as in the covenantal blessings and the Wisdom Literature. At other times, as in the patriarchal narratives and the prophetic apocalypses, God blesses and promises to bless simply because he *wants* to bless, not because the recipients have merited blessing by any principle of retribution. Man is never able to coerce God into blessing him, nor is man able to acquire blessing from a source besides God.

The lexical meanings of the *brk* words in the OT are not all that different from their meanings elsewhere in ancient Syria-Palestine. Blessing in the extra-biblical NW Semitic languages is also largely devoid of magic (see Wehmeier 1970:18-66, Schottroff 1969:178-198). Blessing consists of the gods bestowing children, long life, wealth, etc., upon people. The gods frequently bless in response to prayers for help, and human blessings are benedictions calling upon the gods to bless another person.

There is, therefore, practically no support for the widespread assumption, still held, for example, by Wehmeier (1970:65-66) and Keller (1978:354-355), that the animistic concept of blessing associated with Arabic *baraka* is the original concept of blessing also in NW Semitic. The biblical passages usually cited as evidence for an original animistic concept in Hebrew, such as Isa 65:8 and the passages discussed below, really do not give an animistic picture of *běrākâ* (see further 3.2.2.1, and below). The extra-biblical evidence suggests that the Arabic concept is a parallel development, or perhaps an offshoot, of the theologized[1] blessing concept found in Ugaritic, the Canaanite inscriptions, and the OT.

Pedersen (1926), Mowinckel (1961), Hempel (1961), Westermann (1978), Wehmeier (1970), and Scharbert (1975a:303-304) all see evidence in the Bible of magical or mechanical views of blessing. These authors claim that the originally magical concepts were theologized during the growth of the OT, so that in the latest strata blessing is pictured entirely as a gift of God which cannot be procured by magic.

The first three authors mentioned see the magical conception of blessing as predominant in the OT, while the last three authors consider blessing to have been theologized throughout the Bible except for a few passages, notably Gen 27; 32:22-32, and the Balaam pericope (Num 22-24), where they follow the views of their predecessors. The extreme position of Pedersen, Mowinckel, and Hempel regarding magic is a result of the imposition of their History of Religion approach onto the text, rather than a result of careful exegesis. Their magical interpretations of various verses were discussed above in chapters 3-5, and I have already indicated the major shortcomings of their approach in chapter 2.

Wehmeier (1970:191-193) and Westermann (1978:54-55) use Gen 27 as the basis of their assumption that blessing was originally a transfer of the

---

[1] The term "theologized" is used by many scholars who have written on blessing to denote the view wherein blessing is bestowed only by the gods or God, and blessing is *not* an independent power or entity with its own volition which can operate independently of the gods or God. "Theologized" therefore is antonymous to both "magical" and "animistic," though it is *not* synonymous with "monotheistic."

power of fertility and life from one person to another. God had nothing at all to do with the transfer of this power, and once the blessing was given, the power took effect automatically.

This magical view is based on a fundamental misunderstanding of the purpose of the testamental blessing. Archeological discoveries have shown that societal customs, and not magic, were the basis of the testamental blessing. The testamental blessing was a legal disposition of the father's estate, not a transfer of power (see 4.1.1).

The arguments of Wehmeier (1970:193-194) and Westermann (1978:55) based on Gen 32:22-32 rely on a hypothetical, pre-biblical form of the story. In the extant form of the story, as Wehmeier (194) admits, blessing is freely bestowed by God; Jacob does not wrestle blessing from his opponent against his opponent's will. A hypothetical story which contradicts the extant text concerning the crucial aspect of blessing is hardly a secure basis on which to found a theory of the original meaning of blessing.

Wehmeier (1970:194-196), Scharbert (1975a:296), and Westermann (1978:49-53) view Balaam as a specially endowed person able to impart effective blessings independently from God. The narrative is particularly important because it shows how the former view, wherein blessing could be imparted by gifted persons such as Balaam, was "Yahwistized." The story was reworked so that in the biblical version Yahweh is the sole bestower of blessing. No man can curse those whom Yahweh has blessed, and Balaam's blessing of Israel is simply a declaration of Yahweh's blessing.

But archeological discoveries again make the presumed magical view of blessing in the "pre-Yahwistic" version of the story untenable. Balaam was a diviner (Akkadian bārû) who accurately predicted whether the gods would bless or curse people; he himself denied that he could utter benedictions or curses contrary to the signs which indicated what the gods would do. Balaam's statements are not later Yahwistic additions; they are an essential part of the role of the diviner as described in extra-biblical texts (see 4.1.2).

6.5 The Power of the Spoken Word

Many authors (Pedersen 1926, Hempel 1961, Mowinckel 1961, Lauterbach 1939, Scharbert 1958a:20, 1975a:304, Blank 1950 and 1961) have attributed the power of spoken benedictions to a belief in the magical power of words. The notion that the spoken word was considered a powerful, dynamic entity which inevitably brought to pass what it stated, has been a popular belief among many biblical scholars besides those who have written on blessing, and among many scholars in religious and anthropological fields unrelated to biblical studies (see the authors cited in Thiselton 1974). Many scholars have used blessings and curses to illustrate the self-fulfilling power of the word.

There are two basic reasons why this view of the spoken word inaccurately describes blessing. First, oral blessings and curses are performative or illocutionary speech acts (so also Thiselton 1974, and Austin 1962:159 who list blessings and curses under a subclass of performative utterances called behabitives; on illocutionary utterances see further under 1.1). Illocutionary speech acts are not based on magic, but on societal conventions. The words *must* be spoken in the socially accepted situation, by the proper person, and in the proper form, or else the utterance is invalid; *the words in themselves have no power* (on this point see especially Thiselton 1974). Prov 27:14, for example, says that when a greeting blessing is spoken in a loud voice too early in the morning (an inappropriate form and context), people will respond to it as if it was a curse! Clearly, the blessing words themselves are not self-fulfilling.

But when the speech act is performed properly and in the appropriate context, society accepts the illocutionary utterance as an accomplished act. Isaac's testamental blessing in Gen 27 is a prime example of such an illocutionary speech act. When the patriarch refers to his death, and issues an oral disposition of his estate in the form of a blessing, then the testament is considered legally binding, and it cannot be rescinded. The effective power of the benediction has nothing whatsoever to do with magic words or the transfer of soul power any more than modern legal oaths or a notarized will. As in many modern oaths, Isaac also called upon *God* to enforce the disposition (see 4.1.1).

The second point about the power of words is related. The verses that biblical scholars usually cite to establish the self-fulfilling power of words (for example Gen 1; Jer 1:9-10; Isa 55:10-11) refer to words *spoken by God*. The strength of the words in these verses depends on the fact that God, or a representative of God (a prophet), spoke them. The performative speech is only valid when spoken by the proper person. The words of a false prophet, though spoken in the same form and context as a legitimate prophet's words, are invalid, that is, they are not fulfilled.

When God, or a representative of God, is the speaker, the illocutionary utterance is not wholly dependent on societal conventions for its effectiveness; society may recognize both a true and a false prophet as operating in the accepted manner, or it may not recognize a true prophet (such as Jeremiah) as valid. Nevertheless, the words of a true prophet are still effective (they are still fulfilled), not because of any power inherent in the words, but because God has the power to fulfill the words.

The importance of the identity of the speaker in performative utterances has obvious implications for blessing. The effectiveness of God's promises and benedictions is based on his ability to bestow fertility, wealth, dominion, health, and other benefits. The covenantal blessings outlined by Moses are likewise effective because Moses is God's spokesman, and when the people pronounce the blessings in the covenant renewal ceremony (Josh 8:33-34), the people are speaking according to God's instructions through Moses.

The Priestly blessing is effective because the priests mediate on behalf of God. God promises to honor their benedictions (Num 6:27). God strikingly fulfilled Eli the priest's blessing of Hannah (1 Sam 2:20-21). When the Kings David and Solomon bless the people, they, like the priests, have an effective blessing because of their status as mediators. Balaam's blessings accurately describe God's past and future benefaction toward Israel because Balaam is a competent diviner.

Yet other blessings can be spoken by anyone, not just specially authorized persons. Many of the greetings, thanksgivings, praises and wishes are spoken by ordinary people in everyday situations. However, these blessings are much less effective than those spoken by God or by God's representatives. They are purely social customs, which society, and the speaker, do not expect to be fulfilled immediately or in a dramatic manner.

There are three reasons for the power that these human benedictions do have: 1) God is often invoked in the formula to bless; 2) the blessings rely on God's general retribution; and 3) the blessings rely on God's responsiveness to prayer (on these reasons see 6.2). The benedictions, then, obviously depend on God's power, not on the magical power of the spoken word.

Furthermore, there are biblical passages which explicitly deny the autonomous power of words. Words are no substitute for deeds (Prov 14:23); words cannot alter facts (Prov 24:12; 26:23-28; 28:24); and words cannot compel a response; they are ineffective if the person addressed does not understand them, and sometimes even if he does (Prov 2:3,4; 17:4,10; 29:19; on words in Proverbs see further Kidner 1964:147 and on 11:11 under 3.1.3).

God has the power to annul blessings and curses. He changed Balaam's intended curse into a blessing (Deut 23:6; Josh 24:10; Neh 13:2), and threatened to change the priests' benedictions into curses (Mal 2:2).

Even people have the ability to annul blessings and curses by calling upon God to bless or curse. Micaiah's mother changed her curse into a blessing simply by pronouncing a blessing over her son (Judg 17:2). Pharaoh acknowledged Moses' ability to bless him and so remove God's curse from his land (Exod 12:32), as does David with the Gibeonites (2 Sam 21:3). Solomon declares himself to be *bārûk*, i.e., that he stands in a favorable relationship to God (1 Kgs 2:45), and so Shimei's curse over his dynasty (2 Sam 16:5-13) is ineffective.

There is obviously no room at all for a magical, automatic view of the spoken word. The words are powerful only because they are illocutionary utterances and because they call upon God to act.

6.6   Power Transfer and Blessing

Though God occasionally blesses by bestowing power upon people, God usually blesses through the natural processes. There is no good biblical evidence for a "Segenskraft," a power distinct from God through which blessing is bestowed. Human blessings never transfer power to other people or to God. Human blessings often simply express the speaker's sentiments and do not make the addressee acquire material goods.

Scholars have tended to define God's blessing activity as a transfer of power. Pedersen (1926) especially carries this idea to the extreme and claims that when God blesses someone, God's power and the person's soul combine to such an extent that they are indistinguishable (see 2.1). It is true that God's blessing sometimes does consist of a bestowal of strength or ability and not simply of a bestowal of external material benefits (see especially 6.7). But in those cases the Bible is at pains to distinguish between the strength or ability God gives and the person's natural ability. In a verse discussing the covenantal blessings God warns against thinking, "My own ability and strength brought me this prosperity" (Deut 8:17; see also the criticism of Pedersen's interpretation of Judg 7:13-22 under 2.1).

Most of the time God blesses by promoting the natural processes rather than by bestowing power upon the person. Wehmeier (1970:133-134) reflects Pedersen's ideas when, for example, in verses involving plant and animal fertility, he interprets the statement "Yahweh blessed so-and-so" to mean "Jahwe hat N.N. die Kraft der Vermehrung und des Gedeihens zugeeignet," and talks about the blessing manifesting itself ("ässert sich") in the form of children, etc.

Verses such as Gen 26:12; 30:27,30; 39:5; Job 42:12 make it clear, however, that the plants and animals of those persons blessed reproduced naturally. God did not bestow power, but the rain, sun, food, etc., necessary for the plants and animals to thrive. Though Wehmeier generally argues against the presence of magical and animistic concepts of blessing in the extant text, he still occasionally speaks of God blessing by means of a "Segenskraft" or "Macht" when in fact God blessed using the natural processes (see especially on Lev 25:21 under 3.1.2).

Humans do not transfer power to each other when they bless each other. The assumption that they do is based on a misunderstanding of the purpose of the testamental blessing in Gen 27 (see 4.1.1). Pedersen (1926:202-203), Mowinckel (1961:9), and Westermann 1978:59-63) see greetings as magical transfers of power. Pedersen and Mowinckel base their view on the assumption that because blessing is a transfer of power, greetings must transfer power too, since greetings often contain benedictions. Westermann views greetings, including modern greetings, as magical because he misunderstands the nature of greetings as performative utterances. Just because God is not invoked in a greeting does not mean that the greeting relies on magic to effect what it says.

The greeting is an illocutionary speech act. By pronouncing the socially accepted words of greeting the speaker acknowledges the person's presence and expresses friendly intentions toward him. The person who says "šālôm," or even a greeting invoking God, such as yĕbārekkā yhwh, really does not expect the person greeted suddenly to acquire prosperity or some other blessing; greetings often are not intended to effect what they state. They are simply an expression of the speaker's sentiments. Similarly, thanksgiving and praise blessings frequently are purely social customs intended to make the addressee feel appreciated, rather than to cause him to acquire benefits (see also under 6.5).

On the effective power of human blessings, see 6.2. On the contention that blessing God transfers power to God, see 6.3.

6.7 Deliverance and Blessing

Westermann's (1978) contention that blessing and deliverance denote two distinct activities of God is enthusiastically adopted by Wehmeier (1970:5,218-224, and 1971) and Miller (1975a:247-248), but rejected by Scharbert (1975a:306). Westermann makes two distinctions:

1) Blessing denotes God's continual activity in sustaining creation, while deliverance denotes individual isolated acts of God, and
2) God blesses through the natural processes, but delivers by supernatural or miraculous events.

There certainly are large differences both in the range of meaning and in the range of application between *brk* and the words of deliverance. But both of Westermann's distinctions fail in many passages employing *brk*.

Contrary to Westermann's hypothesis, blessing and deliverance are closely intertwined. The supreme act of deliverance is the Exodus and Conquest. The land is also one of the most important benefits of the patriarchal blessing promises. Many passages promise the land as a result of God's blessing (see 3.1.1).

The blessing theme of dominion/victory is indistinguishable from deliverance. Though dominion is never the sole element of God's blessing, it is a major element of blessing in Gen 1:28-30; 9:1-3; 12:3; 22:17; 27:29; Exod 23:20-33; Deut 7:14-18; 15:6; 28:1; 33:11. In Exod 23:20-33, God's blessing activity (v 25) is an integral part of God enabling Israel to conquer Canaan. Balaam recognizes that Israel is blessed (*bārûk*, Num 22:12), because God is delivering her from Egypt (23:22; 24:8).

Scharbert (1975a:306) justifiably rejects Westermann's hypothesis because dominion/victory is a theme of blessing: dominion "is a blessing that not only guarantees powers of nature and life interwoven with the continuous providence of God . . . but also helps to control extraordinary historical situations."

Blessing and deliverance are even more closely intertwined in the prophetic apocalypses. Westermann (1978) himself recognizes how close the two are (39-40,63-64), and concludes:

> the apocalypses use the language of blessing . . . All powers of destruction . . . are overcome . . . and thus in the culmination there can no longer be any salvation in the sense of rescue, deliverance, or liberation. To speak of "eternal salvation" is to speak of salvation only in the sense of blessing (63).

Since the prophets describe the coming salvation as the inauguration of a state of blessing, Westermann is unjustified in claiming that blessing "cannot be experienced in an event" and that blessing is always a result or "secondary feature" of deliverance (4).

brk occurs in deliverance contexts in Isa 19:24-25; 44:3; 61:9; 65:23; Ezek 34:26; Zech 8:13. Blessing is equated with deliverance also in Pss 3:9; 21:6a (cf. 4a); 28:9; 67:3b (cf. 2a); 109:26b,31b (cf. 28a).

In psalms reciting God's beneficent deeds, such as Pss 106, 107, and Neh 9:5-31, God's acts of blessing are listed beside his acts of deliverance with no indication that the two represent separate types of God's activity.

Incidentally, if *bārûk* did in fact mean "voll Segen" as Wehmeier claims,

Conclusions

then it would provide further evidence against Westermann's hypothesis (adopted whole-heartedly by Wehmeier), since it is often used to praise God for his acts of deliverance.

6.8 Some Close Synonyms of God Blessing Man

During the course of my research I assembled a complete file of all the synonymous and antonymous collocations of the *brk* derivatives. I soon realized the impossibility of comparing and contrasting all of the words in any detail. *brk* is used in a large variety of contexts to denote a wide range of actions, both by God and by man. There are no words which are close synonyms of one of the *brk* derivatives throughout all of its meanings. There are few words which are close synonyms of one of the *brk* derivatives throughout its range of meaning within one of the three areas of God blessing man, man blessing man, or man praising God. However, there is a plethora of words which can become close synonyms of a *brk* derivative in certain specific contexts. I have chosen, therefore, simply to discuss a few close synonyms to the *brk* derivatives in the area of God blessing man (but see also the index of synonyms and antonyms, and below, for other words).

The most important synonyms are other words which denote God's grace and favor, such as ʾāhab, ḥānan and ḥēn, ḥesed, and rāṣâ and rāṣôn, since the connotation of God's favor is that which makes a blessing a blessing (see 6.1).

Although no semantic field study of *brk* has been done, several authors have discussed the relation of some synonyms and antonyms to *brk*. Mowinckel (1961), Hempel (1961), Pedersen (1926), Blank (1950), Scharbert (1958a), Brichto (1963) and Schottroff (1969) have compared curse-words to *brk*. Brichto's study is the most useful. Scharbert's study, though much shorter, is also quite helpful. Pedersen also discusses some words for wisdom, understanding, ability, counsel, and success, but he simply equates these with blessing. Henderson (1977) has a helpful brief discussion of the relation of ʾašrê, šālôm, ṣlḥ, and minḥâ to *brk*. Janzen (1965) gives an excellent discussion of the relation of ʾašrê to blessing. Vetter (1971) offers an excellent analysis of God's presence (God being with, ʾēt or ʿim, someone) as an expression denoting God's blessing.

Semantic field theory is quite helpful for lexicographers. It is unfortunate that the methods are often so difficult to implement, particularly for non-referential words such as the words related to *brk* which resist componential analysis.

Here I will discuss ʾašrê and šālôm. See also the discussions of ḥesed under 4.2.4, *rṣh* and *rāṣôn* in Deut 33 under 4.1.1, *ḥnn* in Num 6:25 under 4.2.1 and in Gen 33:11 under 4.3, the numerous synonyms for praising God under 5.2. and 5.3, and the curse-words on Deut 28 under 3.1.2, under 4.1.2, and under 5.5. I have also made an effort throughout this study to discuss these and other synonyms and antonyms as they co-occurred with *brk*.

The word that is the closest synonym to a form of *brk* is *ʾašrê*. *ʾašrê* denotes a person who has been blessed by God, i.e., a person who is *bārûk*. *ʾašrê* is synonymous with *bārûk* over the entire range of meaning of *ʾašrê*; all that can be called *ʾašrê* can be called *bārûk*. The study of *ʾašrê* reveals that "receipt of that which blessing has to bestow qualifies a person or group to be called *ʾašrê*" (Janzen 1965:223, contra Mowinckel 1961:2). The reference of *ʾašrê* is identical to the reference of *bārûk* applied to man.

However, all that can be called *bārûk* cannot necessarily be called *ʾašrê*. The range of meaning and of application of *bārûk* is much wider. *ʾašrê* is only used in declarative statements describing people, while *bārûk* can be used in both declarative and optative descriptions of people, and of plants, animals, objects, days, abstract qualities, and God. *ʾašrê* is also largely limited to the wisdom literature, while *bārûk* occurs throughout the Bible.

The *ʾašrê* formula is used in three ways. It can: 1) declare that a person already possess blessings (1 Kgs 10:8 = 2 Chr 9:7; Deut 33:29; Ps 144:15); 2) declare that a person will be blessed in the future (Job 5:17; cf. vv 18-26, Prov 29:18); and 3) express declarative praise of the pious, usually an abstract ideal pious person rather than an actual person; a description of the pious person's present and future blessings is often part of the praise (Ps 1:1; 32:1-2; 34:9). The third use is the most common (on this classification compare Janzen 1965: 222-223 note 22). The declarative *bārûk* formula can also be used in each of these three ways, though again, it has many other uses which *ʾašrê* does not have.

There is no word frequently found together with *ʾašrê* in contrast to it. Mowinckel (1961:2,10,11,88) and Wehmeier (1970:105-106) see the pair *ʾašrê/hôy* (or *ʾoy*) as analogous to *bārûk/ʾārûr*. Yet the evidence for *hôy* (*ʾôy*) as a formulaic antonym to *ʾašrê* is limited to 1) emended readings at Isa 3:10-11 and Qoh 10:16-17; 2) *ʾašrê* formulas in Isa 10:18; 32:20 which are in the vicinity of, but are not directly contrasted with, some *hôy* statements, and 3) the *makarios/ouai* pronouncements of Luke 6:20-29. Janzen (1965:220) suggests that it was the Luke passage which gave rise to the *ʾašrê/hôy* hypothesis. Since the biblical evidence is "meagre indeed," he correctly concludes that at most *hôy* was simply one possible

Conclusions 181

antonym to *ʾašrê*, and that the meanings "blessing" and "curse" should not be ascribed to *ʾašrê/hôy* simply by analogy to the word-pair *bārûk/ʾārûr*.

Janzen (1965) feels that because *ʾašrê* and *bārûk* have different etymologies, they must still have some difference in meaning, although they became "nearly identical"; each word still must have a "real essence and irreducible core" of meaning (224). Janzen has succumbed to the "root fallacy" (on which see 1.2).

Janzen postulates that the "core" of *ʾašrê* is "envious desire" (225). This is why *ʾašrê* is never used of God by man, nor of man by God, nor of oneself. Man cannot attain the nature of God, nor could God envy man's condition. Neither could man envy plants or animals.

This hypothesis fails on two counts. First, Janzen fails to give even a single passage in which envy is evident; he merely states his hypothesis. One might expect envy to be present in the use of *ʾašrê* in the Queen of Sheba narrative (1 Kgs 10:8 = 2 Chr 9:7), but there is no mention of it. In other passages, such as Job 5:17 where Eliphaz calls the ailing Job *ʾašrê*, envy is quite out of the question. Secondly, even if *ʾašrê* did connote envy, this would not differentiate it from *brk*. Envy is quite evident in the use of *bārûk* by Abimelek to describe Isaac (Gen 26:29), and in Esau's recognition that Isaac had been blessed (Gen 27, especially v 33; cf. also Laban and Jacob in Gen 30:27).

Comparison of, for example, *bārûk* in Jer 17:7 with *ʾašrê* in Pss 1:1; 40:5 shows that the two words are completely synonymous in these passages. The difference in meaning between the words lies only in the larger ranges of meaning and application of *bārûk*, and its different distribution in the Bible. When *bārûk* is used in one of the three types of statements that can also employ *ʾašrê* (see above), the two words are synonymous.

Hempel (1961:58-61) was the first to suggest that the entire content of blessing is summed up in the term *šālôm*. Many later authors have followed this suggestion (for example, Mowinckel 1962:2.44-45, Beyer 1964:756, Horst 1947:30).

Westermann (1978:29) rejects the idea, claiming that blessing is transmitted diachronically in the patriarchal narratives, while *šālôm* denotes the synchronic well-being of a community. Westermann's distinction, however, is invalid. Diachronic transmission is an essential part of the patriarchal blessing promises because they were *promises*, not because they are promises of blessing (see further 3.1.1). Elsewhere in the OT, God's blessings, unless they were promises, were normally fulfilled in the recipient's lifetime (as they were to some extent in the patriarchal narratives), and the testamental blessings are the only type of blessing regularly passed on to the next generation.

Wehmeier (1970:140) rejects the equation of blessing with šālôm based on Ps 29:11, since šālôm, which Wehmeier there translates "Frieden," is just one of the benefits God can bestow when he blesses. But this is not the meaning of šālôm which Hempel equates with blessing—he defines šālôm in a broader sense as "der Zustand des Unversehrt- und Ungefährdetseins, der Ruhe und Sicherheit, des Glückes und des Heiles im weitesten Umfang" (1961:59).

The natural impulse of any lexicographer is to reject the equation of one word with another. Many semanticists are of the opinion that in any language, two words can never have precisely identical meanings, though they can have identical referents. Hempel (1961), however, merely claims that the benefits bestowed when God blesses comprise that which is denoted by šālôm; he claims that the referents of šālôm and běrākâ are identical, and in this he is basically correct.

Certainly there are some differences. šālôm rarely explicitly includes fertility, a major benefit of blessing. šālôm often denotes military peace which, as Wehmeier points out, is only one benefit that can be included in God's blessing (especially the blessings of dominion and deliverance). But šālôm can be used in a much wider sense. In Deut 29:18, the apostate considers himself blessed (brk, Hithpael) and thinks, "I will have šālôm." šālôm denotes the prosperity, health, longevity, wealth, fertility, security, and peace promised by God in the covenantal blessings. The closing benediction Ps 128:5-6 equates šālôm with the prosperous condition which results from God's blessing:

> May Yahweh bless you from Zion;
> may you see Jerusalem in prosperity (ṭûb) all
> the days of your life.
> May you see your children's children.
> Peace (šālôm) be upon Israel!

Greetings and farewells use šālôm and forms of brk interchangeably. For example, šālôm lěkā (Judg 19:20) is similar to yěbārekkā yhwh (Ruth 2:4b) or bārûk ʾattâ lyhwh (1 Sam 15:13) (cf. also 1 Sam 25:5-6 v.s. v 14; there are many other examples).

Finally, God bestows šālôm out of his favorable attitude toward a person, just as he blesses out of his favor. In the Priestly benediction (Num 6:24-26), the concluding phrase "May he give you peace (šālôm),"

Conclusions

balances the opening phrase, "May Yahweh bless you"; these two general phrases form an *inclusio* around the middle three lines which are specific descriptions of God's favor and graciousness.

Yet šālôm is not the only word that can closely approximate the content of blessing. ṭûb in Ps 128:5 (discussed immediately above) also denotes the state of being blessed. Deut 30:15 equates the benefits of the covenantal blessings with haḥayyîm wehaṭṭôb, and v 19 equates the covenantal blessings, habběrākâ, with haḥayyîm. The verses describe the antonym of God's blessing as hammāwet (v 15,19) and hāraʿ (v 15).

Table 1

The Occurrences of brk "Bless" in the Bible

	Qal	Niph.	Piel	Pual	Hith.	berakâ	Total
Gen	8	3	59	-	2	16	88
Exod	1	-	5	-	-	1	7
Lev	-	-	2	-	-	1	3
Num	2	-	14	1	-	-	17
Deut	9	-	28	1	1	12	51
Josh	-	-	8	-	-	2	10
Judg	1	-	3	2	-	1	7
1 Sam	7	-	4	-	-	2	13
2 Sam	3	-	10	1	-	1	15
1 Kgs	6	-	6	-	-	-	12
2 Kgs	-	-	3	-	-	2	5
Isa	2	-	4	-	2	4	12
Jer	2	-	1	-	1	-	4
Ezek	1	-	-	-	-	3	4
The 12	1	-	1	-	-	4	6
Pss	17	-	52	4	1	9	83
Prov	1	-	3	2	-	8	14
Job	-	-	7	1	-	1	9
Ruth	4	-	1	-	-	-	5
Cant	-	-	-	-	-	-	-
Qoh	-	-	-	-	-	-	-
Lam	-	-	-	-	-	-	-
Esth	-	-	-	-	-	-	-
Dan	1	-	2	1	-	-	4
Ezra	1	-	-	-	-	-	1
Neh	-	-	4	-	-	2	6
1 Chron	2	-	13	1	-	-	16
2 Chron	3	-	5	-	-	2	10
Torah	20	3	108	2	3	30	166
Prophets	23	-	40	3	3	19	88
Writings	29	-	87	9	1	22	148
Total	72	3	235	14	7	71	402

Table 2
The Genesis Niphal and Hithpael Passages and Later Allusions to Them

Passage	Verb	Subject	Means	Addressee
Gen 12:3	wĕnibrĕkû	kōl mišpĕḥōt hāʾădāmâ	bĕkā	Abraham
Gen 18:18	wĕnibrĕkû	kōl gôyê hāʾāreṣ	bô	Abraham
Gen 22:18	wĕhitbārăkû	kōl gôyê hāʾāreṣ	bĕzarʿăkā	Abraham
Gen 26:4	wĕhitbārăkû	kōl gôyê hāʾāreṣ	bĕzarʿăkā	Isaac
Gen 28:14	wĕnibrăkû	kōl mišpĕḥōt hāʾădāmâ	bĕkā ûbĕzarʿekā	Jacob
Jer 4:2	wĕhitbārăkû	gôyim	bô	the nation of Israel
Ps 72:17	wĕyitbārĕkû	kol gôyim	bô	prayer to God

Bibliography

Allis, Oswald T.
1927 "The Blessing of Abraham," *Princeton Theological Review* 25: 263-298.

Anderson, Francis I.
1976 *Job.* Downers Grove: Inter-Varsity Press.

Asensio, Felix
1967 "Trayectoria historico-teológica de la 'Benedición' bíblica de Yahveh en labios del hombre," *Gregorianum* 48: 253-283. (Rome).

Audet, Jean-Paul
1958 "Esquisse historique du genre littéraire de la 'bénédiction' juive et de l'"Eucharistie' chrétienne," *RB* 65: 371-399. Revised English translation:

1959 "Literary Forms and Contents of a Normal *Eucharistia* in the First Century," *Studia Evangelica*, F. L. Cross, ed., Berlin, 643-662.

Austin, John
1962 *How To Do Things With Words.* Oxford: Clarendon Press.

Bach, Kent and Robert Harnish
1979 *Linguistic Communication and Speech Acts.* Cambridge, Mass,: The MIT Press.

Baldwin, Joyce
1972 *Haggai, Zechariah, Malachi.* Downers Grove: Inter-Varsity Press.

Barr, James
1961 *The Semantics of Biblical Language.* Oxford: Oxford University Press.

1968   *Comparative Philology and the Text of the Old Testament.* Oxford: Clarendon Press.

Bauer, Hans and Pontus Leander
1962   *Historische Grammatik der hebräischen Sprache des Alten Testaments.* Hildesheim: Georg Olms.

Bergsträsser, Gotthelf
1962   *Hebäische Grammatik* I/II. Hildesheim: Georg Olms.

Beyer, Hermann W.
1964   "*eulogéo*," *TDNT* 2.754-765.

Bickerman, E. J.
1962   "Bénédiction et prière," *RB* 69: 524-532.

Blachère, Régis: Moustafa Chouémi and Claude Denizeau
1967   *Dictionnaire Arabe-Francais-Anglais.* Paris: G.-P. Maisonneuve et Larose.

Blank, Sheldon
1950   "The Curse, Blasphemy, the Spell and the Oath," *HUCA* 23/1: 73-95.

1961   "Some Observations Concerning Biblical Prayer," *HUCA* 32: 75-90.

Blau, Joshua
1976   *A Grammar of Biblical Hebrew.* Wiesbaden: Otto Harrassowitz.

Boling, Robert G.
1982   *Joshua*, AB 6. Garden City: Doubleday.

Brichto, Herbert
1963   *The Problem of "Curse" in the Hebrew Bible*, JBL Monograph Series 13. Philadelphia: Society of Biblical Literature and Exegesis.

Bright, John
1965   *Jeremiah*, AB 21. Garden City: Doubleday.

Brockelmann, Carl
1913   *Grundriss der vergleichenden Grammatik der semitischen Sprachen* I/II. Berlin: Reuther und Reichard.

1956   *Hebräische Syntax.* Neukirchen Kreis Moers.

Brown, Francis; S. R. Driver and Charles A. Briggs
1953   *A Hebrew and English Lexicon of the Old Testament.* Oxford: Clarendon Press.

Bynon, Theodora
    1977   *Historical Linguistics*. Cambridge: Cambridge University Press.

Campbell, Edward
    1975   *Ruth*, AB 7. Garden City: Doubleday.

Campbell, J. Y.
    1962   "Blessedness," *IDB* 1.445-446.

Cassuto, Umberto
    1967   *A Commentary on the Book of Exodus*. Jerusalem: Magnes Press.

    1978   *A Commentary on the Book of Genesis*. Jerusalem: Magnes Press.

Cazelles, Henri
    1974   "ʾašrê," *TDOT* 1.445-448.

Chelhod, Joseph
    1955   "La baraka chez les Arabes ou l'influence bienfaisante du sacré," *RHR* 148: 68-88.

Childs, Brevard S.
    1974   *Exodus*, OTL. London: SCM Press.

Cohen, Marcel
    1928   "Genou, famille, force dans le monde chamito-sémitique," *Memorial Henri Basset*. Paris: Librairie orientaliste Paul Geuthner, 203-210.

Cooke, G. A.
    1936   *A Critical and Exegetical Commentary on the Book of Ezekiel*, ICC. Edinburgh: T. and T. Clark.

Coppens, J.
    1957   "La Bénédiction de Jacob. Son cadre historique à la lumière des paralleles Ougaritiques," VTSup 4: 97-115.

Corney, Richard W.
    1962   "Obed-edom," *IDB* 3.579-580.

Cowley, A. E.
    1910   *Gesenius' Hebrew Grammar*. Oxford: Clarendon Press.

Craigie, Peter C.
    1976   *The Book of Deuteronomy*, NICOT. Grand Rapids: Eerdmans.

Cross, Frank M., and David N. Freedman
    1948   "The Blessing of Moses," *JBL* 67: 191-210.

Dahood, Mitchell
    1966   *Psalms I*, AB 16. Garden City: Doubleday.

    1968   *Psalms II*, AB 17. Garden City: Doubleday.

    1970   *Psalms III*, AB 17A. Garden City: Doubleday.

Davidson, A. B.
    1901   *Hebrew Syntax*. Edinburgh: T. and T. Clark.

Driver, S. R.
    1905   *The Book of Genesis*. London: Methuen.

Driver, S. R., and George B. Gray
    1921   *A Critical and Exegetical Commentary on the Book of Job*, ICC. New York: Charles Scribner's Sons.

Eichrodt, Walther
    1970   *Ezekiel*, OTL. Philadelphia: Westminster.

Fensham, F. Charles
    1962   "Malediction and Benediction in Ancient Near Eastern Vassal-Treaties and the OT," *ZAW* 74: 1-9.

    1982   *The Books of Ezra and Nehemiah*, NICOT. Grand Rapids: Eerdmans.

Fishbane, Michael
    1983   "Form and Reformulation of the biblical Priestly Blessing," *JAOS* 103: 115-121.

Fodor, Janet Dean
    1980   *Semantics: Theories of Meaning in Generative Grammar*. Cambridge, Mass: Harvard University Press.

Funk, Robert W.; F. Blass and A. Debrunner
    1961   *A Greek Grammar of the New Testament and Other Early Christian Literature*. Chicago: University of Chicago Press.

Gehrke, Ralph D.
    1968   *1 and 2 Samuel*. St. Louis: Concordia.

Gelb, I. J., et alii
    1964   *The Assyrian Dictionary of the Oriental Institute of the University of Chicago*. Chicago: The Oriental Institute.

Gerleman, Gillis
    1965   *Ruth. Das Hohelied*, BKAT. Neukirchener.

Gevirtz, Stanley
    1960   *Curse Motifs in the Old Testament and in the Ancient Near East.* Dissertation, University of Chicago.

    1962   "Curse," *IDB* 1.749-750.

Gray, John
    1964   *1 and 2 Kings.* London: SCM Press.

Guillet, Jacques
    1969   "Le language spontané de la bénédiction dans l'Ancien Testament," *RSR* 57: 163-204.

Hamilton, Victor P.
    1980a   "ʾārar," *TWOT* 1.75-76.

    1980b   "ʾāšar," *TWOT* 1.80-82.

Harrelson, Walter J.
    1962   "Blessings and Cursings," *IDB* 1.446-448.

Harris, R. Laird
    1980   "ḥsd," *TWOT* 1.698-700.

Harrison, Roland K.
    1969   *Introduction to the Old Testament.* Grand Rapids: Eerdmans.

    1973   *Jeremiah and Lamentations.* Downers Grove: Inter-Varsity Press.

Heestermans, H.
    1980   "Some Aspects of Diachronic Semantics," *Proceedings of the Second International Round Table Conference on Historical Lexicography*, W. Pijnenburg and F. de Tollenaere, eds. Cinnaminson, N. J.: Foris Publications.

Hempel, Johannes
    1961   "Die israelitische Anschauungen von Segen und Fluch im Lichte altorientalischer Parallelen," BZAW 81: 30-113, originally published in *ZDMG* 79 (1925): 20-110.

Henderson, Melvin Eugene
    1977   *The Significance of Blessing in Genesis 12-50.* Dissertation, New Orleans Baptist Seminary.

Hertzberg, Hans Wilhelm
1964   *1 and 2 Samuel*, OTL. London: SCM Press.

Hicks, R. Lansing
1962   "Abraham," *IDB* 1.14-21.

Horst, Friedrich
1947   "Segen und Segenshandlungen in der Bibel," *EvT* 7: 23-37, also in *Gottes Recht. Theologische Bücherei* 12 (1961): 188-202.

1968   *Hiob*, BKAT 16. Neukirchener.

Janzen, Waldemar
1965   "ʾašrê in the Old Testament," *HTR* 58/2: 215-226.

Jeffers, Robert, and Ilse Lehiste
1979   *Principles and Methods for Historical Linguistics.* Cambridge, Mass.: The MIT Press.

Jeffrey, Arthur
1938   *The Foreign Vocabulary of the Quran.* Lahore: al-Biruni.

Junker, H.
1959   "Segen als heilsgeschichtliches Motivwort im AT," BETL 12/13: 548-558.

Käser, Walter
1970   "Beobachtungen zum altestamentlichen Makarismus," *ZAW* 82:225-250.

Katz, Jerrold J.
1977   *Propositional Structure and Illocutionary Force: A Study of the Contribution of Sentence Meaning to Speech Acts.* New York: Crowell.

Kedar, Benjamin
1981   *Biblische Semantik.* Stuttgart: W. Kohlhammer.

Keil, C. F., and Franz Delitzsch
1866-   *Commentary on the Old Testament in Ten Volumes.*
1877   Grand Rapids: Eerdmans (cited by biblical book and page number).

Keller, C. A.
1978   "brk," *THAT* 1.353-367.

Kempson, Ruth M.
1977   *Semantic Theory.* Cambridge: Cambridge University Press.

Kidner, Derek
 1964   *Proverbs*. Downers Grove: Inter-Varsity Press.

 1967   *Genesis*. Downers Grove: Inter-Varsity Press.

Koehler, Ludwig and Walter Baumgartner
 1958   *Lexicon in Veteris Testamenti Libros*. Leiden: E. J. Brill.

Kraus, Hans-Joachim
 1961   *Die Psalmen*, BKAT 15. Neukirchener.

Laetsch, Theodore
 1956   *The Minor Prophets*. St. Louis: Concordia.

Landsberger, B.
 1928   "Das 'gute Wort'," *Mitteilungen der Altorientalischen Gesellschaft* 4: 294-321.

Lauterbach, Jacob Z.
 1939   "The Belief in the Power of the Word," *HUCA* 14: 287-302.

Leech, Geoffrey
 1974   *Semantics*. New York: Penguin Books.

Lehrer, Adrianne
 1974   *Semantic Fields and Lexical Structure*. Amsterdam: North-Holland.

Leupold, Herbert C.
 1942   *Exposition of Genesis*. Grand Rapids: Baker Book House.

 1969   *Exposition of the Psalms*. Grand Rapids: Baker Book House.

 1976   *Exposition of Isaiah*. Grand Rapids: Baker Book House.

Liebreich, Leon J.
 1955   "The Songs of Ascent and the Priestly Blessings," *JBL* 74:33-36.

Lipinski, E.
 1968   "Macarismes et psaumes de congratulation," *RB* 75:321-367.

Lyons, John
 1977   *Semantics I/II*. Cambridge: Cambridge University Press.

Mayes, A. D. H.
1979   *Deuteronomy*, NCB. Greenwood, S. C.: Attic Press.

McCarter, P. Keil
1980   *1 Samuel*, AB 8. Garden City: Doubleday.

McComiskey, Thomas
1980   *"nāzîr," TWOT* 2.568.

McKane, William
1970   *Proverbs*, OTL. Philadelphia: Westminster.

Mendelsohn, I.
1959   "On the Preferential Status of the Eldest Son," *BASOR* 156:38-40.

Miller, Patrick
1975   "The Blessing of God: An Interpretation of Num 6:22-27," *Int* 29: 240-251.

Montgomery, James A.
1927   *A Critical and Exegetical Commentary on the Book of Daniel*, ICC. Edinburgh: T. and T. Clark.

Morton, William
1962   "Baca, Valley of," *IDB* 1.338.

Mowinckel, Sigmund
1953   *Religion und Kultus*. Gottingen: Vandenhoek und Ruprecht.

1961   *Segen und Fluch in Israels Kult und Psalmendichtung. Psalmenstudien V*. Amsterdam: P. Schippers. Originally published in 1924.

1962   *The Psalms in Israel's Worship*. Oxford: Basil Blackwell.

Mowvley, Harry
1965   "The Concept and Content of 'Blessing' in the Old Testament," *BT* 16: 74-80.

Muilenberg, James
1965   "Abraham and the Nations: Blessing and World History," *Int* 19: 387-398.

Murtonen, A.
1959   "The Use and Meaning of the Words *lĕbārēk* and *bĕrākāh* in the Old Testament," *VT* 9: 158-177.

Myers, Jacob
  1965   *1 Chronicles*, AB 12. Garden City: Doubleday.

Nida, Eugene
  1972   "Implications of Contemporary Linguistics for Biblical Scholarship," *JBL* 91: 73-89.

  1975   *Componential Analysis of Meaning: An Introduction to Semantic Structures.* The Hague: Mouton.

Noth, Martin
  1928   *Die israelitischen Personennamen im Rahmen der gemeinsemitischen Namengebung*, BWANT 3. Folge, Heft 10. Stuttgart.

  1962   *Exodus*, OTL. Philadelphia: Westminster.

O'Connor, Michael
  1980   *Hebrew Verse Structure.* Winona Lake: Eisenbrauns.

Onians, Richard
  1954   *The Origins of European Thought about the Body, the Mind, the Soul, the World, Time and Fate.* Cambridge: Cambridge University Press.

Oswalt, John N.
  1980   "*bārak*," *TWOT* 1.132-133.

Payne, J. Barton
  1980   "*'abrāhām*," *TWOT* 1.6.

Pedersen, Johannes
  1914   *Der Eid bei den Semiten.* Strassburg.

  1926   *Israel, Its Life and Culture.* London: Oxford. Originally published in Danish in 1920.

Pieper, August
  1979   *Isaiah II.* Milwaukee: Northwestern Publishing House.

Plassmann, Thomas
  1913   *The Signification of bĕrākâ.* New York: Joseph F. Wagner.

  1949   "The Semitic Root *brk*," *CBQ* 11: 445-446.

Pope, Marvin H.
  1962   "Oaths," *IDB* 3.575-577.

  1973   *Job*, AB 15. Garden City: Doubleday.

Quemda, Bernard
  1972   "Lexicology and Lexicography," *Current Trends in Linguistics* 9: 395-475.

von Rad, Gerhard
  1972   *Genesis*, OTL. Philadelphia: Westminster.

Rendsburg, Gary
  1980   "Janus Parallelism in Gen 49:26," *JBL* 99: 291-293.

Robertson, A. T.
  1934   *A Grammar of the Greek New Testament in the Light of Historical Research*. Nashville: Broadman Press.

Rosen, Sanford
  1975   *The Human Blessers and Blessed in the Bible*. Dissertation, Hebrew Union College.

Sarna, Nahum
  1957   "Epic Substratum in the Prose of Job," *JBL* 76: 13-25.

Scharbert, Josef
  1958a   "'Fluchen' und 'Segnen' im Alten Testament," *Bib* 39: 1-36.

  1958b   *Solidarität in Segen und Fluch im Alten Testament und in seiner Umwelt. I, Vaterfluch und Vatersegen*, BBB 14.

  1970   "Blessing," *Sacramentum Verbi* 1.69-75. New York: Herder and Herder.

  1972   Book Review of Wehmeier 1970 in *Theologische Revue* 68: 5-8. (Münster).

  1973   "Die Geschichte der bārûk Formel," *BZ* 17: 1-28.

  1975a   "brk, bĕrākhāh," *TDOT* 2.279-308.

  1975b   "ʾālāh," *TDOT* 1.261-266.

  1975c   "ʾrr," *TDOT* 1.405-418.

Schottroff, Willy
  1969   *Der altisraelitische Fluchspruch*, WMANT 30. Neukirchener.

Schreiner, Josef
  1962   "Segen für die Völker in den Verheissungen an die Väter," *BZ* 6: 1-31.

Scott, R. B. Y.
1965   *Proverbs, Ecclesiastes*, AB 18. Garden City: Doubleday.

Silva, Moises
1983   *Biblical Words and Their Meaning: An Introduction to Lexical Semantics*. Grand Rapids: Zondervan.

Smith, Sidney
1949   "A Note on Blessings," *PEQ* 81: 57.

Snaith, Norman H.
1967   *Leviticus and Numbers*, NCB. London: Thomas Nelson.

von Soden, Wolfram
1965   *Akkadisches Handwörterbuch*. Wiesbaden: Otto Harrassowitz.

Soggin, J. Alberto
1972   *Joshua*, OTL. London: SCM Press.

Speiser, E. A.
1955   "I Know Not The Day of My Death," *JBL* 74: 252-256.

1964   *Genesis*, AB 1. Garden City: Doubleday.

Stoebe, Hans-Joachim
1973   *Das Erste Buch Samuelis*, KAT 8. Gutersloh: Gerd Mohn.

Taylor, John B.
1969   *Ezekiel*. Downers Grove: Inter-Varsity Press.

Thierry, G. J.
1963   "Remarks on Various Passages of the Psalms," *Oudtestamentische Studien* 13, P. A. H. de Boer, ed. Leiden: E. J. Brill.

Thiselton, Anthony C.
1974   "The Supposed Power of Words in the Biblical Writings," *JTS* 25: 283-299.

Thompson, John A.
1974   *Deuteronomy*. Downers Grove: Inter-Varsity Press.

1980   *The Book of Jeremiah*, NICOT. Grand Rapids: Eerdmans.

Toll, Christopher
1982   "Ausdrücke für 'Kraft' im Alten Testament mit besonderer Rücksicht auf die Wurzel BRK," *ZAW* 94: 111-123.

Towner, W. Sibley
1968   "'Blessed be YHWH' and 'Blessed art Thou, YHWH': The Modulation of a Biblical Formula," *CBQ* 30: 386-399.

Tsevat, Matitiahu
1983   "Two Old Testament Stories and Their Hittite Analogues," *JAOS* 103: 321-326.

Ullmann, Stephen
1972   "Semantics," *Current Trends in Linguistics* 9: 343-394.

Vassilyev, L. M.
1974   "The Theory of Semantic Fields: A Survey," *Linguistics* 137:79-93.

Vawter, Bruce
1955   "The Canaanite Background of Gen 49," *CBQ* 17: 1-18.

Vetter, Dieter
1971   *Jahwehs Mitsein - ein Ausdruck des Segens*. Arbeiten zur Theologie 45. Stuttgart: Calwer.

1974   *Seherspruch und Segensschilderung*. Calwer Theologische Monographien 4. Stuttgart: Calwer.

de Vries, Simon J.
1962   "Sarah," *IDB* 4.219-220.

Watts, John D. W.
1944   *A Study of běrākâ in Genesis 12:1-3*. Th.M. thesis, Baptist Bible Institute.

Wehmeier, Gerhard
1970   *Der Segen im Alten Testament*. Theologische Dissertationen 6, Bo Reicke, ed. Basel: Friedrich Reinhardt.

1971   "Deliverance and Blessing in the Old and New Testament," *Indian Journal of Theology* 20: 30-42. (Serampore).

1978   "*brk*," *THAT* 1.367-376.

Weiser, Artur
1962   *The Psalms: A Commentary*, OTL. London: SCM Press.

Bibliography

Wenham, Gordon
- 1979 — *The Book of Leviticus*, NICOT. Grand Rapids: Eerdmans.

Westerman, Claus
- 1957 — "Die Frage nach dem Segen," *Zeichen der Zeit* 11: 244-253.
- 1965 — *The Praise of God in the Psalms.* Richmond: John Knox Press.
- 1969 — *Isaiah 40-66*, OTL. London: SCM Press.
- 1978 — *Blessing in the Bible and the Life of the Church.* Philadelphia: Fortress Press.
- 1980 — *The Promises to the Fathers.* Philadelphia: Fortress Press.
- 1981 — *Genesis*, 2. Teil, Genesis 12-36, BKAT. Neukirchener.
- 1982 — *Genesis*, 3. Teil, Genesis 37-50, BKAT. Neukirchener.

Williams, Ronald J.
- 1976 — *Hebrew Syntax: An Outline.* Toronto: University of Toronto Press.

Wilson, Robert R.
- 1980 — *Prophecy and Society in Ancient Israel.* Philadelphia: Fortress Press.

Wolff, Hans Walter
- 1977 — *Joel and Amos*, Hermeneia. Philadelphia: Fortress Press.

Woudstra, Marten
- 1981 — *The Book of Joshua*, NICOT. Grand Rapids: Eerdmans.

Yamauchi, Edwin
- 1980 — "ḥānan," *TWOT* 1.302-304.

Yaron, Reuven
- 1959 — "The Coptos Decree and 2 Sam XII 14," *VT* 9:89-91.

Young, Edward J.
- 1949 — *The Prophecy of Daniel.* Grand Rapids: Eerdmans.
- 1965 — *The Book of Isaiah*, vol. 1. Grand Rapids: Eerdmans.
- 1969 — *The Book of Isaiah*, vol. 2. Grand Rapids: Eerdmans.

1972 *The Book of Isaiah*, vol. 3. Grand Rapids: Eerdmans.

Zgusta, Ladislav et alii
1971 *Manual of Lexicography*. The Hague: Mouton.

Zimmerli, Walther
1979 *Ezekiel 1*, Hermeneia. Philadelphia: Fortress Press, and
Ezechiel, 2. Teilband, BKAT. Neukirchener.

Index of Synonyms and Antonyms of BRK

Synonyms

In General, 179-180
Praise Synonyms, 126, 135, 138-142, 143, 145, 157-158, 180
ʾhb, 41, 43, 167, 179
ʾašrê, 51-52, 103, 156, 179, 180-181
ʾet, 34, 69, 71, 74, 76, 179
bḥr, 61
ḥayyîm, 42, 76, 183
ḥēn, 45, 74, 179
ḥnn, 74, 122, 126, 167, 179, 180
ḥesed, 73, 74, 96, 100, 101, 110, 111, 112, 139, 143, 151, 157, 160, 167, 179
ṭôb, ṭûb, 42, 45, 47, 49, 51, 73, 119, 182, 183
ydʿ, 71
yšʿ, 57, 60, 119
yēšûʿâ/tēšûʿâ, 46, 74, 119
kbd, 130
minḥâ, 126, 127, 179
nṣl, 57
nšq, 108
ʿzr, 87
ʿim, 34, 69, 71, 76, 93, 105, 107, 179
ʿtr, 104
pll, 103
prh, 62, 63
ṣaddîq, 46, 48
ṣēdāqâ, 46, 52, 114, 167

qdš, 65, 95
rbh, 62, 63
rûaḥ, 17, 56-57, 78, 167
rṣh, 88, 89, 96, 127, 167, 179, 180
rāṣôn, 45, 57, 89, 167, 179, 180
šālôm, 21, 46, 53, 96, 107, 179, 181-183

Antonyms

In General, 179
ʾlh, 42, 70, 112-113, 124, 161
ʾrr, 30, 33, 35, 36, 42, 48, 60, 91, 92, 93-94, 98, 128-129, 161
ʾārûr, 35, 36, 38, 40, 41, 42, 43, 86, 111, 112, 116-117, 153, 180-181
mĕʾērâ, 41, 42-43, 45, 48, 60, 94, 98
zʿm, 48, 92, 93, 161
māwet, 42, 43, 183
nʾṣ, 161, 162, 163, 164
qbb/nqb, 42, 48, 92, 93-94, 161
qll, 30, 33, 36, 42, 43, 47, 53, 93-94, 121, 123, 129-130, 161, 162
qĕlālâ, 41, 42-43, 44, 59, 82, 93-94, 107, 124, 130-131, 162
raʿ, 43, 47, 183
rāšāʿ, 47, 48

Index of Biblical Verses Containing BRK

Genesis
1:22	62, 66, 120
1:28	62-63, 66, 120, 178
2:3	35, 64-65, 95, 120
5:2	35, 63, 66, 120
9:1	62, 63, 178
9:26	41, 153, 154
12:1-3	24, 29
12:1	34, 103
12:2	30, 34, 50, 55, 60, 68, 74, 122
12:3	10, 30, 31, 32, 34, 35-36, 70, 81, 89, 93, 122, 128, 129, 178
14:19-20	16, 116, 137, 153
14:19	115, 116, 117 120, 154, 156, 169
14:20	116, 154, 155
17:16	34, 35, 63, 68, 69, 73, 101
17:20	34, 35, 63, 73, 101
18:18	10, 24, 31, 34, 37
22:17	10, 34, 63, 102, 178
22:18	31, 33, 34, 56
24:1	67
24:27	114, 155, 156, 170
24:31	53, 68, 70, 89, 90, 148
24:35	67-68, 69
24:48	134, 135, 170
24:60	102
25:11	68-69
26:3	34, 69, 76
26:4	10, 31, 33, 34, 56, 63
26:12	69, 176
26:24	34, 37, 63, 69, 74, 76
26:29	53, 68, 69-70, 89, 90, 93, 148, 166, 181
27	23, 24, 80-82, 85, 86, 99, 126, 172-173, 174, 177, 181
27:4	82
27:7	82, 83
27:10	82
27:12	82
27:19	82
27:23	82
27:25	82
27:27	65, 66-67, 76, 82, 83
27:28	66, 75, 81, 82, 83, 87
27:29	30, 33, 35, 41, 81, 82, 89, 128, 147, 178
27:30	82
27:31	82
27:33	82, 181
27:34	82
27:35	82
27:36	82, 109
27:38	82
27:41	82
28:1	99, 101
28:3-4	99, 101
28:3	63, 71, 169
28:6	99, 101
28:14	10, 24, 31, 34, 35, 37, 70, 71, 176, 181
30:27	37, 70, 71, 176, 181
30:30	37, 70, 176
32:1	84, 108-109
32:22-32	24, 35, 109, 172, 173
32:27	90, 109
32:30	109

33:11	126, 180	**Deuteronomy**	
35:9	62, 63, 73, 101	1:11	100
39:1-6	37, 69, 71, 74, 76, 166	2:7	69, 71, 76
39:5	41, 71, 176	7:13	37, 40, 41, 43, 44, 61, 66, 167
47:7, 10	107, 108, 110, 168	7:14	37, 40, 52, 178
48:1-22	14, 22, 83, 85	8:10	135-136
48:3	63	10:8	97-98
48:9	84	11:26-29	44
48:15-16	84, 85	11:26	41, 42, 82
48:20	30, 32, 50, 59, 84, 85, 101	11:27	41, 42
49:1-33	80, 85, 86	11:29	42
49:25-26	86-88, 89	12:7	38, 40, 49
49:25	76, 87, 88	12:15	40, 49
49:26	49, 87, 88	14:24	40, 49
49:28	86	14:29	38
		15:4	37, 44
		15:6	37, 178
Exodus		15:10	38
12:32	104, 110, 112, 176	15:14	40
18:10	156-157, 170	15:18	38
20:11	35, 65, 95	16:10	40, 49
20:24	38, 75	16:15	38, 49
23:25	37, 39, 40, 41, 61, 67, 178	16:17	40, 49
32:29	65, 95	21:5	97-98
39:43	115	23:6	90, 93, 94, 167, 175
		23:21	38, 44
		24:13	114, 167
Leviticus		24:19	38
9:22, 23	97	26:15	100
25:21	38-39, 61, 71, 75, 177	27-28	36, 40
		27:12	42
		28:2	42
Numbers		28:3-6	38, 40, 42, 44
6:23	97, 98	28:3	40
6:24-26	10, 20, 96, 167, 180, 182	28:4	37, 41, 61, 124
6:27	61, 97, 175	28:5	41, 61, 116, 124
22-24	90, 172-173	28:6	41
22:6	48, 90, 91, 92	28:8	38, 39, 44, 61, 71, 75
22:12	48, 63-64, 92, 166, 178	28:12	37, 38, 39, 76, 87
23:11	48, 90, 92	29:18	33, 124, 125, 182
23:20	90, 92, 93	30:1	42, 44, 82, 124
23:25	90, 92	30:16	37, 44, 67
24:1	90, 91, 93	30:19	42, 44, 82, 124, 183
24:9	33, 35, 41, 48, 81, 93, 94, 128, 147	33	80, 85, 86, 88, 180
		33:1	80, 86
24:10	90, 92	33:11	88, 89, 167, 178
		33:13	75, 76, 87, 89, 90, 117, 167

33:20	16, 154	18:28	155
33:23	89, 167	19:40	83, 108-109
33:24	16, 67, 89, 117, 167, 169	21:3	104, 112, 176
		22:47	152

Joshua

8:33	42, 175	**1 Kings**	
8:34	42, 44, 175	1:47	103
14:13	117, 128	1:48	153
15:19	127-128	2:45	72, 75, 94, 125, 147, 176
17:14	71-72	5:21	149, 154, 155
22:6-7	109	8	38, 59, 75, 99, 106, 120
22:33	136	8:14	73, 103, 105
24:10	90, 93, 129, 175	8:15	105, 153
		8:55	73, 103, 105

Judges

1:15	127-128	8:56	153
5:2	16, 145	8:66	103, 108, 110
5:9	16, 145	10:9	114, 116, 147, 152, 154, 156
5:24	16, 117, 134, 169	21:10, 13	162-163
13:24	78, 167		
17:2	94, 111, 112-113, 176	**2 Kings**	
		4:29	107, 108, 168

1 Samuel

2:20	99, 102, 175	5:15	127
9:13	64, 95	10:15	108
13:10	108	18:31	44
15:13	107, 108, 159, 168, 169, 182	**Isaiah**	
23:21	111, 113, 150, 159	19:24-25	24, 55, 57, 122, 167, 178
25:14	108, 168, 182	19:24	30, 50, 55, 60, 64, 74
25:27	126, 127	19:25	55, 64, 166
25:32-33	137, 149, 151, 154	36:16	44
25:33	113, 147, 151, 159	44:3	56, 57, 78, 167, 178
25:39	151	51:2	10, 53, 54, 57
26:25	112-113, 159	61:9	53, 54, 57, 166, 169, 178
30:26	127	65:8	65-66, 172
		65:16	33, 124, 125

2 Samuel

2:5	110, 111, 112, 113, 159	65:23	53, 54, 57, 68, 89, 90, 148, 169, 178
6:11	77, 106	66:3	137, 160
6:12	77, 106		
6:18	73, 98, 105, 106	**Jeremiah**	
6:20	73, 105, 106	4:2	10, 55, 56, 57
7	73, 75, 94, 100, 103, 104, 153	17:7	41, 47, 51, 181
7:29	73, 100-101, 117	20:14	41, 114, 116-117, 124, 147, 152, 156
8:10	103, 116, 117	31:23	122
13:25	109		
14:22	115		

Ezekiel
3:12   149, 158, 160
34:26   30, 50, 52-53, 57,
                      59, 60, 118, 178
44:30   60-61, 72

Joel
2:14   49, 61, 72

Haggai
2:19   58-59, 106

Zechariah
8:13   30, 50, 57, 58, 59-
                  60, 75, 85, 87, 101,
                      106, 118, 178
11:5   154

Malachi
2:2   36, 43, 74, 98, 175
3:10   43, 49, 58, 60, 61,
                 72, 76, 98, 106, 166

Psalms
3:9   119, 178
5:13   45, 51, 167
10:3   163
16:7   138, 139
18:47   152
21:4   72, 73, 178
21:7   60, 72, 73-74
24:5   45-46, 52, 167
26:12   138
28:6   150, 151
28:9   119, 178
29:11   121, 182
31:22   150, 151
34:2   140-141
37:22   46, 51, 52
37:26   30, 50, 52, 53, 59,
                           60, 118
41:14   158
45:3   72, 73, 74
49:19   125
62:5   123
63:5   138, 139
65:11   65-66, 67, 76
66:8   142, 145
66:20   150, 151
67:2   10, 121, 122, 167,
                           178
67:7-8   120
68:20   152
68:27   144, 158, 160
68:36   157, 158, 160
72:15   94, 102-103, 110
72:17   10, 72, 73, 94, 103
72:18   75, 158
72:19   12, 158, 160
84:7   76
89:53   149, 158
96:2   142, 143
100:4   142, 143
103:1-2   82, 144
103:20-22   145
103:22   82
104:1   82, 144
104:35   82, 142, 145
106:48   142, 158
107:38   72
109:17   121, 129, 130
109:28   121-122, 178
112:2   45, 47, 51, 52, 54,
                         166, 167
113:2   12, 135, 148, 152,
                           160
115:12-13   121, 140
115:15   119-120, 156, 169
115:18   138, 139, 140
118:26   38, 98, 105, 123,
                         154
119:12   149, 159
124:6   149, 153
128:4   45, 47, 51, 52, 166
128:5   75, 106, 119, 158,
                     169, 182, 183
129:8   98, 101, 104-105,
                       107, 123
132:15   61, 75
133:3   67, 75, 87
134:1-2   143
134:3   38, 75, 106, 119-120,
                 143, 156, 158, 169
135:19-21   145
135:21   141, 145, 157-
                       158, 160
144:1   152, 159
145:1-2   140-141
145:10   142, 145
145:21   142, 145
147:13   75

Index of Biblical Verses

Job
1:5	163
1:10	77-78
1:11	163
1:21	135, 148, 149, 150, 152, 160
2:5	163
2:9	163
29:13	115
31:20	114
42:12	67, 77, 166, 176

Proverbs
3:33	45, 51, 166
5:18	114, 116, 124, 147, 152, 156
10:6	49, 51, 52
10:7	30, 50, 53, 59, 60, 104, 118
10:22	45, 46, 47, 52, 71
11:11	51, 52, 175
11:25	47, 130
11:26	49, 52, 111, 166
20:21	46, 47, 48, 50, 51, 52
22:9	47, 51, 52, 166
24:25	48, 52, 73, 166
27:14	107, 162, 174
28:20	43, 45, 46, 47-48, 50, 52, 166
30:11	129

Ruth
2:4	105, 106, 107, 108, 168, 169, 182
2:19	111, 114, 116, 134, 147, 152, 156
2:20	110, 111, 114, 135
3:10	110, 111, 113-114, 159
4:14	156, 157

Daniel
2:19	134
2:20	12, 136, 148, 151-152, 160
3:28	156
4:31	134, 136

Ezra
7:27	154

Nehemiah
8:6	137
9:5	4, 136, 141, 142-143, 178
11:2	117-118
13:2	90, 93, 94, 129, 175

1 Chronicles
4:10	76, 101, 104
13:14	77, 106
16:2	73, 98, 105, 106
16:36	137, 158
16:43	73, 105, 106
17:27	100, 101, 117
18:10	103, 116, 117
23:13	97-98
26:5	77
29:10	134, 136, 159, 160
29:20	136, 137, 142

2 Chronicles
2:11	149, 154, 155, 156
6:3	73, 105
6:4	153
9:8	114, 116, 147, 152, 154, 156
20:26	4, 136, 142
30:27	98
31:8	135, 136
31:10	66, 72